Granded with love
from + Sarah

THROUGH THE YEAR WITH WILLIAM BARCLAY

THROUGH THE YEAR
WITH
WILLIAM BARCLAY

Devotional readings for every day

edited by
DENIS DUNCAN

HODDER AND STOUGHTON
LONDON SYDNEY AUCKLAND TORONTO

Contents

Through the Year with William Barclay contains
a Barclay "thought" for each morning or evening.
They originally appeared, in an extended form,
in "Obiter Visa" and "Seen in Passing" in *British
Weekly*, and have been collected and edited into
this form by Denis Duncan, editor of British
Weekly from 1957 to 1970. All appeared in
British Weekly in that period.

William Barclay
the Modern Miracle

I did not find it easy, on my first visit to Trinity College in Glasgow, to find Dr. William Barclay's room. But a passing student made it easy.

"Go up that staircase," he said, "then up the winding stair at the top of it. If you stop and listen for a typewriter in action, you'll find him all right. It's between lectures, so he will be writing."

I found him!

William Barclay is, by any standards, a modern miracle. His work-load and output is phenomenal.

He is a New Testament scholar of fame and distinction.

He is a writer whose output in the New Testament field must exceed that of any other living expositor.

He has himself produced a translation of the New Testament and plans to do the same for the Old Testament.

He is a preacher whose voice is known and loved far beyond his beloved Glasgow.

He is a TV teacher whose broadcasts on the New Testament and other subjects have captivated millions.

He is a journalist whose work has appeared regularly over more than a quarter of a century in newspapers and journals.

He has served as Dean of the Faculty of Divinity in Glasgow University, has directed the college choir for years, and still finds time to take an interest in sport.

Dr. Barclay suffered a serious illness recently, yet his work-load has again built up to one far beyond the range of ordinary men.

How does William Barclay do it—this man who has written a library of over sixty books on his own? this man who has had well over a million copies of his *Daily Study Bible* sold in Britain and more than half a million more in the U.S.A.? this man whose expositions have been translated into many other

9

languages and read in the backwoods of distant continents? As Dr. Barclay would say, if he ever did an "Obiter Visa" on this, "There are, quite simply, two clues."

The first is in the incident in our introduction. There is no time, however tiny, that Dr. Barclay does not use. Whether it is ten minutes or an hour, the Barclay typewriter is turning out something more from the inexhaustible Barclay mind. Never a minute is wasted. Every moment becomes a productive moment.

The second clue is in the Barclay deafness. For years Professor Barclay has worn a hearing aid so visibly that it has become part of the man himself. But don't allow yourself to pity the poor victim of this affliction! Dr. Barclay speaks of it as a blessing. For when he is at work in the study, off comes the aid, and he can hear nothing! The phone rings in vain. The door bell goes unanswered. William Barclay is in the world of silence where concentration is complete and creative writing is at its maximum. This is made possible by his having a wonderful wife—as he himself would be the first to agree!

Professor Barclay was born in Wick in Caithness, Scotland, over sixty years ago. His father was a banker, and his godfather was that famous Scottish laird, Cameron of Lochiel. He was an only child. When he was five, his parents moved to Motherwell, in the heart of the Lanarkshire industrial belt.

He graduated with first-class honours in classics at Glasgow University, gained his B.D. at the same University and continued post-graduate study in Germany.

He was ordained in 1933, his first and only charge being on the fringe of Glasgow in Renfrew on Clydeside. In 1946 he became a lecturer in Trinity College, and was called to the Chair of Biblical Criticism in 1963.

The typical Barclay day bears out the point made earlier about the use of time. He rises at 7.15 a.m. and reaches the University at 8.30. He works at his desk till 1.15. In the afternoon he sees research students from 2.00 to 4.30. The evening he spends reading, writing or out speaking. At 11 p.m. he falls asleep but only for one hour. At midnight he is awake again and works till 2 a.m.

In addition to numerous speaking engagements, Professor Barclay has time to train and conduct the Trinity College Students' Choir. He is an enthusiastic supporter of the Scottish National Orchestra, and a keen supporter of Motherwell Football Club in the Scottish League. He is, too, a railway enthusiast and has a magnificent library of railway books.

Dr. Barclay married the daughter of a minister of Dundonald Parish Church in Ayrshire, the Rev. J. H. Gillespie, in 1933. They have a married son, and a younger daughter, Jane. Their moment of greatest tragedy was the death of their older girl in a yachting accident off the coast of Northern Ireland some years ago.

It is William Barclay's understanding of and involvement in the real hard world of a city like Glasgow that has made this outstanding scholar an interpreter extraordinary of the Word to ordinary people. All Barclay's work has concentrated on the popular field, deliberately. He has been criticised by the academics for this, being told he ought to produce specialist academic work. He could do this far better than many of his critics, but he doesn't see this as his ministry. His aim is to make the New Testament, about which he knows so much more than others, alive and real to ordinary people.

The preparation of this introduction gives me a personal opportunity to pay tribute to Dr. Barclay's extraordinary contribution to *British Weekly* during my period as editor and in my predecessor, Shaun Herron's time too. The effect of "The Barclay Page" in such an extended writing ministry is incalculable.

I also eagerly grasp this chance to say a public and personal word of thanks to the amazing Dr. Barclay who, though one of the "greats" of all time, always has had time for his friends and patience with his editors.

The great are truly humble: the humble are truly great.

This was never more true than in the case of William Barclay, the modern miracle.

Denis Duncan

January

For a happy life, three things are necessary:
Something to hope for.
Something to do.
Someone to love.

Something to hope for

Alexander the Great, in a mood of generosity, was once handing out gifts. To one he gave a fortune, to another a province, to another a position of high honour. A friend said to him, "By doing this you will have nothing to yourself," "Oh yes I have," said Alexander. "I have kept what is greatest of all. I have kept my hopes."

The beginning of the end of life is when we live in memory rather than in hope: when our memories are an escape from prison rather than a stimulus to further living.

Something to do

James Agate tells of the terminal illness of an old charwoman. She wrote when she knew death was near:

> Don't pity me now.
> Don't pity me never.
> I'm going to do nothing
> For ever and ever.

Anyone who can look back to days of unemployment or to a time of enforced inactivity when the hours seemed slow and empty, knows that work is not a curse but a blessing.

13

Someone to love

Browning writes: "He looked at her: she looked at him: suddenly life awoke."

When love enters life, there comes a new thrill; a new humility; a new awareness of possibilities undreamed of. When love is born, life and the world are renewed.

How great is the blessing of someone to love.

RULES FOR LIFE   January 2

I give you three rules for life.

We must never be self-centred in our happiness.

Even while we are happy, there are others whose hearts ache. The time when we want to laugh is for others a time for tears.

A baptism is a time of joy. A new life is being blessed. But for someone, that new life may be a reminder of sadness—a new life taken away all too soon, a loved little one lost through disaster and death.

In our happiness, we must never be so self-centred that we forget others' pain.

We must never be selfish in our prosperity.

The Romans had a proverb which said that riches are like salt water—the more you drink, the more you thirst. How true! Those blessed with much do not always find it easy to give away.

John Wesley's rule was to save all he could and give all he could. When he was at Oxford, he had £30 a year. He lived on £28 and gave £2 away. Then his income increased to £60; £90; £120. But he still lived on £28 and gave the rest away.

It is always wrong for prosperity and selfishness to go hand in hand.

We must never be self-righteous in goodness.

How harmful is the so-called Christian who harps on about his goodness. How little does he realise that the man who is furthest from God is the man who thanks God he is not like others.

Goodness implies humility. It is the one who can say, as the publican in the parable did, "God be merciful to me, a sinner," who is truly justified before God.

TIME (1)   January 3

Nearly all the great men have been haunted by the sense of the shortness of time—and the uncertainty of time.

Denis Mackail in *The Story of J. M. B.* tells of how he used to visit Sir James Barrie. As he left Barrie would say, "Come again. Soon. Just ring up."

Then he would add, "Short notice, you know. I never like any arrangements far ahead."

Barrie was remembering that time is short.

It was Andrew Marvell who said:

> . . . But at my back I always hear
> Time's winged chariot hurrying near.
> And yonder all before us lie
> Deserts of vast eternity.

It was Robert Louis Stevenson who wrote:

> The morning drum-call on my eager ear
> Thrills unforgotten yet; the morning dew
> Lies yet undried along my field of noon.
> But now I pause at whiles in what I do,
> And count the bell, and tremble lest I hear
> (My work untrimmed) the sunset gun too soon.

It was Keats who was haunted by the fear that he might cease to be before his pen had gleaned his teeming brain.

As we grow older, and as time grows ever shorter, there are certain things which we should remember.

We should never leave things half-finished—in case they are never finished.

We should carefully choose what we are going to do—for there is no longer time to do everything, and we should do the things which really matter.

We should never come to the end of a day with a quarrel or a breach between us and any fellow-man—for it may be that the quarrel will never be mended and the breach will never be closed.

TIME (2)   January 4

When we work out how we spend time, the results can be startling. Take three very simple things.

Take the time we spend in eating.

Let's say that we spend 10 minutes at breakfast, 20 minutes at our midday meal, 20 minutes at tea, and 10 minutes at supper; that is 60 minutes or 1 hour per day, 7 hours a week. Put it in another way; this means that we spend one twenty-fourth part of our time eating; that is to say that, every year, we spend the equivalent of about 15 days doing nothing but eat; or to take the long view, it means that in a life of 70 years we will have spent 3 years eating!

15

Take the time we spend sleeping.

Let's say that we sleep for 8 hours every night; 8 hours is one third of the day; one third of our time is spent asleep. That is to say, in a life of 70 years we shall have spent almost 24 years asleep!

Take the case of learning.

There are 365 days in the year. But we do not go to school on Saturdays and Sundays; therefore, 104 days have to come off straightaway; and that leaves 261 days. But there are holidays, say 14 days at Christmas and 14 at Easter and 60 in summer—not to mention the odd days we get here and there throughout the year. That means that another 88 days have to come off; and that leaves 173 days.

But we do not go to school for the whole day. We go for about 6 hours each day. Now 6 hours is one quarter of the time. And one quarter of 173 is about 43. That is to say, we only go to school for the equivalent of 43 days in the year; and remember one third of our time, that is 122 days in each year, is spent asleep: which is to say that, when we are young we spend almost three times as long sleeping as we do learning!

It is startling when we work things out! No wonder we say, *tempus fugit* —time flies.

There are three things we should always remember about time:
We only get so much time, and when that is finished we cannot get any more. None of us knows how much we are going to get.
If there is something to be learned, we must learn it now; for the longer we put it off the harder it will be to learn it.
"Now is the time!"

TIME UP! January 5

In his commentary on 1 Corinthians 14, the chapter in which Paul has to deal with the people who would not stop talking, H. L. Goudge writes: "Not even conscious inspiration gives a man the right to monopolise attention. God's message can be spoken briefly. It is vanity that leads men to make excessive demands upon the time and the attention of other people, not respect for the divine message that they have to deliver."

These are stern words, spoken by a commentator whose usual accent is gentleness. I do not know that he is altogether right about the vanity side of the question. Often a speaker or a preacher is too long through want of preparation!

It is almost a first law of speaking that the shorter a speech or sermon or address has to be, the more careful preparation it demands. In such a case, a man has to know exactly what he wants to say and exactly how he wants to say it.

There are very few sermons which would not be improved by being short-

16

ened. Jesus could say more in a two-minute—yes, a thirty-second—parable, than the wordy speaker can in an hour.

Samuel Johnson wrote in *The Vanity of Human Wishes*: "Superfluous lags the veteran on the stage." No one would wish to eject someone who is doing good work; no one would wish to be hard; everyone will be gratefully aware that there are men who have worked for twenty, thirty, forty, fifty years in the one place—and it has not been one single day too long. But there comes "Time up!"

There is a sense in which change is often good. It is so easy for a man or an institution or a church to become set in his or its ways. It needs a new outlook, new methods, a new surge of energy.

It is one of the tragedies of the ministry that the Church has never made it possible, or been able to make it possible, for a man to retire when he wished. As things are, he has to keep on because it is impossible financially for him to do anything else.

I hope I shall know when it is time to get off the stage.

THE SPIRIT   January 6

The Holy Spirit is not the companion of the hours of mourning alone, although he is that; he is the strength of the soul in every time when life is difficult, when problems are insoluble, when the way ahead is dark, when we are near the breaking-point of life.

The Holy Spirit is the person who enables us to cope with life.

Of course, that is exactly what "Comforter" meant in the seventeenth century; for the word "comforter" has in it the Latin adjective *fortis* which means brave; and a comforter was one who put courage into a man.

I am not forgetting how precious the word "Comforter" is, and I am not forgetting how great a function of the Holy Spirit comfort is, in the modern sense of the word. But to limit the function of the Holy Spirit to that takes much of the strength and iron and virility and gallantry out of the doctrine of the Holy Spirit.

It is very difficult to get an English translation for *parakletos*; it may well be that Moffatt was right when he translated it simply but cogently and beautifully as "The Helper".

I know well how associations gather around any word; but no translation is sacred and immutable and unchangeable; and the translation of *parakletos* by the word "Comforter" is very apt to make the Holy Spirit the refuge of age rather than the inspiration of youth, the consoler of the sad rather than the spur and stimulus to chivalrous and to gallant living. The Holy Spirit is both, and the word "Helper" includes both.

We would add power and relevance to the doctrine of the Spirit, if we once and for all banished the word "Ghost", and if we ceased to limit the work of the Spirit by too much use of the word "Comforter" in relation to him.

B   17

Acquire a *parergon*.

You don't follow me, do you? Well, it is like this.

When I was in Wales once, I met a professor of Applied Mathematics who was the author of a commentary on the Letters to the Corinthians, and a professor of Biochemistry who, Sunday by Sunday, was a most acceptable lay preacher.

In my own university I know two professors who are expert church organists, one a professor of Naval Architecture, the other a professor of Obstetrics.

I know a professor of Mathematics who is an expert on Gaelic, a professor of Italian who is an authority on birds and bird-watching, a professor of Mechanical Engineering who is a poet in the Scots language, a professor of Aeronautics who is an expert actor and dramatic producer.

I knew a professor of Dentistry who, under different names, wrote wonderful children's stories, who was a poet, and who was an expert on Scottish folklore and archaeology. And I know an astronomer who writes the most exciting books of science thriller fiction!

Here is a whole list of men—and it could be expanded many times over—who do two things at once.

The whole point is that they are so distinguished in their own chosen line just because they do two things at once. The extra thing they do is the very thing which keeps them at concert pitch for their main work. And it is that extra thing which is called in Greek a *parergon*.

There is a legend about John the apostle, that one day someone found him playing with a tame partridge and criticised him for not being at work. His answer was, "The bow that is always at full stretch will soon cease to shoot straight." Everyone needs some sort of relaxation, and the more he is dedicated to his own job, the more he needs it.

Acquire a secondary interest in life, a *parergon*. You will work all the better for it, and leisure will become, not a problem, but an integral part of the fullness of life.

THE GENTLE STRONG   January 8

One of the greatest gifts in life is to have strength and gentleness combined.

It is good to have strength of will without being stubborn.

There is a difference between having a strong will and being immovably stubborn. I wonder how often we confuse prejudice with principle, and how often, when we claim to be standing on our principles, we are merely stubborn in our prejudices.

It has been said that consistency is the least of all the virtues. There is greatness in knowing when to change one's mind, when to yield as well as when to stand fast.

It is good to have strength of purpose without being intolerant.

One of the great dangers in life—and it is a danger to which people in churches are particularly prone—is the danger of condemning everything that we do not understand, the danger of thinking that there is only one way of belief and only one way of doing things.

In almost every case we could do better to seek to understand those from whom we differ before we condemn them.

It is good to have strength of faith without being self-righteous.

It is one of the great tragedies of the Christian life that very often those whose faith is strongest and most "evangelical" are quickest to accuse others of heresy, of modernism, of liberalism, and to insist that anyone who has not had the same experience as they have had has had no Christian experience at all.

There are—blessed be God!—many ways to God. No man has any monopoly of belief or of experience.

A man requires both strength and gentleness before he can be a pillar in the house of God.

CONCENTRATION

In concentration there are two essentials.

The first essential is *interest*. No one can really concentrate on anything unless he is interested in it. Given interest, concentration automatically follows.

Interest often comes from *taking the long view of things*.

There are many things which are not in themselves interesting, but which become interesting when they are seen as means towards something beyond themselves. Piano practice is not interesting in itself, but it gives no difficulty to the person whose heart is set on being a great pianist. Athletic training is not in itself interesting, but it will present no difficulty to the person who is determined to excel in athletics.

To take the long view, to see the ultimate effect of a thing, is the way to interest—even in the uninteresting; and that is the way to concentration.

But we can concentrate only if our work is done when it should be done.

The only possible way to concentrate is to do each task when it ought to be done and complete it then, for the sub-conscious memory that there is something which should have been done and has not been done, is itself enough to wreck concentration.

It is the sign of a child that he cannot concentrate for any length of time. It is the sign of a mature adult that he can concentrate.

Concentration in all things is necessary. The greatest concentration of all is the concentrating of the eyes of the soul on Jesus Christ.

Look unto Jesus.

TILL I REST . . . (1)   January 10

C. F. Garbett, who was Archbishop of York, met many important people in his long life. He was in Rome when President Roosevelt of the United States died. He called on the United States ambassador, Alexander Kirk, to express his sympathy.

Garbett tells us what Kirk said. "He spoke very feelingly of Roosevelt. He told me he had great interior powers of recuperation." In 1940 Kirk saw him carried to his cabin on his yacht in a condition of extreme exhaustion, very old and tired. In an hour's time he came out a new man, looking twenty years younger. His daughter remarked: "Father is like that; since his illness [Roosevelt had polio] he has trained himself to rest intensively; that is how he goes on."

To rest intensively—that is a strange and wonderful and a most significant expression. Why is it that, for so many of us, rest is so comparatively ineffective, and that even after rest we are still tired?

What does it mean to rest intensively?

There is no point in resting the body if the mind is not at rest.

There is no point in going to sit down, or to lie down, if the mind is still incessantly active and if thoughts are restlessly chasing each other through it. It is just as necessary to stop the mind thinking as it is to stop the body acting.

We can only rest the mind by making it think of the things which make for peace.

Garbett himself gives us the secret of this rest. Amongst his papers were found notes for personal and private prayer and devotion. His daily prayer began with an act of recollection and adoration. The substance of it was:

God in his Majesty.

God in his Justice.

God high and lifted up, yet ever near.

God in his infinite love in Christ.

The way to rest is to rest in him.

TILL I REST . . . (2)   January 11

Rest does not necessarily mean doing nothing, although there are times when it does. Often the best rest is change of activity.

Few men achieved more work than James Moffatt, the translator of the New Testament. One who knew him well said that, in Moffatt's study, there were three tables. On one was the manuscript of his translation then in progress. On another was the manuscript of a work on Tertullian on which he was then engaged. On a third there was a manuscript of a detective novel which he was writing.

Moffatt's way of resting was to move from one table to another!

Tiredness is often as much staleness as anything else—and the way to defeat it is not to do nothing, but to do something else.

It is almost a law of life that a man is all the better for having more than one thing to do—even if the other thing be no more than a hobby which is dear to his heart.

Real rest must always be contact with power. Clearly, when a man is tired, it means that his own personal resources have been overstrained, and that he must make contact with some source of power other than his own. When a car battery is exhausted, it is obviously not enough merely to take it out of the car; it must also be brought into contact with a new source of electrical power from which it may be recharged.

Real rest must therefore be contact with God so that our strength may be renewed by contact with a power beyond ourselves.

Repeatedly Jesus had to go into a lonely place to meet God— and what was necessary for him must be far more necessary for us.

Real rest is rest in God.

THE WORD (1)   January 12

Dr. F. C. Grant has written a book entitled *How to Read the Bible*. In this book he includes the advice given by Philip Melancthon: "Every good theologian and faithful interpreter of heavenly doctrine must of necessity be first a grammarian, then a dialectician [that is, weighing different interpretations], finally a witness."

Let us look at that programme.

The student of the Bible must be a grammarian.

That is to say, his primary object must be to find out the meaning of the words, to discover what the Bible means.

Canon B. H. Streeter was once asked, 'What do you recommend as a method for the devotional study of the Bible?" His answer was, "The accurate, painstaking critical study of the Bible is its devotional study, for the first thing to enquire of Scripture is its meaning. What could be more important for its devotional interpretation and application than this?"

One of the most serious sins against the light and against the Spirit is the failure to use the helps for Bible study which the great scholars have given us. If we fail to study the meaning of the words of Scripture, then we will be in very serious danger of making Scripture mean what we want it to mean, and not what God wants it to mean.

Once, as Dr. Grant relates, an ancient Rabbi satirised his rival by saying, "When Rabbi Eliezer expounds, he begins by saying, 'Scripture, be silent while I am interpreting'."

It is impossible not to be amazed at the staggering arrogance of those who either preach or expound Scripture without making an attempt to find out what the great and devoted scholars have to say to us. It is true that every man cannot know Greek and Hebrew, but he can at least know what the scholars who know these languages can tell him. And he can be humble enough to admit his own need of help.

THE WORD (2)   January 13

The student of the Bible must be a dialectician.

That is to say, he must be willing to weigh one interpretation against another. There are many so-called students of Scripture who would strenuously deny the doctrine of Papal Infallibility, but who claim a like infallibility for their own interpretations.

No man ever became a scholar by assuming that he was always right. There is nothing in this world more beneficial spiritually and intellectually than listening to someone with whom you disagree!

In the study of the Bible it is a duty to listen to every side of the question, and not to be deliberately blind to that which it does not suit us to see.

The student of Scripture must be a witness.

The Nestlé editions of the Greek New Testament, to which New Testament students have for so long owed so much, begin their prefaces by printing at the top of the page that saying of Bengel, the prince of commentators: "*Te totum applica ad textum; rem totam applica ad te,*" which translated means: "Apply yourself wholly to the text, then apply the whole to yourself."

It is quite true that we must study the Bible as we study any other book, applying it to the same stringent methods and tests of study which we would apply to any other book. But we do not study the Bible for the same reason and purpose as that for which we study any other book.

We study the Bible to find in it the picture of Jesus Christ, his offer of salvation for our souls, and his guidance and his commands and demands for our life.

The study of the Bible is not a pleasant intellectual exercise in which we are stimulated by what someone called a "mental hike". The study of the Bible ought to be a putting of ourselves before the pages of that book with the question on our lips, "Lord, what wilt thou have me to do?"

SPEAK!   January 14

If ever we see a man who is on the wrong way, if ever we see a man who is making a mess of things, if ever we see a man who is clearly going to shipwreck his own life and damage the lives of others or break the hearts of others, it is a terrible mistake to do nothing about it.

It is a duty to speak.

We must speak in time.

There comes a time when it is too late to speak, and the damage is done. Prevention is always better than cure.

I think it was Fosdick who said that it was always a better plan to build a fence at a dangerous bend with a steep drop than to keep an ambulance waiting at the bottom of the drop to pick up the bodies after the smash.

We must speak at the right time.

A word spoken at the wrong time can do very much more harm than good. We must have the wisdom to choose our time; and any word of warning must always be spoken in private, and never flung out in public, when it can produce nothing but resentment.

We must speak in the right way.

Certainly we must speak the truth, but equally certainly we must speak the truth in love (Eph. 4:15). Whenever the truth is spoken in such a way as to hurt and wound, whenever the main accent of the voice is criticism, whenever we seem to speak down to the other person, then warning and rebuke and advice are bound to fail.

The kinder the warning the more effective it will be.

The duty of being our brother's keeper is laid upon us (Gen. 4.9), and that means that we can never allow any man to ruin his own life or to hurt others without speaking the word of warning that we are able to speak.

At such a time, speech, not silence, is golden!

OPTIMISTS AND PESSIMISTS   January 15

"It is an excellent thing to have an optimist at the front provided there is a pessimist at the rear."

There is wisdom in this observation by Lord Asquith, the famous British Prime Minister. If you were to embark on some great operation, it would do no harm to have both sorts of men in your company.

There is value in the kind of man who sees possibilities in everything.

He is the kind of man who, when faced with a problem, is creating all kinds of ingenious solutions. They may not all be practical, but they are always worth a look.

There is the kind of man who is willing to plunge into anything with the sketchiest of preparations.

There is the kind of man who is confident that "everything will be all right on the night", who looks on a bad rehearsal as the inevitable forerunner of a good performance.

There is the kind of man who, in his own idiom, will "have a bash at it" and see what happens.

These sorts of men are not unuseful when things are going badly.

There is, however, also the man who sees difficulties in everything.

He refuses to make a move until the last detail is prepared and under control.

He must see his way clearly, not only to the next step but also to the one after that.

He is cautious, slow to commit himself, prone to see the possibility that all will end in failure.

The Greeks liked to divide men into two kinds—those who need the spur and those who need the rein. Both kinds were found in the apostolic company

There was Peter and there was Thomas.

Both played a part in Jesus' band.

The good leader can use both kinds complementarily.

ABOUT TURN! January 16

It is quite a handicap not to be able to turn round!

The Bible is clear that to turn round is just about the most essential action in this life.

The promise of the Law is happiness and prosperity "if thou turn unto the Lord thy God with all thine heart and with all thy soul" (Deut. 30:10).

In Antioch a great number believed and turned unto the Lord (Acts 11:21). Paul's God-given task was to turn the Gentiles from darkness to light and from the power of Satan to God (Acts 26:18). It was Paul's joy that the Thessalonians had turned to God from idols to serve the living and true God (1 Thess. 1:9).

The Bible is full of the word "turn". And how could it be otherwise? The word "conversion" is derived from the Latin verb *convertere* which simply means "to turn".

In life there are certain turnings which are essential.

We must turn from ourselves to others.

The Christian life cannot be the selfish and the self-centred life; it must be the life of care and concern. The great quality of the Christian life is mercy. To be really Christian, we must care so much for others that we forget ourselves and get right into them until we can see with their eyes and feel with their hearts and think with their minds.

We must turn so that we are looking outward and not inward.

We must turn from the past to the future.

The Christian characteristically looks forward. He is well aware of the sins and failures of the past; his penitence is real and heartfelt; and yet he knows that, in the grace of God, for the Christian the best is always yet to be.

We must turn to look forward and not backward.

We must turn from the world and look to God.

The Stoics used to say that the only way to live was *sub specie aeternitatis*, that is, under the shadow of eternity. It is easy to slip into a life where God is hardly ever remembered, and yet, because man is mortal, one day he must meet God, and, therefore, he cannot dare to forget God.

We must turn so that we are looking upward, not downward.

THE PERFECT BLEND   January 17

Swoppets are little toy figures. Mostly they are cowboys and Indians on foot and on horseback. But the thrilling thing about them is that they all come to pieces; and you can take one figure's head off and put it on to another figure's body. Or you can take one rider off one horse and put him on another.

Whenever I see Swoppets I begin to wish that you could do the same with human beings. I begin to wish that it was possible to take one part from one person and another part from another person, and so to make up a combination that was far better and far more complete than either was alone.

I wish we could join together A's determination and B's gentleness.

There are some people who know what they want and who know where they are going—which is a good thing—but, if anyone gets in the way, he simply gets knocked down or knocked aside without the slightest regard for his feelings—which is a bad thing.

I wish we could join together C's cold and impeccable goodness with D's warm-hearted recklessness.

There are some people who are morally almost without fault, but who are cold-hearted and without sympathy; there are others who have all kinds of faults from the moral point of view, but who have a great kindliness and generosity.

It is when purity and love go hand in hand that the finest character is born.

Our trouble so often is that we are half good. If only we could put the best of two people together we would get real and total goodness.

People aren't Swoppets and we can't take bits from each of them and add them together. But Jesus Christ can make new men.

BARRIERS (1)   January 18

I have come across, in an old notebook, a copy of a certain prayer. Years

25

ago I think that I must have copied this prayer from W. H. Elliott's autobiography *Undiscovered Ends*.

W. H. Elliott was one of the most famous and effective of early religious broadcasters, and there was a time when the weekly service from his church in London was one of the great religious events of the week on the wireless. The service went on for years, and through the years a very real unseen fellowship of listeners was built up.

Out of that fellowship there grew the League of Prayer which had a prayer that all its members were pledged to pray. It ran like this:

O God, who hast made of one blood all nations of men, mercifully receive the prayers that we offer for our anxious and troubled world.
Send Thy light into our darkness, and guide the nations as one family into the ways of peace.
Take away all prejudice and hatred and fear.
Strengthen in us day by day the will to understand.
And to those who by their counsels lead the peoples of the Earth grant a right judgment, that so through them and us Thy will be done.
Through Jesus Christ Our Lord, Amen.

If ever we needed to pray that prayer, we need to pray it today. It is a prayer that God may guide men at last to live in a world where the barriers are down.

We have our international barriers.
When we look at the world calmly and sanely, it is incredible that the nations are busily engaged in bankrupting themselves and threatening the health of mankind in an attempt to build up a store of weapons the use of which would make the earth uninhabitable.
Such barrier erecting is devilish.

BARRIERS (2)   January 19
We have our ecclesiastical barriers.
It is not very logical to fulminate against political *apartheid* and to practise ecclesiastical *apartheid*. So long as the Church is disunited within herself, she can have little influence as an advocate of unity amongst men.

J. L. Hodson, in a war book, told how a naval officer on a destroyer reported a desperate situation to the flagship, by a signal. Immediately back came the Admiral's acknowledgement and the return signal: "Repeat to God". The naval formula for the passing of a message to a higher authority is "Repeat to so and so". And in that moment there had come a situation which human wit was insufficient to deal with. It had to be reported to God.

We are rapidly coming to a situation in which man-made defences are nothing better than man-made destructions, and in which men seek to ensure the safety of the future by methods which may well blast the future out of existence. We are coming to a situation in which man-made compromises can do no more than momentarily stem a rising tide which ultimately cannot be stayed.

Nothing is more certain than that the world must either become one world or perish.

As far as the Christian is concerned, the supreme tragedy of the whole situation is that the Church, as it stands just now, is quite unfitted to take the lead in the great crusade for unity under God, for very certainly it will not heal the divisions of the world until it heals its own.

If the leaders of the Churches can find no way to unity, then we must pray that there will come such an upsurge towards unity from the ordinary people that the instinct of the heart may achieve what the arguments of the mind have failed to achieve.

Down with these barriers!

READ! (1) January 20

There came into my hands recently a book which is not new, but which I had never seen before. It interested me greatly. It is a book called *The Book Room*, in which Frank Cumbers tells the story of the Methodist Publishing House and the Epworth Press.

What interested me more than anything else was the attitude of John Wesley to books. One Methodist historian credits John Wesley with the publication of no fewer than 371 works, thirty of them jointly with Charles Wesley; and it is to be remembered that this was the work of the man who travelled more miles and preached more sermons every year than any man has ever done.

It was said of Southey that he was never happy except when he was reading or writing a book. That is not far from being true of John Wesley.

He insisted that his helpers and preachers should read, and read constantly. "Steadily spend all morning in this employ," he writes, "or at least five hours in the twenty-four."

Someone objects, "But I have no taste for reading." Wesley answers with a certain violence, "Then contract a taste for it, or return to your trade!"

Wesley knew well that the man has not yet been born who can continue to give out as a preacher without taking in as a student and scholar. But Wesley insisted that not only his helpers and preachers should be readers, but that all his people should read. "The work of grace would die out in one generation," he wrote, "if the Methodists were not a reading people." "Reading Christians," he said, "will be knowing Christians."

In the Standing Orders there was the question: "What is the business of an assistant?" And part of the answer was: "To take care that every society is duly supplied with books."

It is difficult to think of a world without books—theological works and detective stories too!

There are great values in constant and wide reading.

The man who reads will never be lonely.

Between the covers of books he will find people who will become very real to him; and thoughts which will ever keep his mind employed.

The man who reads will never be bored.

The man who finds pleasure in a book has a pleasure which is open to him at any time. No man can use his leisure with profit and without boredom who never reads a book.

The man who reads will never be ignorant.

He will be in constant touch with minds far greater than his own. A preacher without a library is like a workman with no tools. The preacher who ceases to read will also soon cease to preach in any real sense of the term. He is a bold man who thinks that he can afford to neglect what the great minds of the past and of the present have left to him.

Perhaps the decline in preaching is due to the fact that so many of us spend too much time at committees and too little time in our studies.

The man who reads will never be circumscribed.

By means of books he can live in any century, move in any society, travel in any country, match himself with and against any thought.

Reading will save a man from parochialism, from small-mindedness, from forgetting world issues because he is immersed in local politics at "parish pump" level.

To read is to have the horizons widened and the mind stored.

To the Christian there is always the Book of all books, the Bible, to be read.

He may study it for a lifetime but he will never exhaust it. The more strenuously and determinedly he studies it, the more it will give him.

I once heard the famous Scottish preacher, Dr. Johnstone Jeffrey, speak of the good you can do with a stamp. That is indeed true. Perhaps we ought to write more letters than we do.

A letter can convey our congratulations.

When we have some success, or when something good happens to us, one of the happiest things is to know that there are others who are sharing our joy and who are wishing us well.

It has been said, rightly I think, that it is much easier to weep with those that weep than it is to rejoice with those that rejoice. In a world where envy and jealousy are far too common, a stamp can do a lot of good if it tells our friends that we are glad some success or some happiness has come to them.

A letter can convey appreciation.

There are few things which uplift a man's heart like a word of appreciation and of praise. Such a word does not make a man proud or conceited; it is much more likely to keep him humble because he is well aware how little he deserves it.

Most people have the experience of being depressed and discouraged because they try so hard and seem to achieve so little. A stamp used to tell some one we appreciate his work could often do a power of good.

A letter can convey sympathy.

There is a sense in which a man must bear his own sorrow and no one can really help him to bear it. "Truly", said Jeremiah, "this is a grief and I must bear it" (Jer. 10:19). No man could bear it for him; he had to bear it himself. Nevertheless it is also true that, in the day of sorrow, there is comfort in the awareness that others are thinking of us and remembering us and sharing sorrow with us in so far as it is humanly possible to do so. A stamp should certainly be used to send our sympathy to someone who is surrounded by sorrows.

A letter can convey remembrance.

"A man," said Dr. Johnson, "should keep his friendships in constant repair."

A stamp has power!

LETTERS AGAIN   January 23

I have just had a letter from America. I do not know the lady who sent it, but across the flap she had written:

> Dear Letter, go on your way o'er mountain, plain or sea;
> God bless all who speed your flight to where I wish you to be.
> And bless all those beneath the roof
> where I would bid you rest;
> But bless even more the one to whom this letter is addressed.

It is not poetry; it is not even good verse. But it warms the heart to get a message like that.

It also made me want to set down some rules for letter writers!

Write at once, answer at once.

I talked earlier about the word of sympathy, of thanks, of congratulation. It should be written at once, so do it at once! If you don't do it at once, you probably won't do it at all!

Write legibly—especially your name and address.

Illegible writing is discourtesy. You can't answer a letter if you don't know who and where it came from!

Say whether you are Mrs. or Miss! The number of ladies who simply sign their name and put no status is amazing! It has landed me in a lot of trouble!

There is a text in the New Testament about letters which no Christian should ever forget. Paul wrote to his Corinthian friends, "You are a letter from Christ" (2 Cor. 3:3). It is through us that Jesus Christ communicates with men.

Jesus is God's word, and we are Jesus' letters.

This is the privilege and the responsibility of the Christian.

TO LIVE IS . . . ! (1)   January 24

Some years ago there was, in Glasgow at Hampden Park, one of the greatest matches of the century, the final of the European Cup between the German team Eintracht and Real Madrid, the greatest club team in the world.

Of all Real Madrid's famous players none was greater and none more famous than Puskas, the Hungarian. It was he who was usually the architect of victory and the scorer of goals.

On the morning after the great European Cup Final, Puskas was interviewed by one of the great newspapers. And Puskas was very willing to talk, for, he told the reporter, "When I don't play football, I talk football. When I don't talk football, I think football."

For Puskas football was the ruling passion; football was his life. That is why Puskas was the master footballer.

In this life there are many ruling passions which may grip and drive and govern a man. It was said of Southey, the author, that he was never happy except when he was writing or reading a book.

The golfer will spend hour after hour almost fanatically trying to get some part of his game just right. The cricketer will walk around with a ball in his hand, even as he goes about his business, strengthening his fingers by gripping.

The gambler can have such a passion for gambling that he will denude his house of all his possessions and starve his family to get money to stake.

The alcoholic will come to a stage when he cannot exist without his liquor.

The man who is out for money will spend all day trying to find ways of making and saving it, and his nights in dreaming of it.

It is true that a man will never become outstandingly good at anything

30

unless that thing is his ruling passion. There must be something of which he can say, "For me to live is this."

TO LIVE IS . . .! (2)   January 25

What does it mean to say, "For me to live is Christ"?

It means that we never forget his Cross and all that he did and suffered for us.
There is more than a little to be said for the Roman Catholic custom of carrying a crucifix, in order that we may never forget the Man upon the Cross, and how on the Cross he suffered for us men and for our salvation.

It means that we never forget his presence.
It means that at morning, at midday and at evening, night and day, we are conscious that we are in his sight, and that he is with us. Everyone feels the presence of Jesus Christ at some special moment in life. Everyone feels him near in the church, at some sacred spot, at prayer. But for true Christians it must be true, as it was true for Brother Lawrence, that he feels Jesus Christ as near when he washes the dishes and does the most menial task as at the Blessed Sacrament.

It means that we take no step without submitting our action for his approval.
Men act from many motives in this life—the desire for gain, the eagerness for honour and prestige, the love of comfort, the desire for safety, from motives of prudence, of ambition, of self-protection. The Christian motive can be no other than the approval of Jesus Christ. We would act very differently, and life would be very different, if we never acted without placing every decision and every word and every thought in the presence of the eyes of Jesus Christ.

For me to live is—?
Christ!

THIS IS YOUR LIFE   January 26

Last Sunday I had the joy of preaching in my old church and of baptising the baby daughter of my successor in the ministry there. Yesterday I had the sorrow of officiating at the funeral of the mother of the wife of one of my closest friends in the ministry. And in the course of the week I had the pleasure of being at three different celebrations dedicated to the immortal memory of our great Scottish poet, Robert Burns, whose birthday, January 25, is celebrated by Scots all over the world with Burns Suppers during this week.

The week has been a kind of summary of life, for circumstances have brought me into close contact with what may be called the three great universal realities in life—Birth, Death and Memory.

There was the baptism which reminds us of birth.

There is nothing in the world so moving as to hold a little child in one's arms. There in one's arms there rests an amazing bundle of possibilities for good or for ill. And the challenging thing is that the realisation of these possibilities rests almost entirely in the hands of the parents.

Every person in this world is a dream of God; for every person sent into this world by the gate of birth, God has a plan and a purpose; and it depends almost entirely on the teaching, the training, and the example the parents can give the child whether or not God's plan and purpose will be realised.

There was the funeral to remind us of death.

As Epicurus said long ago, "In regard to death everyone of us lives in an unfortified city." Here is the assault against which we have no defence; here is the end which we cannot escape.

There is nothing here for complaint or regret or fear; for this is part of the essential human situation into which every human being enters. But again there is challenge, the challenge to be ready whenever the call comes for us, at morning, at midday, or at evening.

There were the Burns celebrations to remind us of memory.

One of the great questions in life is, By what will a man be remembered, when he has passed on?

When a man passes on, and when others speak of him, again and again someone sums up his life in one sentence, for every man leaves behind him some dominant impression of himself. We must seek so to live that men will remember our names with pleasure when our presence is gone.

May we so live that the memory we leave is a fragrant and abiding possession.

GOALS   January 27

There are many possible ends in life. A man's goal may be money, or knowledge, or prestige, or position, or discovery.

Leslie Weatherhead in his book *A Private House of Prayer* tells of a conversation which took place in a university common room. Someone posed the question, "What do you want to be?" Many answers were given, many of them not unworthy—academic distinction, an athletic prize, a professor's chair. Then one quiet, shy, sensitive man spoke. "You fellows will laugh at me," he said, "but I want to be a saint."

Here are three definitions of a saint:

A saint is someone in whom Christ lives again.

A saint is someone who makes it easier to believe in God.

A saint is someone who lets the light shine through.

To be a saint is simply to walk the way of life with Christ— and that indeed is the true end of life.

We must always remember that life is not finished until it comes to its end.

The danger of life is that, to the very last moment of it, disaster can come. A famous man absolutely refused to allow his biography to be written during his lifetime, although his achievements would well have justified the telling of its story. He always said, "I have seen too many men fall out on the last lap."

In life there is never any time for relaxation. As John Bunyan saw in his vision, there is a road even from the very gates of heaven to hell. It is he who endures to the end who is saved. To the end of the day there is the possibility of falling to temptation, there is the possibility of undoing in one rash and unguarded moment all that the years have built up.

"Eternal vigilance is the price of liberty."

Eternal watchfulness is the price of honour. That watchfulness must last to the end.

LEARNERS   January 28

Real teaching is not teaching a pupil what to think; it is teaching him *how* to think. Any teacher who is out to make the pupil think and believe the same as himself is a bad teacher. The good teacher is out to help the pupil to think for himself.

True education is not so much putting things into the pupil as it is drawing things out of the pupil.

One of the greatest mistakes is to confuse teaching and indoctrination. Teaching builds up character and independence; indoctrination destroys both. What then do we have to do to help our education?

We have to be ready to learn from advice.

There are many people who go to others for advice. But for all that, they do not really want advice. They want to be told that they are doing well; that they ought to go right ahead and do as they are doing.

To ask advice, and to be ready to learn from advice are two very different things.

We have to be ready to learn from example.

This is particularly true of what we might call bad example. We see or hear of someone who has made a mess of things, and whose downfall was due to something which has some part in our own lives. Instead of taking warning, we so often in effect say, "It can't happen to me," and go on doing as we are doing. That is the way to trouble.

We have to be ready to learn from our mistakes.

The wise man is the man who never makes the same mistake twice. Most of us unfortunately go on making the same mistakes over and over again.

c   33

That is why we are never any further forward!

OUT OF PROPORTION January 29

How tragic it is that, in life, we get so much out of proportion.

It happens over the things on which we expend time and trouble.
Have you ever watched someone studying "the pools", or the racing supplement? Yet those are people who would certainly grudge time spent reading a book.

How much more time is given by some to entertainment and sport rather than work? People run themselves into the ground to get more "possessions"—another car, a colour TV, expensive holidays—and yet have no time at all for the things that really matter. Yes, and many a social worker—or even a minister—will spend hours on other people's families and little on his own.

If one had but one prayer to pray, he might best pray that God would make him sensitive enough to see the difference between the things that matter and the things that don't: or to put it the other way, to cultivate a sense of proportion.

It happens over the things that interest people.
Lloyd George, the famous British Prime Minister, once invited Ramsay Macdonald, also a Prime Minister during his political career, to discuss some important issues—especially unemployment. "Did you make any progress?" Lloyd George was asked. The fiery Welshman blazed with indignation. "Progress?" he said; "he insisted on discussing the old Dutch masters!"

Well, the Dutch masters are worth discussing— but at the right time. Lloyd George, overwhelmed by the mass unemployment he faced, felt this was fiddling while Rome burned.

How necessary it is to put first things first in life!
How essential it is to cultivate and operate a sense of proportion!

TAKE PRIDE! January 30

One of the happiest men I ever knew, a man who took the greatest pride in his job, was a man in a garage in a town where I used to live. He was not a mechanic; nothing so high up as that. His job, six days a week, was to wash dirty motor cars.

What a pride he took in that job! He washed them with such thoroughness and such pride that you could run your hand along the inside of the mudguard on the wing and withdraw it spotless!

His gift was the gift of washing cars!
But how he used it and gloried in it!

Someone has said that what the world needs, and what God needs, is not so much people who can do extraordinary things, as people who can do ordinary things extraordinarily well. A bus conductor or conductress can take your fare in a way that lights up the whole day. A shop assistant can serve you in a way that makes this world a better place.

One of the commonest things in life is the fact that many a person who is much in the public eye could not do his work for a single day without someone who, all unseen, does the greatest task that God ever gave anyone to do—the task of making a home which is really a home.

We should never envy anyone his gift. Everyone of us has a gift. The duty of life is to use that gift, whether it be a gift that all the world can see or a gift that blooms, almost unseen.

Sometimes Jesus told us little bits of his autobiography. Once he said, as he told a story, that the master of all good life said to one of his servants: "You have been faithful over a few things, I will make you master over many" (Matt. 25:21, 23).

Take pride in whatever you have to do!

INFECTION   January 31

One of the oddest features of the society of the middle twentieth century is the amount of advertising which is nothing other than an invitation to acquire the worst possible habits. The characteristic of modern advertising is that it does not only announce the things which a firm has for sale; it does not only aim to satisfy a need; it aims to create a need. And there are cases in which the need which it seeks to create is a need which can cause nothing but trouble.

One of the worst possible features of modern life is the flood of thoroughly bad literature which issues from the printing presses. There are few towns in which you cannot discover without difficulty a bookshop which deals in books which are barely on this side of pornography and sometimes not on the right side at all. There is a deliberate stimulation of that which is worst.

Life is full of infection. In modern life it is quite impossible that the young person should escape contact with this infection.

It is neither possible nor is it desirable to isolate the young person from life.

There is therefore laid upon parents a very great responsibility in these dangerous days.

There is the responsibility of real education not only in letters, but in life.

One of the saddest and most tragic of all situations is that which arises when a young person comes back to a parent or a teacher with life in ruins, and says, "I would never have been in this mess, if you had only told me what you ought to have told me."

There is above all the responsibility of making Jesus Christ a living presence in life.

If we can introduce our young people to Jesus Christ, and if we can teach and train and enable them to walk every way of life in his company and aware of his presence, then they will have a prophylactic which will preserve them from any infection which may attack them.

The more civilised and the more sophisticated the world becomes, the more the world needs Jesus Christ.

February

Leadership is a gift. Some men have it. Others don't. But most of us could have more of the capacity to lead if we understood the secrets of leadership.

The leader whom men will respect is the one who is himself involved in the job.

George VI was a king who had an impediment in his speech. It was not a stutter. It was really a stop.

One day he was seeing over a certain film studio. By an unfortunate coincidence, the engineer who was showing him round had exactly the same impediment. In his nervousness the engineer found he was becoming worse and worse.

King George put his hand on the man's shoulder. "It's all right, friend," he said. "I know what it's like."

The same King's brother, the Duke of Kent, was killed in a wartime plane crash. That same King's home, Buckingham Palace, was bombed.

When the leaders are involved, the supporters find it easier to follow.

The leader for whom men will work is the one with the personal touch.

One of the things that made Field Marshal Montgomery a great leader was simply that his men practically knew him by sight. He did not sit in headquarters issuing directions. He came and met them.

Letters are no substitute for personal contacts. The man who leads is the man who is near and known.

The leader for whom men will work is the one who asks for co-operation more than he issues orders.

There are leaders who are so anxious to show their authority that they provoke instinctive opposition and resentment. The leadership which invites help will generate much more help than the leadership which demands service.

A good many years ago now one of my favourite books was Adams Bron's *A Creed for Free Men*. Looking at notes I had made from it, I find that I had noted a passage in it which sets out the qualifications of leadership.

It is so good that I would like to pass it, or at least its headings, on.

A leader must have insight to see what ought to be done.

Half the battle is won when we discover what is wrong and what needs to be done. Some of us drive motor cars without any idea of what is going on under the bonnet. When something goes wrong and the car stops, we are helpless. We have to send for the motor mechanic; he opens the bonnet; he immediately diagnoses the trouble; and often it is so simple that, if we had been able to see what was wrong, we could have fixed it for ourselves!

In life we can only see what needs to be done by looking at things with the eyes of Jesus Christ, and in the light which he supplies. It may well be said that the first step towards mending any situation is nothing other than praying about it.

A leader must have resourcefulness to devise a way of doing what needs to be done.

It is far too common a reaction to a bad situation that nothing can be done. Cavour said that the first essential of a statement is "the sense of the impossible". As P. G. Wodehouse's famous Jeeves used to say, "There is always a way."

We may well remain defeatist when we tackle things in our own strength, but the grace of God in Jesus Christ is sufficient for all things.

A leader must have wisdom to know when to do what needs to be done.

George Bernard Shaw described Fabian doctrine which takes its name from the famous Roman general, Quintus Fabius Cunctator. "For the right moment you must wait, as Fabius did most patiently when warring against Hannibal, though many censured his delays; but when the time comes, you must strike hard, as Fabius did, or your waiting will be vain and fruitless."

Many a man's work is spoiled because he is in too big a hurry. There are few dangers like the danger of being a new broom. No man can make sweeping changes until he gains the confidence and the affection of people.

Many a man's work is spoiled because he waits too long before he acts, and the time for action and for cure is past. There is no greater gift than to know when to act.

A leader must have the courage to risk it.

Few people like the truth, and few people like reformations. "Truth," said the Cynics, "is like the light to sore eyes." Therefore, the man who speaks the truth always takes a risk. Most people prefer to remain comfortably undisturbed. Therefore, the reformer always incurs dislike.

George Bernard Shaw said, "If you do not say a thing in an irritating way, you may just as well not say it at all, since nobody will trouble themselves about anything that does not trouble them."

They killed Socrates because he was like a human gadfly. The leader must be prepared to take a risk.

It is a divine command to "launch out into the deep"—and the deep is never safe. There is no greater risk than to give a man freedom— and that is precisely the risk that God himself took.

A leader must have magnetism to fire his followers.

That magnetism comes from only one source. It comes from a burning conviction of the rightness of the cause and a transparent sincerity of purpose. No one can kindle men to enthusiasm unless he is on fire himself. No one can light a flame in the hearts of other men unless he has a fire in his own bones. And no one will follow a leader whose sincerity he does not trust. The time-server, the man who is dominated by personal ambition, is always seen through but men will admire the burning enthusiast even if they feel that he is wrong.

It can be seen at once that leadership is a costly thing. It begins with self-dedication to Christ, for real leadership is based not on the exaltation of self, but on the obliteration of self.

TRADITION   February 4

Tradition is important.
Let us see why.

Tradition preserves what is fine.

To enter into the tradition of a great school, or a great ministry, or a great congregation, is one of the most inspiring things of life. Here is something to live up to. Here is something one must not let down.

I have been told that, even on the retreat from Dunkirk in the Second World War, the Guards held a kit inspection on the beaches, then landed in England and marched off as if they were on ceremonial parade.

Other units arrived disorganised and in disintegration. But for the Guards, tradition must be maintained.

This is good and fine.

But tradition can fossilise something that has lost all point.

Even today a bride is on a bridegroom's left arm in order to leave his right arm—the sword arm—free to meet a crisis! Even today a man walks on the outside of a lady on a pavement because, in past days, before roads were surfaced, he walked there to shield her from the mud thrown up by horses' hooves and carriage wheels! The dress of the Moderator of the General Assembly of the Church of Scotland is still, for some extraordinary reason, a fossilised version of eighteenth-century court dress!

There is many a tradition that is meaningless now because its origin has been forgotten. Yet it goes on!

This can be bad!

Tradition can therefore be an inspiration or a handicap.

A man can be lifted up by it—there are times when even to put on a certain uniform does something to a man: or it can become a barrier to progress—"we never did that here!"

Encourage traditions that are fine.
Discourage those that are fossilising.

UNSHOCKABLE   February 5

If there is a virtue that a teacher and a parent and any kind of friend should have, it is that of never being shocked.

This does not for a moment mean that you have to agree with everything that everyone, perhaps especially young people, says.

It does not mean that, when they make some outrageous suggestion, and when they want society to be completely permissive, you say, "That's quite all right. Go ahead!" It will in fact mean that you often find yourself in strenuous and violent disagreement with them, and that you often find yourself arguing for a precisely opposite point of view.

Argument is the great activity of friendship.

It does mean that you willingly and freely grant to the other person the right to think for himself. The last thing you want to do is to stop anyone thinking for himself.

People don't think too much; they think too little. If they thought a little more strenuously and a little more clearly, they would probably think themselves out of the things which are wrong.

Wrong ways and decisions are the result of too little, not too much, thinking. So when people start thinking for themselves, the last reaction we ought to have is to be shocked.

It also means that you have to give everyone the right of free speech.

The days when young people had to be seen and not heard are long past. The child has won the right to speak.

Jesus was the friend of tax-gatherers and sinners; he wasn't shocked; all he wanted to do was to listen and to help.

We should do likewise.

THE GAPS   February 6

How wonderful it would be if parents could always be called the friends of our children. There is so often an almost unbridgeable gap between parent and children. They become strangers to each other.

There are reasons for that gap.

There is the inevitable gap between the generations.

There is the gap between the "then" and the "now". Parents do not bridge that gap by being determinedly "with it". There is, in fact, nothing more embarrassing than, in the old phrase, "mutton trying to look like lamb."

A gap there is, but each generation must be itself. Age trying to behave like youth is worse than youth aping age. We must be ourselves.

There is the gap produced by the whole concept of authority.

No one likes the feeling of being subject to authority. There was a time when a child had to obey, and, if he asked why, he was told by the parent, "Because I said so".

Nothing but trouble can come from an attitude like that. There must always be a genuine attempt to understand the other's point of view. There must always be communication.

The parent who is a dictator is simply insulting his child's intelligence and personality by demanding a blind and unreasoning obedience.

The parent who is a guide and a counsellor in the business of life is at least treating the child as a person—and that is the first essential.

If a parent is to be a friend to his child, there must be communication.

The tragedy of modern family life is that so very often parents and children drift so far apart from each other that, in the end, they cannot even make conversation; they have nothing to say to each other. This is a situation which must not arise.

Happy is the child whose parents are not only his parents, but his friends too.

I REMEMBER, I REMEMBER . . .   February 7

I remember the time when an aeroplane was an incredible sight.

I remember when motor cars were rarities.

I remember the first wireless sets.

I remember the first ball-point pens—how rare they were and how expensive!

I remember when you could buy cigarettes for eightpence for twenty and petrol at one shilling and twopence for a gallon.

Do I feel nostalgic about all this? Would I put the clock back if I could? Certainly not!

For there are other things I remember.

I remember when there was no health service.

I remember when people could not have proper medical attention because they could not pay for it.

I remember when my work, week after week, included visits to sanatoria, for tuberculosis *was* a scourge then!

I remember children with rickets and diphtheria. I don't want to go back to that!

I remember the days of terrible unemployment in the middle 'thirties, when nineteen out of my twenty-six elders were out of work, and when the Queen Mary was lying unfinished on the stocks in Clydebank across the river.

I saw respectable poverty then—and no one would want to go back to that.

I remember the days when half the population had, and half had not; when only the very wealthy could have a car; when a restaurant meal for the ordinary person was an event; when people often could not have a holiday at all: when a fortnight in Spain would have seemed a wild and incredible dream.

No one would want to go back to a time when the good things of life were so ill distributed.

That great teacher and preacher, A. J. Gossip, jumped on someone who once said that things could never be the same again. "Thank God," said Gossip, 'that things can never be the same again."

ONE FARTHING   February 8

St. John's-Renfield Church in Glasgow celebrated its one hundred and fiftieth anniversary in 1969. A very interesting brochure, with a brief but vivid history of the congregation, was issued to mark the event.

Among the many interesting things in that account is the story of the opening of Free St. John's Church in George Street on June 8, 1845. The collection that day was made up as follows:

Banknotes: 2 at £100, 22 at £20, 7 at £10, 95 at £5, 444 at £1.

Gold: 1 old guinea, 10 sovereigns, 23 half-sovereigns.

Silver: 52 crowns, 1 American dollar, 420 half-crowns, 627 shillings, 393 sixpences, 53 fourpences, 2 threepences, 1 twopence.

Copper: 48 pennies, 42 halfpennies, and 1 farthing.

To this had to be added £12.3.4d in the evening collection and £8.2.9d. of donations from people who were absent—a grand total of £1779.17.10d.—*and one farthing.*

This farthing fascinates me. Who gave it and why did he give it?

There are three possibilities.

Perhaps someone was so incredibly mean that, into the collection, he put the smallest coin of the realm.

If so, the farthing stands for those who give to the Church and to Jesus Christ and to their fellow men, the irreducible minimum. There are people who give the least of their time, their talents and their substance to their Lord and to mankind.

It could stand for a modern version of the widow's mite (Luke 21 :1–4).

Perhaps it was all that some poor person had to give. If so it was worth more than the £100 notes.

There are some people who give what they can, and no one can give more.

Perhaps on that memorable Sunday someone literally turned out his pockets giving the notes, the silver, the copper that was in them—to the uttermost farthing.

If so, this stands for the person who gives everything he has got to his Lord, and keeps nothing back.

Happy is the man who gives himself and his all—to the uttermost *farthing.*

One farthing.

In which group are you?

What is the Highway Code?

The Highway Code is what you might call "the distillation of driving experience". It is a summary of the things that years of experience have shown to be necessary and even essential for driving that is safe for the driver and for other users of the road.

Before you may drive, you must know what experience has taught and discovered, and you must agree to accept it and to abide by it.

In life there must be a correct balance between adventurous experiment and respect for experience.

Young people are natural experimenters; it would be wrong if they were not. But they cannot neglect the wisdom and the voice of experience unless at their peril.

The Highway Code is not about that which is advisable. It is something which has to be observed if chaos on the roads is not to occur. Similarly the code of the Christian ethic must be observed, if life is not to become a jungle.

The Highway Code is not, however, law. It is the statement of the principles which must govern the use of the roads, if life on the roads is to be safe.

The Christian ethic is not rules and regulations concocted to limit and to circumscribe Christian freedom. It is a presentation of principles, which in each circumstance, the individual must work out and apply for himself, on the principle that the Christian must live and love as Jesus Christ lived and loved.

There is a Highway Code ; no sane driver neglects it. There is a Christian code of living.

Permissiveness is no virtue, if it permits that which experience has proved to be fatal.

The church should never hesitate to say that society neglects this code for life at its peril.

THE FOUNDATIONS

I know a couple who live in a village.

The husband was taken suddenly and seriously ill. He was removed to an infirmary. Daily his wife visited him and we always asked how he was getting on.

One night his wife said to me, "Do you know what he said to me today?" I said, "Tell me." "Well", she said, "when I asked him if there was anything I could bring him, he said, 'All I would like is a drink of water from the pump that draws water from the well in the village street.' "

If anyone knows his Bible, straightaway his thoughts will go to David, hiding in the cave of Adullam and wanting nothing in the world so much as a drink of water from the well that was beside the gate (2 Sam. 23; 13–17).

When we are up against it, it is the simple things we want, like water from the village well.

This is true of religion.

It is my job to teach in a university. I know well how essential scholarship is. But I sometimes wonder if religion is really as difficult and as complicated as all that, and I sometimes wonder how much of our "technical" scholarship is really relevant to the human situation.

When we are up against it, our minds and memories go back to childhood's days.

Thomas Carlyle travelled far from the little village of Ecclefechan, in the south of Scotland, but he used to say that what kept him right was his mother's voice across the years: "Trust in God, and do the right."

You remember Jesus, and his dying prayer, "Father, into thy hands I commit my spirit!" (Luke 23:46). That is a quotation from Psalm 31:5, with the word "Father" added. It was the first good-night prayer that every Jewish mother taught her child to say before going to sleep, just as many of us were taught "Now I lay me down to sleep".

Jesus died with his boyhood's prayer on his lips. Happy is the man who has a childhood's faith on which to look back—for no life is stronger than its foundations.

The simple things, the foundations—these are the things that matter when the hard times come.

NOBODY

I heard recently about a certain lady. She was a quiet, gentle, unobtrusive person.

One day she said, "You know, when I see the people who are somebody, I'm very grateful that I'm a nobody."

What did she mean? I offer my guesses!

She was perhaps thinking of the people whom success has spoiled.

Abraham Lincoln once said cynically, "You can see what God thinks of money, when you see the people he gives it to."

You are perfectly right to magnify your office—but not to magnify yourself! When you get a step up in life, ask yourself a question: "Do I regard this advancement as a means of exercising more power or as a means of rendering more service? Do I regard this as a means of getting more or of giving more?"

If you remember that a Christian is among his fellow men as one who *serves*, then success will not spoil you!

The higher you go in your trade or profession, the harder you have to work.

Higher posts do not bring *less* work. They always bring *more* work.

It is much easier to be a nobody than to be a somebody, but if a man has the inescapable conviction that his contribution to life must be proportionate to the gifts and talents God has given him, then he will not complain of life's demands.

If we accept the Christian view of man, then there is no such person in life as a nobody.

As a workman of any kind, there is no doubt that we could be more or less readily replaced. But if there is anyone in this world who loves us, there is someone in whose heart we cannot be replaced. We matter to someone. And even if on earth we know that loneliness which has none to love and none to care, we matter to God.

You can lose everything and still have God.

If you have God, you cannot be a nobody.

45

We may never acquire a grasp of foreign languages but, if we are going to help people, there are certain languages which we need to be able to speak.

We must be able to speak the language of doubt.

It is very difficult for a man who has never experienced a twinge of doubt to talk to a man whose mind and heart are tortured by questions.

A faith is not the highest kind of faith until it has been tested. We should never be ashamed of having doubts. They are the way to real certainty.

Tennyson said rightly that there is often more faith in honest doubt than in the unthinking acceptance of a conventional creed.

We must be able to speak the language of temptation.

Wesley said of a certain man that he was a good man but a stranger to much temptation. For that very reason he was unable really to help others.

The way to real goodness lies through the victorious battle with temptation.

One of the greatest things about Jesus is that he was tempted, for that gave him his power both to sympathise with and to help others who are tempted.

We must be able to speak the language of sorrow.

Barrie told how his mother lost the son she loved. "That is where my mother got her soft eyes," he said, "and that is why other mothers ran to her when they lost their child."

The ability to comfort others is a costly thing. It comes through having sorrowed oneself.

To help the doubter, we must have experienced doubt. To help the tempted, we must have experienced temptation. To help the sorrowing, we must have experienced sorrow.

Ezekiel said, "I sat where they sat."

That is the way of help.

QUESTIONS   February 13

The great characteristic of the teaching of Jesus is the parable.

The parable is a story which invites a question. At the end of a parable there always comes the question, spoken or implied: "Well, what do you think?"

The question method has two great virtues. First, it compels a man to *discover* the truth. It does not tell him the truth; it leads him to discover the truth for himself.

It is only when truth is discovered that it is appropriated. When a man is simply told the truth, it remains external to him and he can quite easily forget it. When he is led to discover the truth for himself, it becomes an integral part of him, and he never forgets it.

What set me off on this line of thought was a section in Dr. H. Cecil Paw-son's excellent little book *Personal Evangelism*. Basing his selection on a B.B.C. panel game in which the panel have to identify a person by a series of questions, he devised, for his Men's Club, a series of questions by which they could identify themselves.

Some of them are questions; some of them are sentences which must be concluded. Here they are:

(1) Church-going is to me . . .
(2) So far as Sunday is concerned, I . . .
(3) Total abstinence is to me . . .
(4) Can you conceive of a condition in your life in which it would be true to say "I've lost everything"?
(5) When I am depressed I . . .
(6) It's my belief that . . .
(7) If I hear of someone who has spoken critically behind my back, I . . .
(8) What are the sins which delay the coming of a better world?
(9) I wish I could . . .
(10) My greatest ambition is . . .

There are Professor Pawson's questions. If we try to answer them, and are honest in doing so, it could be a revealing and salutary experience.

You try it!

A MAGNIFYING GLASS   February 14

There is a magnifying glass in the mind, not just in old age but at all ages.

There are people who magnify the amount of work they have to do.

To meet them you would think that they had the whole world on their shoulders; that no one ever had so much to do or had to work such long hours.

It is not really a wise occupation, for the more work we have to do, the more necessary it is to stop talking about it and to get on with the job.

There are people who magnify the hardness of life.

They have a permanent chip on their shoulder. Their battle-cry is, "Why did this have to happen to me? What have I done to deserve a situation like this?"

Paul has something to say to these people. Whatever happens to you, he said, remember it has happened to plenty of other people before, and it will happen to plenty of other people again. It is only part of the human situation. God will always send you a way out (1 Cor. 10:13), he adds.

There are people who magnify slights and insults.

In many ways they are the most difficult people in life to deal with. If, in

47

any group of people, there is someone of whose feelings we have always got to be careful, if we have always got to watch what we are saying, if anything we do say has every chance of being twisted into something we never meant, then there is a tension which is quite intolerable.

The whole atmosphere of a group can be spoiled by one of these people with a magnifying glass for insults in their minds.

Keep that sense of proportion we have thought about already. If you really like your job, and if you really see that it is important, then nothing will be too hard to do.

Some people really work for themselves.

It is a hard thing to say, but almost every church and every voluntary and charitable organisation contains a certain number of people who seek for office and for place because they have no chance of any prominence in the world and the church, or the voluntary organisation, is the one place where they can be somebody.

People who work for themselves and for their own honour and glory very seldom find any real joy in their work.

There are those who work for a person.

This is better, but there is a very real danger here. There are people who work for the minister, because they like him and admire him.

The danger is this. If a person is working in a church for the sake of the minister, then what is to happen when the minister goes?

It would be quite wrong to eliminate the personal influence of the minister, but there is always a danger in making the service of the church dependent on the attraction of a person. A ministry is not really successful when it is dependent on the attraction of one man.

There are those who work for the church.

This is still better, but there are dangers here too. It is quite possible for a person who works for his church to become a congregationalist in the wrong sense of the term. He wants to see his congregation at the top, his church full, his organisations flourishing.

Of course we must love our congregation and our denomination, but the body of Christ is bigger than that.

In the end there is only one way to work, and that is to work for Jesus.

Always our question must be, "Lord, what do you want me to do?" Always our work must be taken and shown to him. The only thing which should matter to us is his "Well done!"

When we work for him, then all pride and all resentment will be ended, and we will find our joy, not in what men say, and not in what happens to us, but by serving him by serving others; if need be, unnoticed and unseen.

THE BIBLE (1)   February 16

What you get out of the Bible depends on what you bring to the Bible. The Bible has an extraordinary way of providing a personal message to each of its readers.

The Bible speaks to our interests and our abilities.
One of the curious things about the Bible is that so many craftsmen will find things about *their* skill and *their* crafts in it.
The doctor finds his skills discussed in Leviticus.
The lawyer and the judge will feel at home in Deuteronomy.
The preacher can study the message of the teaching of the prophets.
The soldier and the military leader will find battles and campaigns to analyse.
The traveller . . .
The archaeologist . . .
The geographer . . .
The builder . . . Why, the description of the detail of the Temple is a fascinating mine of information for any craftsman to wonder at!
The housewife will find herself in the parables of our Lord.

What a wonderful book to touch life at so many points!
No one need ever feel the Bible irrelevant.
For it deals with what we know and do.

THE BIBLE (2)   February 17

What you get out of the Bible depends on what you bring to it (we said). The Bible touches life at so many points that there is hardly anyone who will not find something relevant to his own life and work in it (we said).

The Bible speaks to our needs whatever they may be.
The Bible gives comfort in a time of sorrow, guidance in a time of difficulty, challenge when we have lost the place, the means to praise when we want to rejoice.
You cannot find an area of life that does not find, in the Bible, a relevant comment on our needs.
This is the wonder of this wonderful book.

D   **49**

The more we take to the Bible the more it will give us.

The Bible can give to the simplest soul and the most uninstructed a word for the way, but delve deeply into it and there is matter and meaning that will stretch the greatest intellectual. A means to simple worship, it is also a mine of information—archaeological, historical, geographical, biological and so on.

It was said of the Persians that they never gave their young men a meal until they had broken sweat. The more, in toil and thought, that we give to the Bible, the more it will give to us in riches and wealth.

The story of the Bible is that there is no one who goes to it in need and in faith whom it does not find.

THE GOD WHO HEARS   February 18

The wonderful thing about God is that he can listen to all men's prayers at the same time.

It is never too late and never too early to pray to God.

Sometimes we fear to visit a person too early in the morning or too late at night or during their busy time, lest we be nothing better than a nuisance to them, lest we interrupt their work, and lest they be too busy to see us.

It can never be like this with God. Early in the morning, late at night, in the rush of the midday, God will hear.

No one is too small and no one is too great to pray to God.

There is no importance and unimportance in the sight of God. He is accessible at any time to the greatest and to the smallest; for in the sight of God there is no great or small.

No one is too young and no one is too old to pray to God.

Sometimes we say of children that they should be seen and not heard, to quote that old Victorian tag again. But Jesus said, "Let the little children come to me."

Sometimes people grow old and all their loved ones and their friends pass on and they have no one to talk to. Loneliness is one of the supreme problems of age.

No child is too small to talk to God; no aged one is too forgotten to talk to God. The fears of childhood, the problems of youth, the weariness of the middle years, the loneliness of age—they can every one of them be brought to God, and God will hear.

That is precisely why prayer should be not only a thing of the crisis and the emergency, but of the daily life of every man.

The wonder of God is that he listens to each one of us as if there was only one of us to listen to. He is the hearer of prayer—the world's prayer, and my prayer.

PRAYER (1)   February 19

A great many people stop praying because they think that prayer does not work. But this happens because they have a wrong idea of prayer.

Prayer has its laws.

Here are two of them.

Prayer is not God doing things for us: prayer is God helping us to do things for ourselves.

It is a first law of prayer that God will never do anything for us that we can do very well for ourselves. God is not the easy way out.

Very often a child brings an exercise home from school and asks his parents to help him with it. Every wise parent knows that, while it is far easier to do the exercise for the child, that it is no help to the child at all. The real help is to guide, explain, encourage until the child can do it for himself.

Prayer is not simply unloading our tasks on to God. Prayer is the means by which God enables us to do them for ourselves.

Prayer does not change circumstances. It changes us.

The circumstances are the same, but we approach them with new courage, new strength and a new ability to cope with them.

Epictetus said, long ago, that everything in this world had two handles, one of lead and one of gold, so that how we faced a situation depended wholly on the handle by which we picked it up.

Prayer helps us meet difficulties in a new way.

PRAYER (2)   February 20

Prayer is not God doing things for us. It is God helping us to do things for ourselves.

Prayer does not change circumstances. It changes us.

These are the two "rules of prayer" we have already laid down.

Here are two more.

Prayer is not escape. It is conquest.

Prayer is not a mechanism for helping us to avoid a demanding situation. It helps us to face and overcome that situation.

Suppose we are in a difficulty. Suppose we go to some trusted friend for help and guidance. When we leave that friend, we have not escaped from the situation, for it is still there to be faced, but somehow that time with our friend has made the situation less daunting and more tolerable.

Similarly prayer never offered any man escape from a difficult set of circumstances. It offered him strength to face those circumstances and to conquer or to endure them.

Prayer is not so much talking to God as listening to God. It is not so much telling God what we want him to do, as listening to see what he wants us to do.

In prayer, we have, of course, to begin by talking, but we always have to end by listening. Prayer is literally saying, "God, what wilt thou have me to do?"

So many people stop praying because they have looked for so many wrong things from prayer. Follow the rules, and see what God can do for—and with —you.

PRAYER (3)   February 21

Here is the prayer which a small boy actually wrote: "O God, help us to be good and to help other people." In many ways it is the perfect prayer.

It does not say "Make us"; it says "Help us".

The boy has grasped the fact that prayer is not getting things done for us; prayer is getting the strength to do them for ourselves.

The prayer does not say, "Help me"; it says, "Help us".

Our prayers would be very much more effective if they had in them less of the "me" and more of the "us".

The prayer asks simply for help to be good.

If things are right at the centre, they will be right at the circumference. There may be many things we need, but we need to be made good most of all; and, if we are good, all other things will take their proper place.

It does not say "Help others", it says, "Help me to help others".

When we pray for others, we must always at once try to answer our own prayers.

There is no good praying for the aged and the lonely without visiting them; or for the poor without helping them; or for the work of the church in the mission fields without giving something to help it. Far oftener than we realise, we could do much to answer our own prayers.

The best prayer of all is, "Help me to help".

KIOSK AND CATHEDRAL   February 22

Sir Giles Gilbert Scott, the great English architect, had an extraordinary distinction. He designed Liverpool Cathedral *and* the street telephone kiosk!

Vast grandeur and unadorned utility came from the same man.

No truly great man ever despises small things.
Giles Gilbert Scott gave his genius to a great modern cathedral, but was equally dedicated in producing a telephone kiosk.

How true this attitude of mind is of our Lord. Carpenter and Saviour! He who saved mankind hammered into shape yokes for the oxen.

To be faithful in little things is a great qualification for great tasks.

But isn't there another great truth here? I think so.

In a cathedral men talk to God : in a telephone kiosk, they talk to each other.
The man who is at variance with his brother can't be in fellowship with God. The man who is in fellowship with God will be in fellowship with his brother man.

The kiosk and the cathedral stand for communication between man with man and man with God. We cannot have the one without the other.

Whatever we do, we must do it with our might. It is often easy to get people to do the public thing, and hard to find people to do the humble task.

But, in the service of God, there is no great and small, no important and unimportant.

Kiosk or cathedral—do it with all your might!

ACT! February 23

Confession, so they say, is good for the soul. I am one of those people who are no good about the house.

When there is a job to be done about the house, I regret to say that I am not amongst those present. And I am the worst kind of "no good", because it is not that I am handless and cannot do things. I can, but I just don't do them—because I am so busy writing and things like this that I make the excuse that I haven't time!

Sometimes, however, I can be propelled into action, and what really alarms me is that something has just shown me that I am propelled into action at the wrong time and from the wrong motives altogether.

What happened was this. A painting job had to be done in a room in our house and another member of the family decided on a do-it-yourself policy. Well, the job was done and, in my view, it was not well done.

I was, therefore, as I said, forced into action, and promptly—after some well-chosen words of criticism—did the job myself over again. And, though I say it myself, did it very well indeed!

That, I can now see, is exactly and precisely the wrong way to do things. *It is always wrong to delay action until something goes wrong.* It is always

53

wrong to be lazy and selfish enough to do nothing until in the end something has to be done. It is far better to act in time, before things go wrong.

Prevention is better than cure every time.

ACT IN LOVE! February 24

I remember reading a tale about D. L. Moody. A man came to him with a very sorry story. "What would you do, Mr. Moody," he asked, "if you had got into a mess like that?" "Man," said Moody, "I would never have got into it." (All the same he helped the man to the utmost.)

There are so many things which need never have happened, if action had been taken in time.

Many a labour and industrial dispute would never arise, if some grievance were personally dealt with in time. Many an international crisis and even a war would be averted, if someone had the sense to act in time. Many a situation in a church has been allowed to grow to serious proportions, when, if it had been dealt with in Christian love and charity and prayer at the beginning, it could have been cured straightaway. Many a young person has made shipwreck simply because a parent or older friend did not want the trouble and the unpleasantness of speaking a word of warning and rebuke in time.

It is wrong to leave things till we have to clear up the mess when there need never have been a mess at all—if we had acted in time.

It is always wrong to be propelled into action from motives of criticism. Action which is really the result of criticism, whether the criticism is expressed or whether it is unexpressed, is always the action of superiority and conscious superiority at that. And we get nowhere that way. Action must always be in love and in sympathy. So long as we stand above people, we cannot really help them. We can do something for them, but that is a very different story from helping them.

The action which is fundamentally the action of criticism may be efficient enough, but it can never speak to the heart.

I hope that I have learned my lesson.

SEE IT THROUGH (1) February 25

I told you of my experiment in house painting. Now the paint which I was using was a rather special kind of paint which is guaranteed not to drip. That, of course, is a very useful quality in a paint. But it is thick, not liquid, almost like a jelly, and there are right ways and wrong ways of using it.

From that paint I learned certain lessons, and they are lessons not only for painting but for life.

I learned that you must know how to do a thing or your work will be quite ineffective.
I had to learn how to use this paint.

Normally, in painting, you can sweep the brush backwards and forwards like a pendulum. But you couldn't do that with this paint. If you drew the brush in one direction, you laid it on; but if you swept the brush backwards in the reverse direction, you promptly brushed it off again, and so you "got nowhere fast". But if you kept laying it on, always in the same direction, you got a wonderful job.

It is always necessary to learn how to do a thing. Somehow or other the word "technique" has become a word which many people rather despise, but whatever we are doing, from painting a room to preaching a sermon, if we neglect and despise technique, we may well ruin the most excellent material, and get the poorest results when we might have had the best.

It is very essential to get knowledge, but it is at least as essential to learn how to use knowledge in the right way.

I learned that you cannot paint in a hurry.

If you hurried it might look all right when the paint was still wet, but when it dried, it was streaky instead of even, and the underpaint showed through. It was a thoroughly unsatisfactory job.

Haste was hopeless!

SEE IT THROUGH! (2)   February 26

Perhaps the greatest fault of our age is that we are in too big a hurry.

A man who was a frequent visitor to America said that the first time he visited America, he thought that the main aim of Americans was money; the second time he thought that the main aim was power; and the third time he thought that the main aim was speed, and that third impression remained. And I am quite sure that is not true only of America.

Alan Walker tells of a man from the backwoods who came for the first time to the city of Sydney. His first question was, "Why is everyone running?"

After all, it is not much good doing things in a hurry, if they only have to be done over again. And the great question is, If you do save two minutes by rushing as fast as you can, what are you going to do with the two minutes you have saved?

The prophet has it: "He who believes will not be in haste" (Isaiah 28:16). Work would improve and temper would improve, if there were more repose and quiet, and less haste and rush in life.

I learned from my painting that you cannot leave a job half done.

If you left it half done and then began again, the join was quite easy to see. If you began a job, you had to finish it.

One of the sorriest things in life is the number of things which we begin and never finish. Life is littered with things half done. Most of us are much better starters than finishers. When we were young, we used to begin a collection of this or that or the next thing, and we would be enthusiastic for a week or two, and then the thing would be thrown into a cupboard or pushed away into a drawer and forgotten. That may be all right for a child, for a child has not yet learned to have any concentration, but it certainly will not do for a person who is supposed to be a mature man or woman.

"Blessed is he who endures to the end" (Matthew 24:13). It is the man who sees things through who comes to happiness and to success in the end.

FIRST THINGS FIRST! (1)   February 27

One of the most dangerous jobs in the war was sailing in convoys; and the worst danger of all was sailing in the convoys bound for Russia, for then, if a ship was torpedoed, a man perished quickly in the icy waters, unless help came at once. Every man in those Russian convoys was a hero.

One day a chaplain came to a man who was sailing in those convoys and asked him for any special impressions. "I don't think," said that man, "that there is anything I can tell." "But," said the chaplain, "I know that you have been bombed and torpedoed and machine-gunned. There must be something." "That was all in the day's work," the man said. "But there must be something," said the chaplain, "that has made some lasting impression on you, something that you will remember all your life." "Yes," said the man, "there is something, or rather, there are two things that I shall always remember. The first is the sound of men's voices in the sea at night, when you can't stop to pick them up . . . and the other is the sound of people's voices complaining in the shops at home."

Into the man's mind there had burned itself the contrast between men dying in icy waters and men and women complaining about trifling and petty inconveniences. People grumbled at quite unimportant things while men were dying at sea, and sacrificing their lives.

One of the most tragic things in life is that lack of proportion in it, that I have mentioned so often.

I heard the other day of a woman who knew all the latest local sensations in the newspapers and who had never heard that there was such a place as Vietnam or that there was trouble there. She avidly read the local news and was unaware of the conflict which might set the world aflame.

There is hardly anything so necessary as the ability to distinguish between that which is important and that which is not.

FIRST THINGS FIRST! (2)   February 28

There can be that tragic lack of proportion in the things to which people give their effort and their strength.

Many a man will spend hours studying a form-book or filling up a football pool, and never spend five minutes on a book that matters.

Many a man will expend far more energy on a game than he will on his work.

Many a man will run himself into debt and will scrimp and save to get something for the house—a new television set, a new car, a new gadget—while his home is utterly impoverished in the things which really matter.

Many a social worker will spend hours on other people's families and no time on his own.

Many a man will spend his whole strength and thought and energy on this world and forget completely that there is a God and that there is a world to come.

Perhaps there never was an age in which there is such a lack of sense of proportion as there is today. It is easy to say, "We never had it so good," if you are thinking only in material terms. If you are thinking in spiritual terms, it is a very different story.

If a man had one prayer to pray, he might well pray that God would keep him vividly awake and alive in mind and spirit so that he can see the difference between the things that matter and the things that, in the long run, do not matter at all.

THREATS   February 29

So the day seems to be coming when work will be able to be done with no more effort than sitting and watching. If that day comes, there will be trouble.

Juvenal, the famous Roman satirist, prayed the famous prayer for *mens sana in corpore sano*, a sound mind in a sound body. Now we cannot have a sound body without exercise. The health problems of *homo sedentarius* are already well enough known. And we cannot have a sound mind if there is absolutely no interest at all in work, and if it can produce nothing but boredom.

At the moment there is a balance. It may be difficult to get at one and the same time a sound mind and a sound body. But there are those whose work is so mentally interesting that they can forget the lack of physical effort, and there are those whose work is so physically demanding that they can forget its repetitive nature. But when work becomes physically immobile and mentally boring then the trouble will come.

I have seen it written that one of the great social tasks of this generation may be to prepare men for idleness, the idleness which will come of robots, computers and automation. It seems that we must control progress before progress destroys us.

It seems that the more complex and sophisticated living becomes, the harder it will be to find real life.

March

The most God-like thing in the world is the passion to help others.

You remember the four lines of doggerel that C. T. Studd, the prince of missionaries, loved:

> Some want to work within the sound
>> Of church or chapel bell;
> I want to run a rescue shop
>> Within a yard of hell.

There is a phrase in the creed. I know that it is a difficult phrase, and that even the exact meaning of it is far from certain— "He descended into hell." Whatever may be the exact and precise meaning of it, here is a picture of Jesus Christ scouring even the depths of hell with the message of salvation, going to the literal utmost to help and to save men.

Life is for ever full of the contrast between divine selflessness and human selfishness. When Paul wishes to describe Jesus in all his Godhead, it is not in terms of glory that he describes him; it is in terms of the abandonment of glory, the acceptance of the humiliation of humanity, the toil of servitude, the agony of the Cross (Phil. 2:5-11). It is precisely there that the God-likeness of Jesus essentially lies.

So much of the trouble in life is due to the division of our own lives into emotion and action. It is not that we do not feel pity and compassion; it is that so often the pity and the compassion remain untranslated into action, because so often we are not prepared to make the sacrifice which action involves.

Almost all of us lie under this condemnation, for in many ways selfishness and self-centredness are the essential human sins. Maybe something might happen if we remembered that we are never nearer God, and we are never

59

more kin to God, than when we are sharing someone's trouble, bearing some one's burden, and helping someone's need.

The young man I had to examine had graduated Master of Arts with Honours in Mental Philosophy. It was as he entered his course of study for the ministry that I marked his Greek and English Bible papers.

He scored 94 per cent in the first and 86 per cent in the second.

What I have not yet told you is that he is totally blind.

Handicaps are meant to be overcome.

How often seriously handicapped people have done great work and so won great victories.

Julius Caesar was an epileptic.

Augustus, the great Roman Emperer, had a stomach ulcer, so some historians believe.

Douglas Bader, that wartime flying ace supreme, won his greatest triumphs after he lost his legs and had to use artificial ones.

This is victory!

All handicaps bring compensations.

I am almost completely deaf. But this means I can sleep without trouble in a noisy hotel by a railway station! And I can concentrate far better on work and study for I have no distractions. And at boring committee meetings, I can switch off my hearing-aid!

A handicap has its compensations. His attitude to these can make or break a man.

If you are determined to overcome a handicap, nature becomes your ally and helps you to victory.

The sightless become sensitive in hearing and touch. The physically handicapped develop a versatility of other movements and methods which the normal would neither attempt nor achieve.

Nature loves the person who will not give in! That is why no one is beaten till he decides to give in. And that he need never do and must never do, if he wants the victory.

If a man has a handicap and is determined to conquer it, nature becomes his ally.

I know a person who had to have a very delicate and serious eye operation.

For a long time this involved lying in a hospital bed with her eyes bandaged so that not a ray of light might come near them.

This friend told me that, in less than a week, she could tell exactly what nurse was walking along the corridor simply by the sound of her feet, and could even identify a person by the person's touch on the bedclothes. It was as if all the other faculties sharpened and strengthened themselves to make up for the faculty which had ceased to function.

Nature loves the person who refuses to give in. No man is beaten by a handicap until he admits defeat, and he need never do that.

The one thing which will enable a man not to admit defeat is some kind of aim and purpose in life.

He did not tell me so, but I should not be surprised if my student examinee's brave victory was in no small measure due to the fact that he had set his heart on entering the ministry of the Church.

The determination never to be useless, the determination somehow to do a job for men and for God. the determination to make some contribution to life, the determination to achieve some measure of independence will take a man a very long way.

The greatest of them all was Paul with that terrible thorn—that stake, as it might well be translated—turning and twisting in his tortured body. He beat it because he brought two things to it. He brought his own determination and he brought that amazing grace of God in which he was able to do all things, because his weakness was made strong in the strength of God (2 Cor. 12:9; Phil. 4:14).

If we have some handicap, we and God can do something about it together.

REALITY!   March 4

Tillotson, the great Archbishop of Canterbury, was one day talking to Betterton, the great actor in the eighteenth century. Tillotson asked Betterton, "Why is it that I, when I am preaching about the greatest things, leave people quite unmoved, while you, when you are acting in what is nothing more than a play, can move them to the depths of their hearts?" "Sir," said Betterton, "you are telling them stories, while I am showing them facts."

What a condemnation of human nature, what a commentary on the human heart, that the action of a play should be more real to people than the working out of the eternal drama of the love of God!

What is the reason for this?

There are two reasons, I think.

There is the deadening influence of familiarity.

Most of us have heard the story so often that the cutting edge of it is gone.

There is the strange fact that for so many people the Bible stories happen in a kind of land of make-believe.

They happen in the same twilight land as the fairy tales do; they lack the reality of events which are sharply historical.

How can this be amended?

It can be amended by new methods of presentation and communication.

Too often the Church is dying of dignity, and perishing in the perfection of some noble liturgy. New things are apt to shock us, and we do not like being shocked. We much prefer to remain comfortably half-awake.

We need re-expression of the Christian gospel; but, maybe even more than that, we need re-realisation of the Christian gospel.

The re-expression is not an end in itself; it is only the means towards an end, and the end is the awakened realisation of what this gospel means.

It is when we face ourselves and face Christ, that we are lost in wonder, love and praise. We need to rediscover the almost lost discipline of self-examination; and then a re-awakened sense of sin will beget a re-awakened sense of wonder.

Perhaps then God will no longer have to say, "Is it nothing to you, all you who pass by?" (Lam. 1:12).

THERE IS GOOD . . .   March 5

Owing to a certain traffic problem in the avenue where we live in Glasgow, I wrote to the local police; and almost by return post there came back a very charming and courteous letter, actually thanking me for complaining and saying that something would be done—and it was done, and at once.

Over a rather unsatisfactory matter in Post Office practice here in our Cathcart area I wrote to the local postmaster. In a very few days I had a letter back, again actually thanking me for complaining, and saying that the matter had been attended to.

The last instance is almost beyond belief! I had certain correspondence with the Inspector of Taxes! Now I want to admit that I had been very dilatory in dealing with this correspondence and I deserved a sharp rebuke. But when I did answer, and when I did state my claims, the Inspector of Taxes actually wrote back expressing the opinion that in my claims I had been "rather harsh on myself" and suggesting that I should claim far more than I did.

It is the fashion to criticise the Post Office; it is the fashion to criticise the operation of income tax and those who administer it. I can only say that my own experience was that of a courtesy and a friendliness and a helpfulness which made a pleasure out of what might have been a trial.

From all this certain truths emerge:

We should never allow the bad incidents in life to blind us to the vast amount of good that there is in life.
We should never allow the conduct of one bad or discourteous person to make us condemn the whole institution to which he belongs.
We should never condemn a man or a woman on the strength of one action.

Anyone can make a mistake; anyone can fall to an attack of temptation; anyone can be momentarily discourteous or impolite or selfish. We should always look on a person as a whole.

There is so much that is good about.

I hope you find it, too.

CAUTION! March 6

We must be very cautious, very careful, how we touch and handle and treat things which are very precious.

How carefully a teacher or a parent should touch and handle the mind and the innocence of a child! How carefully we ought to touch and handle friendship and love lest the loveliest of human relationships should be hurt or damaged or impaired!

The lovely things of life must be handled with all care.

We must be very cautious how we meet the dangerous things in life.

It is to warn of approaching danger that most signs on the roads are erected. It is very easy to play with fire, to flirt with danger.

I read in the correspondence columns of a newspaper a very wise story. An old lady in the old days advertised for a new coachman. There were three applicants. She asked each of them the same question. "How near," she asked the first, "could you drive to the edge of a precipice?" He answered that he could drive within an inch of the edge. She asked the second the same question. He also claimed that he could drive to within an inch of the edge. She asked the third the same question. "Madam," he said, "I cannot tell you, because I always keep as far away from danger as I possibly can."

The third man got the job.

We must be very cautious how we use things which have great potentialities for good and for evil, things which can equally well bring ruin and blessing.

There are things in life which have an unlimited potentiality for good or for evil. There is, for instance, human speech, as James long ago saw (Jas. 3). We can use our tongues to do great good and we can use them to work infinite harm. The tongue can persuade men to good and seduce them to evil; the tongue can cement friendship and bring peace in strife; the tongue can divide men in anger and destroy personal relationships. The tongue can witness to the truth and can spread all falsehood.

63

He is a wise man who handles the precious things with care, who avoids the dangerous things with care, and who uses with care the things which have great potential for good and for evil.

Two women were overheard talking on the top of a tram car. The first was bemoaning the fact that she found it desperately hard to make ends meet, that she could never get anything new, and that she could never get any of the things she wanted for the house. The second said, "Well, you know, I've taken a part-time job, and from it I managed to save enough to get a new carpet for the sitting-room."

The first woman said enviously, "Yes, but you were always one of the lucky ones." The second woman said with a smile, "Yes, I suppose that's true. But I have noticed that the harder I work, the luckier I seem to be!"

No man can take a chance when it comes to him unless he has made himself ready to take it when it does come.

One of the grim things in life is that there are any number of people today who wish that they had worked a bit harder and studied a bit harder when they were young, because now they are passed over for promotion because—to use a colloquial phrase—they have not got what it takes.

This is true of the far greater things too. No man can ever hope to enter into a great friendship or a lasting love unless he has made himself, through his own efforts and through the grace of God, the kind of person for whom a real relationship and real love are possible.

No man can take a chance when it comes unless he is there to take it.

A man will wait for long enough, if he waits for inspiration to come to him. Inspiration comes to the man who is prepared to work until it comes to him. The preacher, the writer, the student will find that the likeliest place to find inspiration is at his desk. He must avoid the habit of not going to his desk until inspiration has come; he must go, and inspiration will come—out of mental perspiration!

The man who refuses to blame himself will seldom get anywhere.

There is a kind of person who blames everyone but himself. He lives in a world in which everything seems to be permanently against him. The weather, the boss, the other man, some specially malignant collection of circumstances, the general stupidity and even dishonesty of other people—this kind of person can produce them all as reasons why he has not done better than he has done, and why he has not gone further than he has gone.

There comes a time when a man should stop explaining what is wrong with circumstances and what is wrong with other people, and should start asking:

"What is wrong with me?" For self-examination would often be the best way to a change of what is called luck.

DO IT NOW!   March 8

There is a law of life. There are some things you can do and see any time; there are other things which you only get the chance to do and see once; and if you are ever going to see and do them, you must take that chance, or it does not come back.

If a word of praise or thanks has to be spoken, it had better be spoken now—for life is an uncertain business, and you may never get the chance to speak it again.

> If with pleasure you are viewing
>   any work a man is doing,
> If you like him and you trust him, tell him now.
> Don't withhold your approbation,
>   till the person makes oration,
> And he lies with snowy lillies o'er his brow;
> For no matter how you shout it,
>   he won't know a thing about it,
> For he cannot read his tombstone, when he's dead.

While we have them, we ought to tell them of our love and gratitude.

Very often a word of warning should be spoken now.
One of the tragedies of life is when someone slips into some ruinous mistake because those who might have warned him did not speak in time. It is quite true that we may be rebuffed, and it is quite true that we must be careful how we speak, for there is a hard way of speaking that will do more harm than good, but it is better to speak and be rebuffed than not to speak at all. We have said this before, but it is worth emphasising again.

Very often there are gifts which should be given now.
There is an old Latin proverb which says *qui cito dat bis dat*, which means, "He who gives quickly gives twice." A gift which is given in the moment of need is of double value. If we put off giving it, it may be too late to give it at all.
Too many serious impulses are allowed to die at birth, when they should have been acted on at once.

There are decisions which ought to be taken here and now.
As Lowell had it:

Once to every man and nation comes the moment to decide,
In the strife of Truth with Falsehood, for the good or evil side.

The fine impulse comes to a man; he postpones it; it never comes back. "Choose you this day whom you will serve" (Joshua 24:15).

If you keep steadily on at a thing with repeated efforts, even if each effort is not much in itself, it can do big things in the end.

In Glasgow University, the famous Lord Kelvin used to illustrate the effect of small forces on large masses. In his classroom he would have a huge heavy lump of metal weighing as much as a hundredweight and more suspended from the ceiling. He would have a basket full of paper pellets; and, to the great joy of the class, he would begin to bombard the heavy iron mass with the little pellets of paper.

At first nothing happened; then after a time the iron mass would begin to tremble; then it would begin to move; and finally it would begin to swing in a wide arc, and all through the effect of repeated blows with the little paper pellets.

The little things can achieve the big things, if we keep on—but you have to keep on, for, if you stopped bombarding the iron mass with the paper pellets, it would stop moving.

It is the little, constantly repeated efforts which count.

If you keep steadily at a thing, it is amazing what changes you can, in the end, achieve.

There is another experiment which demonstrates this. A very large beaker of clear water is taken, and a little phial of dye. Drop by drop the dye is dropped into the clear water. At first there is no alteration at all; the water remains quite unaffected to the eye. Then, bit by bit, the colour begins faintly and dimly to show; then the colour begins to darken and to deepen; and, in the end, the whole beaker of clear water is transformed into the colour of the dye.

It was drop by drop that the change was effected.

It is a commonplace to say that it is out of little things that perfection is achieved.

"Who has despised the day of small things?" said Zechariah (Zech. 4:10).

There may be a time to rid ourselves of trifles, and not to get lost in the details, but the man who disregards the little things will often lose the big things too. The man who carefully does the little things will end with something really great.

The important thing is not that something should be done perfectly, but that it should be done as well as we can do it.

Very often we don't try to do something, on the excuse that we cannot do it very well. But our first duty is not to do the thing very well, but to do it as well as we can do it.

When Henry VIII asked Miles Coverdale to produce an English translation of the Bible, Coverdale knew very well his own limitations and his lack of the necessary scholarship in Hebrew and Greek. "Considering how excellent knowledge and learning an interpreter of scripture ought to have in the tongues, and pondering also mine own insufficiency therein, and how weak I am to perform the office of translator, I was the more loath to meddle with this work."

But then he goes on: "But to say the truth before God, it was neither my labour or desire to have this work put in my hand; nevertheless it grieved me that other nations should be more plenteously provided for with the scripture in their mother tongue than we; therefore when I was instantly required, though I could not do as well as I would, I thought it my duty to do my best, and that with a good will."

Coverdale knew that he was but ill-equipped; but he did his best, and his best became a masterpiece.

It is not so much the efficiency with which a thing is done that matters, as the spirit in which it is done.

There are times when a really valuable gift can leave you with a sore heart in the taking of it, and when it is more of an insult than a gift, and there are times when a very small gift warms the heart and brings delight. When it is given in love and good will, a little thing becomes great. When it is given without love, the greatest becomes valueless.

God is not nearly so interested in how much we give as in how hard we try.

God is very gentle to the man who brings him something that is very inadequate, if it is the best the man can bring. God is like an earthly father who welcomes a child's gift, not because of its value, but because of the love in the heart which gave it.

OUR FRIEND GOD   March 11

The most precious thing in the world is a friend to whom we can go at any time, and never feel a nuisance; someone to whom we can turn just whenever we need them; someone to whom we can talk about anything; someone who will never laugh at our dreams or mock at our failures; to say it again, someone to whom we are never a nuisance.

We all know the person who is really half-watching the clock all the time we are there; the kind of person who implies, if he does not actually say it, that he can give us ten minutes and no more; the kind of person who, all the time, is quite obviously thinking of his next appointment and his next engagement; the kind of person to whom we are really more of a nuisance and a bother than anything else.

There is a wonderful incident in the life of Jesus (Mark 6: 31–34). The crowds were so pressing and so insistent that Jesus and his friends could not even get peace to eat a meal. So Jesus took his friends into the boat and they went across the lake to a lonely place to rest awhile, to get a little peace and quiet. But the people saw him go and they raced round the lake and they were there when he arrived.

So many people would have found the crowd an unmitigated nuisance and would have left them in no doubt that it was so. But when Jesus saw them, he was moved with compassion for they were "as sheep without a shepherd". He was tired and harassed and hungry; he wanted peace; but even then the people who needed him were not a nuisance.

It is so with God.

A VISIBLE SIGN   March 12

I remember being in Newcastle-upon-Tyne once. In that city, at a very busy junction where many roads met, there was a monument to the famous Earl Grey of the Reform Bill. It was on a tall pillar which soared hundreds of feet into the air.

When you looked up to the top of that pillar, you saw two bright lights outstretched on metal arms, shining at the top of it; and if you looked a little more closely, you saw that there were two other arms with two other unlit lights upon them.

I wondered what this meant.

Whenever there was a fatal road accident in Newcastle, then the two white lights were switched off and two red lights switched on. So in Newcastle they knew when someone died on the road. The red lights meant that a life had been lost.

This seems to me an extremely wise and effective method of impressing a fact upon the people's minds.

Indeed this is what Jesus did too, when he took bread and wine and used them as symbols of his body broken and his blood shed for men.

The Newcastle light was a reminder.

It was meant forcibly to remind people that another had been added to the terrible toll of death upon the roads. Jesus said of the broken bread and the poured out wine, "This do in remembrance of me."

The Newcastle light was a warning.

When people saw it shining red, it was a reminder that another had died on the roads, and it was meant to warn every motorist who saw it to drive more carefully and every pedestrian to walk more watchfully. So the broken bread and the poured out wine are the symbols of the broken body and the shed blood of Christ, and are therefore the supreme warning of what sin can do.

The Newcastle light was a challenge.

It was a challenge to see to it that things like that did not happen in that city, a challenge to motorists and pedestrians and every road-user so to live and move that that light would not shine again.

In the sacrament we see the symbols and the signs of the agony of Christ, and there must come to us the challenge, "You were worth all that. God thought you worth the life and the death and the suffering of his son. And, if you are worth all that, you cannot waste and soil your life. You cannot spurn that love and break your heart. You must seek for ever to be worthy of that sacrifice and of that love."

ONE MAN'S MEAT   March 13

T. R. Glover used to say that one of the first laws of life was to remember that "whatever you think, someone thinks differently".

This is true in all kinds of ways in the Church.

It is true of worship, with the great prayers of the Church, and with language sonorous, dignified and ecclesiastical.

Other people like a simple form of worship where there is more room for spontaneity and for extempore prayer. In this there is no right or wrong.

The liturgists must not despise the simple folk, and the simple folk must not go about saying that anyone who likes liturgy and ritual is half way to Rome! Let each worship God as he finds God and let him not criticise or despise the other.

It is true of the life of the Church.

Some people think that the Church should have a highly organised social life. They like to find their parties and their socials, and their dances and their entertainment in the Church, as they love to find their worship on the Sunday. Others have a much more austere view of the Church and think that these things are out of place in the Church and think that the Church's activities should be confined to "religious" meetings in the narrower sense of the term.

There is room for both. Those who like everything in the Church must not inveigh against the "narrowness" of the others. Those who do not like these things must not in a superior way criticise the "worldliness" of their brethren.

It is true of the Bible.

There are those whom we label fundamentalists, for whom the Bible contains no error of any kind, for whom every word in the Bible is the word of God without qualification and who can settle every argument by saying "The Bible says". There are those whom we call liberals, who cannot accept every word of the Bible as equally inspired, who do not believe that the Bible is the last word on history or on science, and who are much freer in their handling of the Bible.

There is a lot to be said for both. But let not the fundamentalists talk of the liberals as if they were not Christians at all, and let not the liberals grow irritated and annoyed at the unyielding attitude of the fundamentalists. They can, if they have the grace of Christ, quite well live together.

CHALLENGE AND CHANCE   March 14

We live in a world in which values have gone mad. But from all this one basic fact emerges—the world sets its highest value on that which entertains.

No preacher—even if he wanted it—would ever receive, for a sermon, the amount which a comedian receives for one performance. No serious writer will ever receive for a book what a popular novelist will receive. And it would appear that no one in the world is worth quite so much as a footballer or a film star.

What the world is willing to pay for is entertainment. Men will pay anything to be amused.

There are certain things that follow from this.

There is the strangest parallel with the Roman society of the time when Christianity came into this world.

It would be difficult to find any age in world history when so much was spent on food as it was then. Tacitus tells us of single banquets which cost as much as £500. Seneca tells us of dinner at which the dishes included peacocks' brains and nightingales' tongues. Suetonius tells us that the Emperor Vitellius set on the table at one banquet 2,000 fish and 7,000 birds and that in a reign of less than a year he managed to spend more than £3,000,000 on food. The elder Pliny tells of seeing a Roman bride, Lollia Paulina, dressed in a bridal dress which was so richly jewelled that it cost £423,000.

An age which pours out money on its pleasures is a decadent age.

There is no doubt what that Roman world was trying to do. It was trying to escape, to escape from the weariness and the boredom which had it in its grip.

Matthew Arnold well described its mood.

> In that hard pagan world disgust
> And secret loathing fell;

Deep weariness and sated lust
　　Made human life a shell.
In his cool hall, with haggard eyes,
　　The Roman noble lay:
He drove abroad in furious guise
　　Along the Appian Way;
He made a feast, drank fierce and fast,
　　And crowned his hair with flowers—
Nor easier nor quicker passed
　　The impracticable hours.

Extravagance is always a sign of the desire to escape.

It is hard to avoid the conclusion that *we* are living in an age of decadence and of escapism. And as Christians, there lies our challenge and our chance.

Sir John Reith once said, "I do not like crises, but I like the opportunities they bring."

The Church has the chance today to lead men to that which is life and life indeed.

Once Buddha was in a town where there was a conflict of warring theological views between the monks. Some believed one thing and some another, and each of them believed that he alone was right and that all the others were wrong. So Buddha told them the parable of the Rajah, the blind men and the elephant.

One day the Rajah called a servant, and bade him assemble, at his palace, all the men in the town who had been born blind. Then he commanded that an elephant should be brought in. Then the Rajah made one blind man touch the head of the elephant, another the ear, another the trunk, a tusk, a foot, the back, the tail, and the tuft of the tail; and to each one the Rajah said that he was touching the elephant.

When they had all felt the elephant, the Rajah said to them, "Have you all studied the elephant? Now tell me your conclusion." The man who had touched the head said, "It is like a pot." The one who had touched the ear said, "It is like a fan." And for the others the trunk became a plough; a tusk, a ploughshare; a foot, a pillar; the back, a granary; the tail, a pestle; the tuft of the tail, a besom. And each blind man thought that what he had touched was an elephant.

They began therefore to argue with each other and to quarrel, saying, "An elephant is like this"—"No, it is like this"—"I tell you it is not"—and so on until, in the end, they came to blows.

That, said Buddha, is what men are like about the truth.

Just as each blind man insisted that the part of the elephant he had touched was the whole elephant, so men insist that the little bit of truth that they have seen and grasped is the whole truth.

It is extraordinary that any man should think that he has grasped the whole truth. Such a confidence can do no other than indicate an arrogance of spirit.

The world would be a more gracious place, if those who claim to worship God had something more of the wideness of the mercy of God and the gentleness of the patience of God.

SPRING   March 16

It will be winter so long as we put a wall around our life, and it will be spring when we take the wall away.

Some people put up a wall against their fellow-men.

Sometimes they do it because they are too proud to mix with common people. Sometimes they do it because they are so obsessed with ambition and with "getting on" that every man becomes a competitor and a potential enemy.

Sometimes they do it because they are intolerant. They will have nothing to do with those who think in other ways. They brand them as heretics and people to avoid. Sometimes it is just shyness that puts up the wall—and so often shyness comes from thinking too much about ourselves and too little about others.

Life is always winter where there is no friendship and fellowship in it.

Aristotle in a great phrase called a friend "another self", an *alter ego*.

Springtime comes when friendship comes.

Some people put up a wall against God and Jesus Christ.

"Behold", said Jesus, "I stand at the door and knock" (Rev. 3:20). And when Holman Hunt painted his famous picture of the knocking Christ, he was right to show that there is no handle on the outside of the door of the human heart; it has to be opened from the inside.

It is always winter when we try to live alone; but when we open the door and receive Christ into our hearts, we too will say with the old hymn, "There is springtime in my soul today".

RECIPE FOR REFORM (1)   March 17

I am bound to say that I never realised what a truly great man William Booth, the founder of the Salvation Army, was. I had, of course, always set him high in my admiration as a man of God, but the reading of the book, *The Founder Speaks Again*, has been something of a revelation to me of his amazing greatness.

This is a book published by the Salvationist Publishing Company and contains a selection of William Booth's own writings.

Two things amaze me about this book—first, the entirely contemporary character of this man's writing. I do not think that there is a sentence of it that is out of date. Secondly, the amount of common sense that this saint packed into his writings and statements leaves me astonished.

It was as long ago as 1890 that William Booth published *In Darkest England and The Way Out* and it is as relevant today as on the day when it first saw the light.

William Booth saw that the social gospel is not an addendum to the Christian message, an optional extra; he saw that it is an essential part of the Christian message.

"What is the use," he said, "of preaching the gospel to men whose whole attention is concentrated upon a mad, desperate struggle to keep themselves alive? You might as well give a tract to a shipwrecked sailor who is battling with the surf which has drowned his comrades and threatens to drown him. He will not listen to you. Nay, he cannot hear you any more than a man whose head is under water can listen to a sermon. The first thing to do is to get him at least a footing on firm ground, and to give him room to live."

Booth was one of the first men to see that salvation is total salvation, salvation of body and soul.

He went on to lay down some essentials in any plan for reformation.

First, it is essential that any scheme put forward must change the man when it is his character and conduct which constitutes the reasons for his failure in the battle of life.

Booth saw quite clearly that the essential aim is the creation of new men and women.

None the less, the remedy, to be effectual, must change the circumstances of the individual, when these circumstances are the cause of his wretched condition, and lie beyond his control.

Booth saw clearly what environment can do.

RECIPE FOR REFORM (2)   March 18

Here are the five other principles laid down by William Booth.

Any remedy must be commensurate with the evil with which it proposes to deal.

So often attempts to do something do no more than scratch the surface.

Today for instance, the problem of the teenager cannot be solved by the running of clubs by voluntary, under-financed, under-staffed, inadequately equipped organisations. It is a national problem which only the government of a country can deal with. That same government can find millions for potential destruction while the youth of the country is being slowly destroyed morally and spiritually.

Any such scheme must be capable of being permanent.

Little is to be gained by monetary emergency measures. Something has to be done which can become part of life permanently.

Any such scheme must not only be permanent. It must be immediately practicable.

It must not be a dream; it must be something which is capable of being put into operation now.

Any such scheme must not indirectly injure the very people it was meant to help.

For instance, indiscriminate charity can, in the end, sap the moral fibre of the people it is intended to help. Entertainment without discipline could in the end do more harm than good.

Any assistance given to one section of the community, must not interfere with the needs and interests of another.

Concentration on the need and interests of any one age, or section, or class of society must never be at the cost of the neglect of any other parts of the community.

These were Booth's items in the "recipe for reformation". They are as relevant today as they were in 1890. If somehow all the churches and all the resources of the state were to get together on these lines, things might happen. Things *would* happen.

Is it impossible?

RECIPE FOR THE INDIVIDUAL (1) March 19

I have been drawing again on the magnificent advice of William Booth as we find it in the selection of his writings called *The Founder Speaks Again*. Now we come to the centre of the circle, the individual person.

As Harold Begbie tells, when Booth was twenty years of age, on December 6, 1849, he drew up a series of resolutions. I quote them in full.

"I do promise," he wrote, "my God helping:

"Firstly, that I will rise every morning sufficiently early (say twenty minutes before seven o'clock) to wash, dress, and have a few minutes, not less than five, in private prayer.

'Secondly, that I will, as much as possible, avoid all that babbling and idle talk in which I have lately so sinfully indulged.

"Thirdly, that I will endeavour in my conduct and deportment before the world and my fellow servants especially to conduct myself as a humble, meek and zealous follower of the bleeding Lamb, and, by serious conversation and warning, endeavour to lead them to think of their immortal souls.

"Fourthly, that I will not read less than four chapters in God's word every day.

"Fifthly, that I will strive to live closer to God, and to seek after holiness of heart, and leave providential events with God.

"Sixthly, that I will read this over every day or at least twice a week. God help me, enable me to cultivate a spirit of self-denial and to yield myself a prisoner of love to the Redeemer of the world. Amen and Amen. William Booth. I feel my own weakness, and without God's help I shall not keep these resolutions a day. The Lord have mercy on my guilty soul."

Here is a list of resolutions which any man who desires to walk the Christian way might well take as his own.

RECIPE FOR THE INDIVIDUAL (2)   March 20

I now put some of Booth's resolutions into my own version. Here they are:

Begin the day with God.
It is bound to make a very great difference to our life and conduct, if we go out to the presence of God, for then we will take something of heaven with us into the affairs of earth, and we shall see time in the light of eternity. Only then will we see everything in its true importance and in its true proportion.

Avoid gossip.
One of the grim facts of life is that most people prefer to pass on something bad about other people than something good. There are people whose main recreation is the assassination of the good name of others over the teacups.

Be a witness and a missionary for Christ.
The only true advertisement for Christianity is a Christian, and, conversely as it has been said, "The greatest handicap that the Church has is the unsatisfactory lives of professing Christians." Those who are Christians must at least try to live as lights in the world.

Study the Word of God.
No traveller sets out on a journey without having studied the map of the way. The Bible is the Christian guide-book for life, and the Christian must study it to find God's word for him.

Booth's next resolution involves two things:
(a) *Keep growing.*
The New Testament word for sanctification is *hagiasmos*. All Greek nouns which end in *-asmos* describe a process; and sanctification is "the road to holiness".

75

(b) *Don't worry.*

We have to leave the providential ordering of things to God. All that worry does is to unfit us to deal with a situation when it actually comes. In any event, God can give us the strength to deal with any situation when it does come.

Renew your resolutions every day.

We often make our resolutions and then forget them, as if the making of them was all that mattered. To review them every day is to confront ourselves daily with the challenge and the condemnation which will lead to progress.

And Jesus will give us the strength to do this.

Nothing is ever quite so good the second time it is done. This is part of the human situation, it is part of the "set-up" of life; and it is something which the Church is very prone to forget.

If we try to repeat a success, it means that we are living in the past.

Many a church, somewhere in the past, has had a great ministry, and, for the rest of its days, it spends its time talking about that great ministry and trying to repeat it.

Many a time some kind of experiment, some kind of method has proved successful, and then the tendency has been to do it again, and to expect the same spectacular results.

Harnack said that the danger of all great institutions is that they begin to worship their own past. You cannot go back; you must either go forward or perish.

We can use the past for inspiration, and we can use the past for guidance, but we can seldom or never use the past as a pattern for the present.

To try to repeat a success is to forget that you can never get the same combination of circumstances twice.

Life never repeats itself; and for that very reason there can be no formula for success there.

The question always is not, "What succeeded a generation or two ago?" but, "What does the present generation demand?"

The logical conclusion of this is that, if there is one thing the Church should never fear, it is change.

H. F. Lyte's famous hymn has it: "Change and decay in all around I see", but in point of fact that line might well be rewritten: "Change *or* decay in all around I see".

Unless a living organism changes, it necessarily dies. The one thing which does not change is a fossil—and a fossil has been dead for a very long time.

76

One of the causes of the Church's failure is its consistent attempt to repeat the successes of the past, for, in attempting that, it is attempting the impossible.

There are three qualities without which any civilisation is bound to disintegrate. They are the cement which holds any society together.

There is honesty, without which all business, all trade, all commerce, all human relationships must simply disintegrate.
Now there are any number of people who are prepared to take a dishonest chance or to put through a dishonest deal themselves, and who yet depend on the core of decent honourable people to hold society together and to make life possible.

There is the spirit of service.
Unless there are those who are prepared to do something for their fellow-men without pay, without gain, and without hope of reward, that is to say, unless there are at least some people who are prepared to live unselfishly, the whole structure of social welfare and social responsibility breaks down.

There is chastity.
Unless there is chastity and purity and fidelity, there must follow the destruction of the home, and the destruction of the home would mean the end of society as we know it.
There are any number of people prepared to live lives which flout all moral standards, and who yet at the same time depend on the hundreds of decent, ordinary people who live according to the standards of Christian morality.
There are thousands of people who themselves abandon all Christian standards and who quite consciously depend on those who do accept Christian standards to hold society and civilisation together. That is why the responsibility of the Church to be the leaven of society was never greater than it is today.

The Church is the custodian of those standards. Not even those who break them would wish to see them destroyed.

Is it not true that we can all afford what we want to afford?
It is very easy to find that we cannot afford to do what we do not want to do and to give what we do not want to give.
It is very easy to find reasons why it is really an economy to buy what we want to buy.

Is it not true that we can afford for ourselves what we find it quite impossible to afford for others?

Expenditure on self is always possible even when expenditure on others is impossible.

How much do we give of our time to our Church?

Apart from our attendance at church on Sunday, do we give to the work of Christ and his Church as much time as we give to television, to the cinema, to golf, to tennis, to gardening, to a motor run to the coast? Are there some of us who from Sunday to Sunday give literally no time to the work of the Church and to the service of Christ and his people?

How much do we give of our talents?

Do we give at all of such talents of hand and mind and voice as we possess to Christ and his Church? If we sing, do we sing for Christ? If we teach, do we teach for Christ? Do we give as much of our talents to the Church and to Christ and his people as we give to our favourite hobby?

How much do we give of our money?

There must be very few who give one twentieth of their income to the Church and to its Master. Many people think that they are being generous if they give 15 pence a week to the Church, and in many cases that must be less than one hundred and fiftieth part of their income.

It may be time that we began thinking of the things which, if Jesus Christ is right, we cannot afford not to do.

THE SECOND PLACE   March 24

A friend has just sent me a little poem which is a prayer, and which I like very much indeed.

> Lord, bless the folk who somehow never got there,
> The people who intended something fine;
> The folk who might have lived a little nobler,
> The men who somehow always failed to shine;
> The people who have tried to keep their temper,
> And yet who seemed to lose it all the more,
> The ones who haven't made their name at business,
> Who should be rich, yet always will be poor;
> The folk who aren't as clever as they might be,
> Who aren't as good, and feel their efforts vain,
> Lord, bless all these, and Lord, bless me among them,
> And give us all the heart to try again.

Here is a prayer for all those who somehow or other have to take the second place, those who are to the end of the day second bests.

Almost always behind some brilliant, scintillating, publicised character there is someone standing in support.

During the war one of the most colourful generals was the American General Patton. He swept through Europe like a gale of wind with his pearl-handled revolver and his flair for publicity. Someone once asked him, "How do you do it? Where on earth does the petrol come from to feed your motorised columns?" "I don't know," said Patton—"I've got a chap who looks after that."

Behind the vivid Patton there was a quiet man, whose name no one knows, who kept the whole army moving. It is like that in the most varied walks of life.

It is not the job that matters. What matters is how we do it.

The question is not, What is your work? but, Is your work your absolute best? The old hackneyed poem is right when it says that the point is not whether you won or lost, but how you played the game. Here if ever it is true that "all service ranks the same with God".

Most of us will never see the first place. Most of us will have to be content with the second place. Most of us will never have the spotlight on us; most of us will have to work behind the scenes. But at the end of the day there is not a doubt that the unseen work will be seen, and the unrewarded work will be rewarded—and then it may well be that many that were first will be last, and many that were last will be first.

Whatever our task is, God needs it and God needs us; the point of life is not the task, *but how the task is done.*

GREATNESS   March 25

I remember once doing some work for the Royal Army Chaplain's Department in Germany and going to a place called Ostenwalde where there was a church house in which excellent work was being done. And when I was there I remember being thrilled because the bed in which I slept had once been—as he then was—General Montgomery's bed!

And I remember still another thing. I remember playing football once and the jerseys on this occasion had been lent to us by a famous Scottish football club. And I remember the thrill of pulling over my head a jersey which had often been worn by the captain of Scotland and which bore his number in the team upon it.

What gives these things their special thrill? The special thrill of course lay in the fact that each of these occasions gave to me, a very ordinary person, a contact with greatness, however distant and remote.

This is the idea which lies behind museums and houses which have been preserved and which we can visit because some famous person lived there. To look at old relics, sometimes even to touch and handle them, to visit such houses and to go into such rooms, gives to ordinary people a contact with greatness, and such a contact is always a thrill. And, for the Christian, such a contact is always possible.

Every time we enter a church and worship there, we are putting ourselves in touch with the saints and the heroes and the prophets and the martyrs. We can say to ourselves, "I belong to that fellowship to which those who loved and died for their faith in every age and generation belonged". When we sit at the sacrament, we can say to ourselves, "I am doing exactly what Jesus did with his disciples in the upper room long ago".

For the Christian this contact with greatness is even more universal. We live in the world which is the work of God. The men and women amongst whom we live and move are the children of God.

The world in which we live is the handiwork of God. Everywhere we go, we can say, "Here is God".

MORE THAN COMMUNISM (1)   March 26

A new charter of the Russian Communist Party was prepared, laying down what a Communist should believe and how he should behave. It was reported that that charter had seven points, and the seven points are more than worth setting down.

The first demand is loyalty to the cause of Communism both in Russia and in other countries.

The second is conscientious labour for the benefit of society.

The third is collectivism and comradely mutual assistance. "One for all and all for one."

The fourth principle is honesty and truthfulness, moral purity, unpretentiousness, and modesty in public and personal life.

The fifth demand is for mutual respect within the family circle, and concern for the upbringing of children.

The sixth principle is intolerance of injustice, parasitism, dishonesty and careerism.

The last demand is for fraternal solidarity with the working people of all countries.

Here is nothing, except the demand for loyalty to Communism, which a Christian could not accept and which, in fact, a Christian is bound to do. In face of this very remarkable document there are certain things to be said.

The Communist can state in a few intelligent and intelligible words what he believes and on what broad principles he believes that life ought to be lived.

If he is asked for what he stands, he is able to say so. Can the Christian do the same?

It is impossible to fail to see that this Communist creed is a social creed.

It is clearly designed to be worked out in life and living. For instance, it sets before a man a standard of workmanship in the shop, the office, the factory, the workshop wherever he may be. It sets before him the attitude he ought to have to his work and to other people and to himself.

Does the Christian take his Christianity to the office and the factory with him as the Communist takes his Communism?

I very much doubt it.

MORE THAN COMMUNISM (2) March 27

Behind the Communist creed there are two basic principles.

There is the principle that a way must be found in which people can live together. And above all, there is the principle of responsibility. Apart from anything else this creed clearly lays down the duty of every man to be the best possible workman that he can be, and to do the best possible day's work that he can do.

There are very, very few people who accept that duty and obligation in our so-called Christian Western society. With us it has become almost a principle that a man does as little as he can and gets as much as he can.

If this Communist creed is carried out in practice, it actually provides a more Christian philosophy of work and responsibility than exists in alleged Christian countries.

The conclusion is clear and challenging. It is simply this : to put it colloquially, the Christian has "got to go some" to beat this creed.

In the last analysis, there is a simple test of any creed. The test of any creed is the kind of life which it produces. Christianity can only prove its superiority to Communism by proving that Christianity produces better and happier men and women.

THE BOOK WHICH LEADS TO TRUTH March 28

It is only in the Bible that truth is clearly revealed and clearly seen. Wherein is that specially true?

The Bible gives us the true view of man.

There is no book so realistic as the Bible. The Bible is clear that there can be no higher purpose than that with which man was created, but it is also clear that something has gone badly wrong.

So the Bible clearly sees man's high destiny and man's sad failure; and then the Bible goes on to say that the cure for the situation lies alone in Jesus Christ.

The Bible sees three stages in the human story: God made man in his own image; sin entered in and wrecked that plan; Jesus Christ came, and only in Christ can men be what they are meant to be.

The Bible gives us the true view of the world.

As the Bible sees it, the world is neither to be despised nor is it to be worshipped. Earth is neither a desert drear, nor is it the paradise of God. Parable after parable of Jesus shows us the world as the training and the testing ground of eternity.

This life is the arena where a man fits or unfits himself for the life which is to come. As the Bible sees it, no man can withdraw from the life of this world. There is no man in the New Testament who is more sternly condemned than the man who failed to use his one talent (Matt. 25:24–30). No man can dedicate himself to the world.

In the New Testament no man's folly is more sternly revealed than the folly of the Rich Fool who never saw beyond the goods he had acquired (Luke 12:13–21). The wise man neither withdraws from the world nor dedicates himself to the world. He sees the world as the school of soul-making.

The Bible gives us the true view of God.

Or rather it is truer to say that the Bible tells how in Jesus Christ the true view of God came to me. There was a time when men were terrified of God. But then there came Jesus Christ to say, "He who has seen me has seen the Father" (John 14:9); and men saw that above and beyond all else God is the lover of the souls of men.

Any thinking man is bound to ask three questions: Who am I? What kind of world is this in which I live? Who and what is the power behind the changing scene of things?

If a man will turn to the Bible, he will find these basic questions answered— and answered above all in Jesus Christ.

FIRE!   March 29

One day recently my minister friend was telling me that his niece was giving him advice on how to preach! And her advice was: "If you can't put fire into your sermon, put your sermon in the fire!"

A better epigram and better advice it would be hard to find!

Fire can warm a person.

On the great day in Aldersgate which changed John Wesley's life, Wesley said: "I felt my heart strangely warmed."

A great German critic said of the First Letter of Peter that its outstanding characteristic is warmth.

There can be no great preaching without warmth, nor can there be any real teaching without warmth. Warmth does not mean that a man will rant and shout and gesticulate and generally throw himself about. There can be a quietness and a stillness which have in them a white-hot intensity which no one can mistake.

Fire can melt the hardest metal.

Keri Evans in his book, *My Spiritual Pilgrimage*, remembers that Finney, the great evangelist, calls the atmosphere which is created by the Holy Spirit "a melting atmosphere", producing what our fathers used to describe as "a tender frame of mind".

It was said of a certain person: "She was like a well-laid fire to whom no one had ever put a match." All the equipment of life was there—except warmth—and therefore although in a sense everything was there, in another sense everything was lacking.

Heat fuses things together.

Usually an alloy will be made out of two metals by heat. There is a lesson there. If ever there is to be union amongst us, that union must come not so much from cold logic as from the warmth of the loving heart. When our hearts reach out to each other in love, we will get further than ever the arguments did.

It is only the warmth of love that can fuse two personalities or two churches or two congregations together.

DYNAMITE?   March 30

What is the difference between fireworks and dynamite?

Both of them make a noise.

But in the one case the noise is what you might call an ineffective noise; it has no discernible result. In the other case the noise is an extremely effective noise, for with the noise things happen.

There can be a kind of preaching which, as Shakespeare once said of life, is "full of sound and fury, signifying nothing".

Now what are the ineffective and the effective noises? To put it very shortly: when the preacher is airing his own personal views on this, that and the next thing, the preaching is less effective, for after all the preacher is a man amongst men. He has just as much chance of being wrong in his views as the next man has; but when the preacher is proclaiming the word of God, then he has at least the chance of being mightily effective.

Fireworks amuse, dynamite terrifies.

It is perfectly true that there is a sense in which preaching must entertain, for the attention of the congregation must be caught. It is quite true, as Jesus so well showed us, that a sunny shaft of humour is often very necessary and very effective. No one would hear Jesus talking about a man with a plank in his own eye trying to take a speck of dust out of another man's eye without a smile or even a roar of laughter.

It will be a sad day when a congregation is shocked by laughter. But what is important is the ultimate effect; and there is something wrong with a sermon of which the jokes are remembered and retailed when the message is forgotten.

Preaching must leave a man facing his own sin and the holiness of God and the grace of the Lord Jesus Christ.

The greatest danger of fireworks is to those who play with them, not realising their potentialities for harm.

The greatest danger of the firework type of preaching is to the man who becomes a slave to it. He loses the conception of what preaching is.

To preach is in Greek *kerussein*, which is the word which is used for a herald's proclamation on behalf of the king.

Let a preacher remember that he is the herald of God and he cannot then go far wrong.

BEAUTY   March 31

As the years go on, we make ourselves a certain kind of face. An expression assumed often enough leaves permanent marks on the face.

Worry will leave its mark upon a face in the vertical lines etched upon the forehead.

You can always tell a worried man by his face. Yet we forget that a worried Christian is a contradiction in terms. For the Christian, there is a way to the peace that passeth understanding.

Discontent will leave its mark upon a face.

Many a pretty face has been spoiled by a permanent look of discontent. Yet the Christian will count his blessings—and he will always have some blessings to count.

A friend of mine used to say: "If you have a pain in the neck, thank God you are not a giraffe!"

Resentment will leave its mark upon a face.

There are some people who are resentful against life, against their fellow-men, against God. They live life in the permanent conviction that they have never had a square deal from anything or anyone.

But joy, too, leaves its mark upon a face.

There are those who always look as if they are going to smile. "A happy man,"

84

said Robert Louis Stevenson, "is a better thing to find than a five pound note."

"When you looked into my mother's eyes you knew, as if he had told you, why God sent her into the world—it was to open the minds of all who looked, to beautiful thought. And that is the beginning and end of literature. These eyes that I could not see till I was six years old have guided me through life, and I pray God that they may remain my only earthly judge to the last."

That is what a face can be and do.

Easter Day

HE IS RISEN!

It is one of the strange things in the modern Church that we think of the Easter faith only at Easter time.

It is at Easter time almost alone that we think of the Resurrection and of the life to come; it is at Easter time almost alone that we sing the hymns of the Easter faith.

This is so wrong. I think that we have forgotten the origin of Sunday, the Lord's Day. The Sabbath, the Jewish holy day, commemorated the rest of God after the labour of the six days of creation; the Sunday, the Lord's Day, commemorates the Resurrection of our Lord, for it was on that day that he rose from the dead.

In the early Church the Resurrection was the star in the firmament of the Church. The Resurrection was the one glorious fact on which all worship and all life were founded. To that centrality of the Easter faith, the Resurrection faith, we would do well to return continually.

It is the Easter faith, the faith in the risen and living Lord, which makes us able to meet life.

For if we believe that Jesus Christ is risen and living, then we must believe that all life is lived in his presence, that we are literally never alone, that we are called upon to make no effort, to endure no sorrow, to face no temptation without him.

It is the Easter faith, the faith in the risen and living Lord, which makes us able to meet death.

It is the Easter faith that we have a friend and a companion who lived and who died and who is alive for evermore, who is the conqueror of death. The presence which is with us in life is with us in death and beyond.

A writer tells how his father died. His father was old and ill. One morning the writer tells how he went up to his father's bedroom to waken him. The old man said, "Pull up the blinds so that I can see the morning light." The son pulled up the blind and even as the light entered the room, the old man sank back on his pillows dead. Death was the coming of the morning light.

The Easter faith should be in our thoughts not simply at a certain season of the Christian year; it ought to be the faith in which Christians daily live, and in which in the end they die, only to live again.

April

I have always loved the story of Dean Ramsey. The good Dean loved his roses and it was a high mark of favour when he would say to a guest, "Come into the garden; I would like you to see my roses".

But one day a very lovely lady was visiting him. "Come into the garden," he said, "I would like my roses to see you!"—which is one of the loveliest compliments ever paid.

Still it does make one wonder why people will flock in crowds for aids to beauty which is skin deep, and remain quite indifferent to the beauty of the soul which makes life lovely.

Beauty which is skin deep is not very difficult to acquire, if you have the money.

You can buy it in a box or in a bottle, at the shop of a hairdresser or a beautician. On the other hand, the loveliness of the soul, the great inward graces of life, which make all life beautiful, are not easy to come by. They need to be paid for in self-discipline, in self-denial, in effort, in struggle, in prayer. It is so much easier to get the thing in the box.

There are things which are not so satisfactory about the beauty that is skin deep.

For one thing, it only masks the reality beneath it. You can paint and powder-on a lovely complexion, but that does not change the dull, lack-lustre skin beneath the coating.

For another thing it is very impermanent. It has to come off at night, if only to put a mud-pack on! Soap and water will soon remove it. But the great graces of the heart and mind are an indelible part of life which nothing can remove.

Skin-deep beauty is sought to impress others.

Maybe it does— for a moment; maybe it does make others turn in the street and look—and even whistle! But when the years go by, the people we really remember are the people who are gentle and gracious and wise and kind. Real loveliness outlasts synthetic beauty.

Even if it is outward beauty we are looking for (and why shouldn't we?), it is impossible to get it without the inward beauty.

Inner discontent will etch upon the face lines that the beautician cannot remove. Crossness and irritability and bad temper will mark a face with wrinkles that a plastic surgeon cannot remove.

If we really want beauty, it must begin from inside. There can never be a permanently lovely face without a lovely soul.

THINGS COULD HAPPEN IF . . . !   April 2

Paul said: I am not ashamed of the gospel of Christ (Rom. 1:16). This actually says more in Greek; for Greek has a way of saying things in a negative form when it really wants to express a very strong positive. It is a way of using an understatement as a very strong statement. And we would really get the meaning of this better, if we translated it: "I am proud of the gospel of Jesus Christ."

Once G. K. Chesterton was criticised because, it was said, after he had become a Roman Catholic, he could not write a book which did not somewhere or other show that he was a Roman Catholic. His answer was: "Indeed, I hope that's true."

The Christian should always be proud to show that he is a Christian—and that not simply in church but everywhere.

A man's Christianity should emerge in his work, by making him, in a slack and shoddy age, a man who takes a pride in craftsmanship; who is always conscientious, who is concerned not to do a job as quickly and easily as it can be done, but as well as it can be done.

A man's Christianity should be demonstrated in his pleasure, in that he refuses any pleasure which would soil him in body, mind or spirit. or which would threaten someone else's welfare or innocence.

A man's Christianity should be obvious in his sport. When I was younger, I played almost every game that can be played. Nowadays the thing that strikes me most when I watch sport, is that gamesmanship has ousted sportsmanship. In every game the Christian should be an honourable sportsman—and the crowd would love it.

A man's Christianity should emerge in the fact that he has a social conscience. It is a Christian duty to take a full share in political matters in trade union matters, in local government—not in one party but in every party.

Things could happen, if every Christian could say and would say, "I am proud of the gospel of Jesus Christ".

The Syro-Phoenician woman wanted Jesus to heal her sick daughter (Mark 7:24-30); but she was not a Jew and Jesus' mission was in the first place to the Jews, and he told her that his help was not at the moment for her.

"You can't take the children's bread," he said, "and throw it to the dogs." "True," she replied, "but, sir, even the dogs under the table eat the children's scraps!" "For saying that," said Jesus, "you may go home content." And she went home to find her daughter healed.

For saying that.

The Syro-Phoenician woman would not take "No" for an answer.

Columbus would not take "No" for an answer. For eighteen years he tramped round the courts and the great houses seeking for financial help to fit out a squadron to discover the new worlds on the other side of the seas.

Booker Washington would not take "No" for an answer. He wanted a university education. He heard of a college which would accept Negroes. He walked there, hundred of miles. When he arrived there, the college was full up; but he pleaded so hard that they gave him a job sweeping the floors and making the beds and cleaning the windows, and in the end he got in as a student, because he would not take "No" for an answer. Once, seeking to find a way to do something, he carried out more than seven hundred experiments, all of which ended in failure. "Now," he said cheerfully, "we know seven hundred ways not to do it," and carried on until he got the right way.

If we want really to get somewhere, we must be of those people who won't take "No" for an answer.

The Syro-Phoenician woman found the value of a cheerful answer.

We very often fail to get something because we meet a first refusal with a burst of bad temper or with black looks or with obvious resentment, and because we turn away with every line of our body showing how angry we are. If instead of that, we answered with a laugh and a jest, we might very well get what we want.

Perseverance plus cheerfulness will get a man almost anywhere. Even if they don't get him all the way, they will still make him laugh wherever he arrives.

The world needs people like that.

THE TRAPPINGS April 4

There is an old Roman story which tells how one of the Emperors was celebrating a triumph and was leading his victorious troops through the streets of Rome.

The streets were crowded with people, and at a certain point on the route a platform had been erected from which the Empress and the Enperor's family might see this scene.

The route was lined with great tall Roman legionaries fully armed. When the procession was coming near the platform where the Empress and the children were, the Emperor's little son jumped down off the platform, burrowed his way through the crowd and was just about to run out on the road to intercept his father's imperial chariot.

One of the legionaries who were lining the road, picked him up and held him. "You can't run out there," he said. "Don't you know who that is who is just about to ride by? That's the Emperor. You can't run out to him." The little lad laughed at the legionary. "He may be your Emperor," he said, "but he's my father."

This kind of thing has a two-way effect.

It is the loveliest thing in the world to have someone who likes you and loves you and knows you for what you are, and who never even thinks of the labels and the values the world puts on you.

But in the second place, there is something else which is much more alarming. When you take off the labels, when you take off the disguise, when you take off the importance which the world attaches to you, what is left? What is the real person who is beneath them all? Here is the acid test. What are we, stripped of everything except ourselves?

That is the way in which God sees us. He sees us stripped of the externals and the labels and the rank which the world attaches to us.

And it is just exactly that that ought to make us think of what we are doing with life.

WATCH IT!   April 5

What kind of example are we setting our children?

What are we making our children think of marriage and of the relationship of husband and wife within the home?

Do we make them think of marriage as a relationship in which two people are for ever bickering and quarrelling about this, that and the next thing, a relationship in which two people spend their lives snapping at each other? Or do we make them think of marriage as a relationship in which two people are in perfect harmony and perfect accord with one another?

Is the child being brought up all unconsciously to think of marriage as an uneasy and unhappy and uncomfortable relationship and to think of the home as the arena of a series of squabbles and fights? Or is he being brought up to think of marriage as the most perfect of relationships and the home as a place of comradeship and togetherness and peace?

That is the question; each of us must answer it for ourselves.

What are we making our children think of work?

Are we making them think of work as something in which it is the right thing to do as little as possible and to expect as much reward as possible? Are we teaching them to think of work as something in which it is a clever thing to "pull a fast one" on our employer or our boss? Are we teaching them that profitable little dishonesties are clever and praiseworthy so long as you get away with them?

Or are we teaching them that there is in fact no satisfaction like the satisfaction of a task well done, that there are people who are more concerned to do a job well, than to watch the clock and to count the wage, that petty dishonesty is something with which a Christian must have nothing to do?

This is the question; each of us must answer it for ourselves.

What are we making our children think of the Church?

Are we making them think of the Church as something to which we have to be grudgingly compelled every now and then to make some gift? Or are we making them think of the Church as a place to which, like the Psalmist, we are glad to "go up", a place where we find our friends, and to help which is a pleasure and a privilege?

Imitation is a God-given faculty for it is by imitating that we learn. We who are parents must remember the responsibility of being imitated by the children whom God has entrusted to our care.

LIGHT   April 6

In the primitive districts of India there are, of course, no lights in the streets or in the houses. The lighting is still with the simple little oil lamps that people were using back in the time when Jesus lived in the flesh.

In one of these country districts of India is a temple. And hanging from the roof of it there is a great brass structure with one hundred different places in it into which the little lamps may fit. There are no lamps in it, and until lamps are put into it the temple is dark.

When the people come in the dark to worship, each of them comes with his little lamp to guide him along the dark roads and streets. When they come to the temple, and when they enter it, they each of them take their own lamps and carry them to the great brass fitting and fix them into a place there.

At first the temple is dark; but, as each worshipper comes and places his lamp, bit by bit the temple grows lighter and lighter, until, when all the hundred places are filled with the lamps which the worshippers bring, the temple is a blaze of light.

There is a parable there. It is the worshippers who bring the light to that temple; and every congregation brings—or fails to bring—something to church with them.

It is not the minister alone who makes or unmakes a church service. The congregation has just as much to do with it as any minister has.

There are churches where there is such an atmosphere of eagerness and expectation that the preacher is fired by it as he enters his pulpit; there are churches with such an atmosphere of listlessness and apathy and disinterest that the preacher feels he is battering against a brick wall.

There are churches where the atmosphere is so warm in heart that the preacher cannot help kindling in response; there are churches with such a spiritual chill in them that they cause a shiver in the heart.

There are churches where the atmosphere is so kindly that the preacher finds that even a poor sermon somehow aquires a radiance; there are churches where the atmosphere is so critical and unsympathetic that even a sermon written in a man's heart's blood falls lifeless and dead from his lips.

Any preacher knows that it is the congregation which makes a service, it is the congregation which preaches more than half the sermon for better or worse.

BE PREPARED!   April 7

It would make a tremendous difference if every congregation would do certain things.

When we come to church, we ought to come prepared.

There are so very few people who make any preparation for worship at all. They have to hurry to get ready; they have to hurry down the road; they take their places almost at the last moment; and there is no preparation at all.

If every person who comes to church would, before he comes, or even on the road there, think of God for just a moment or two, and say a prayer for himself and for the preacher and the people who will meet in worship, it would make a whole world of difference.

We should come seeking.

To come to the services of the church should never be simply a matter of habit, a burden of duty, a hallmark of respectability, the satisfying of a convention. It should be a deliberate attempt to come out of the world and to find contact with God.

One of the great secrets of success in any of the business of life is to know what we want, when we are doing a thing; and when we come to church we should want God.

We should come determined to give all of ourselves.

He who comes to church only to get will, in the end, get nothing. We should come determined to give our interest, our prayer, our devotion, our sympathy. The success of any gathering, the happiness of any party, is always dependent on the people who are prepared to give themselves to the fellowship of the occasion.

So with the church. Sometimes we hear people say, "I've stopped going to church, because I don't get anything out of the services". We might well ask them, "What have you tried to give to the services in loving devotion and in humble fellowship with your fellow-men?"

If we bring, not only our physical bodies, but also our hearts, our love, our devotion, our prayers to the services of the church, we shall certainly go out again in the company of him who is "the Light of the World".

MODERATION BUT . . .   April 8

There is a great deal of value and a great deal of truth in the advice which tells us to avoid extremes, to study moderation in all things, and always to seek the golden mean.

The person who oscillates between glowing enthusiasm and complete despair is an unsatisfactory person. The person who plunges from radiant joy to unrelieved gloom is a difficult person. We say of such people that they have no halfway house. Such people are often at the mercy of trifles, and they rocket their way through life swinging from one extreme to the other.

It is quite true that the man who pursues a steady, even course, the man whom nothing uplifts too much, and nothing casts down too much, the solid and imperturbable, and—to use a modern vivid coinage—the "unflappable" man, is indeed a valuable person to have beside you in any undertaking.

But although there is truth in the advice which bids us to seek the golden mean and to avoid extremes, it is by no means the whole truth. The Greek suspected enthusiasm; the one man whom the Greek could not understand was the fanatic.

There is a sense in which for the Christian enthusiasm is the one essential quality, and the fanatic is the man who matters most of all.

The great point at issue is this—the attitude of mind behind the advice to avoid extremes is the attitude of mind which regards playing safe as the most important thing in life. If, for instance, we always pursue a cautious prudence in speech, we will certainly never offend anyone else, and we will certainly never get into trouble ourselves. But, at the same time, we will never be able to say the things which rebuke men's sins and challenge their minds, and stir their hearts.

If we insist on following the middle and the cautious course of action, we will quite possibly make no glaring mistakes, but we will never at any time produce the heroic and the sacrificial actions which really matter in their effect on men. The one thing that the Christian cannot ever do is to play safe.

"All things in moderation" is prudent advice, and it has its value; but all things for Christ with an even reckless extravagance is the law of the Christian way.

95

Charm is one of the greatest of all gifts.

You remember how Maggie, in Barrie's play *What Every Woman Knows*, describes charm: "Oh, it's—it's a sort of bloom on a woman. If you have it, you don't need to have anything else; and if you don't have it, it doesn't matter what else you have."

Everyone knows the people who have charm. To meet people with charm is a happy experience. They can bring the sunshine on a rainy day. They can make other people their willing servants. They can persuade people to do what anyone would have thought they could never dream of doing.

There is a strength in charm like the strength of the sun which melts the ice.

But charm is one of the most dangerous gifts that any person can have.

There are two dangers in charm.

The first is that a person should use it to get away with something they have done. So often a person with charm can talk and smile and "blarney" his way out of any situation, so that there comes a time when he comes to depend on that. He thinks that he can talk his way out of any trouble he has got into or any mistake that he has made.

The second danger is that a person with charm should try to make his charm a substitute for deeds, that he should try to make pleasant words and attractive mannerisms and fascinating smiles take the place of the things he ought to do.

Pitt, the great Prime Minister, had as a friend a Scotsman called Dundas. He had grown to depend on Dundas very greatly. He said of Dundas: "Dundas is no orator; Dundas is not even a speaker; but Dundas will go out with you in any kind of weather."

Dundas had none of the showy qualities and little of the superficial charm which fascinates and attracts, but he had something greater—you could depend on him hail, rain or shine!

Goodness *and* cleverness, charm *and* efficiency—a Christian ought to have all these qualities.

"NO" April 10

A good test of a person is whether or not he instinctively says "No" when he is asked to do something.

Men and women can be classified into two groups—those who instinctively say "Yes" when they are asked for help, and those who instinctively say "No". I sometimes think that if I were choosing a colleague to work with, the first thing I would ask about would not be his university degrees and certificates, and his academic distinctions, but, "Is he obliging or disobliging?"

By far the best kind of person to have around is the kind of person who is always ready to say "Yes" when you ask him to do something.

But the tragedy of life is that it is not only to our fellow-men that we so often say "No"; we so often say "No" to God. We know that conscience is directing us somewhere; we know, in our heart of hearts, that there is a call to do something, but so often we say "No".

You can see this happening even with our prayers. So many people try to use prayer in the wrong way altogether. They continuously try to use prayer as a way of escape, as a way of averting something that they believe is going to happen. Their whole attitude in prayer, conscious or unconscious, is that they are always begging God to change his mind to suit them.

For them, prayer is a way of saying to God, "Your will be changed." It is not a way of saying to God, "Your will be done."

There can be no real happiness in life, there can be nothing but discontent and resentment and bitterness, until we learn to say "Yes" to God.

This is really another way of saying that there is one person to whom it is often right to say "No"; and that one person is ourselves. "If any man will come after me", Jesus said, "let him deny himself" (Matt. 16:24). Let him say "No" to himself.

The New English Bible translates this very well: "He must leave self behind". We must learn to say "Yes" to men's appeal for help, to say "Yes" to God's ordering of our lives, but to say "No" to ourselves.

EARLY TO RISE   April 11

George Johnstone Jeffrey (whom I have already quoted) was a saint and a man of devotion. His advice is most practical. He had a favourite text—he quotes it twice in his lectures—"Hast thou commanded the morning?" (Job 38:12).

He uses this text in the most down to earth way. "I am weighing my words," he says, "when I say that if there is one habit more than another that has been of value in the art of preaching it is that of early rising."

A minister is his own master as far as time is concerned; and there is no profession in which it is so fatally easy to waste time.
The office-worker has to be at his desk at a set time; the factory worker has to be at his bench or his machine at a given time. There is no one and nothing to compel the minister to start work at any time—except his conscience.

The minister should be as meticulous in getting to his desk at a fixed time as any office or factory worker is.

The minister is at everyone's beck and call, not eight hours a day, but twenty-four hours a day.

His job is comparable with the job of the doctor, in that it is never done. He can never close his door and he can never refuse an appeal for help. Meticulous he must be as to when he begins, but he has no claim at all as to when he is to end.

No work that is done in a hurry is well done.
Chaucer, as Johnstone Jeffrey reminds us, said:

> There is workeman
> That can both worken well and hastilie.
> This must be done at leisure, par-faitilie.

Neither can a sermon be flung together at the last minute.
A. J. Gossip used to commend to us, his students, the example of a certain famous preacher who always rose early, dressed fully, and immediately after breakfast, put on his boots. He knew the psychological effect of slippers, and he avoided them!
"Hast thou commanded the morning?"
Happy is the man who can answer, "Yes!"

J. H. Jowett said, "I have been greatly impressed in recent years by one refrain which I have found running through many biographies. Dr. Parker repeated again and again, 'Preach to broken hearts'."
Ian Maclaren said, "The chief end of preaching is comfort."
Dr. Dale said, "People want to be comforted ... They need consolation— really need it, and do not merely long for it."
Johnstone Jeffrey, to quote this saintly man again, tells how George Eliot found a healing power in Thomas à Kempis's *Imitation of Christ* in that "it was not written by one reclining on velvet cushions, for those walking the hard, stony way with bleeding feet".

People need comfort in sorrow.
There would be one way to ensure that sorrow never entered into life, and that would be never to love anyone. Wherever there is love, there will also be sorrow. This means that almost everyone in this world will at some time, know tears and a broken heart.
There is no congregation in the world where there is not someone who is sad. It is the preacher's duty to bring comfort to them.

People need comfort in sin.
In every congregation, there are those who are suffering from a sense of sin —in some, an acute agony, in some a dull hopelessness, in some a vague

dispeace. But it is there. There are those in whom realisation of, and penitence for, sin has never been awakened. It must be awakened. But, in their case, too, after the awakening, there must come the message of comfort.

"Comfort ye, comfort ye, my people, says your God," Isaiah wrote (Isa. 40:1). The Greek word for "to comfort", a great word, is the verb *parakalein*. Besides meaning to comfort, it means to exhort, to encourage, to make men able to stand upon their own two feet and meet life undefeated and unbowed.

ADVERTISEMENTS   April 13

The Christian is a living epistle known and read of all men, an open letter, an advertisement for Christianity (2 Cor. 3:2, 3).

We are so to live that when people see the good we do they may give praise to our Father in heaven (Matt. 5:16).

Just how do we measure up to this demand that the Christian life should be the only effective advertisement for Christianity?

Advertising consists in making a claim.

Christianity claims that it gives rest and joy and peace and power. Is there in our lives a calm serenity, a radiant happiness, a power to cope with life that the non-Christian does not possess? Or are we just as worried and anxious, just as gloomy and grumbling, just as liable to collapse as the next man?

We cannot expect others to want Christianity, if it apparently makes no difference at all.

Advertising makes comparisons.

By implication one product is compared with another so that by the comparision its superior quality may be seen.

We say that Christianity alone can save the world; we claim that it is better than any other religion. You can only judge a religion by the people it produces; there is no other standard available.

How, for instance does the devotion of the Christian to his Church compare with the devotion of the Communist to his party?

When we compare the churchman with the person who never goes to church at all, is there any discernible difference? If not, how can we really expect anyone who is not a Christian to want to be a Christian?

Advertising makes promises.

It promises that the article advertised will provide this or that service or give this or that satisfaction.

The Christian Church promises to supply fellowship, human and divine. Does it? Does the outside world really look upon the Church as a society of friends with an open door and an open heart and an open hand for all who will come in?

Are *you* a good advertisement for Jesus Christ?

THE PROPHET

The prophet is a man with a seeing eye.

In the Old Testament, the prophets were the men who could see what was happening. They could see the way history was shaping. Others would be busy dashing about trying to arrange alliances and treaties with Egypt, with Syria, or with some other power. The prophet was the man who saw deeper than superficial power relationships. He saw the nation's destiny.

Every country in the world needs its prophet.

The prophet is the man with the listening ear.

The first thing Samuel had to say was, "Speak, Lord, for thy servant heareth!"

We are often so busy talking, discussing and arguing that we have no time for listening. Even when we pray we are so busy telling God what we want him to do that we have no time to listen to what he wants us to do.

The prophet had the listening ear.

We need that too.

The prophet has a courageous voice.

He tells the truth whatever the cost. "We cannot but speak the things we have seen and heard," said Peter and John to the Sanhedrin. The prophet never buys security with a cowardly silence.

The prophet has a dedicated life.

Said Isaiah to God when he learned there was work to be done, "Here am I, send me." He had to do not what he himself wanted to do, but what God needed him to do.

God needs people of dedication, like the prophets.

The prophet is a man with a dangerous occupation.

Jerusalem was the city that stoned the prophets (Matt. 23:37). Stephen told the Jews that they had consistently stoned the prophets (Acts 7:52).

No one can be a prophet who is not prepared to take a risk for God.

THERE'S POWER IN THE WORD!

Tokichi Ishii had a record of savage and beastly cruelty that was almost without equal. With almost fiendish brutality he had murdered men, women and even children, and had pitilessly and cold-bloodedly removed anyone who stood in his way. At last the law caught up with him. He was captured; he was in prison awaiting execution.

While he was in prison, he was visited by two Canadian ladies who tried to talk to him through the prison bars. They were unable to make even the very slightest impression on him. He merely glowered back at them like a wild animal.

In the end they left a Bible with him, in the faint hope that the Bible might be able to make the appeal that no human words had been able to make.

Then the thing happened. He began to read, and the story so gripped him that he could not stop. He read on until he came at last to the story of the Crucifixion. It was the words, "Father, forgive them, for they know not what they do," that broke down his last resistance. "I stopped, he said. "I was stabbed to the heart, as if pierced by a five-inch nail. Shall I call it the love of Christ? Shall I call it his compassion? I do not know what to call it. I only know that I believed and that the hardness of my heart was changed."

Later, says A. M. Chirgwin, as he retells the story in *The Bible in World Evangelism*, when the jailer came to lead the doomed man to the scaffold, he found, not the surly, hardened brute he expected, but a smiling, radiant man, for Ishii the murderer had been born again!

The power of Scripture to make its own effect is something which has been demonstrated again and again.

The unique thing about the Bible is that it does all three things. It informs us about Jesus, for it is the only book with a first-hand account of the life of Jesus upon earth. It reforms us, for in it we find the ideal and the standard by which we ought to live; in it we find the law of God by which life must be lived. It shows us ourselves as we are and life as it should be, and it shames and challenges us into reformation. It transforms us because in it we are brought face to face with that grace and that power in which all things are made new.

Information, reformation, transformation—the Bible has them all.

THE HAND OF GOD   April 16

A story is told of John Ruskin, the famous art critic and artist. One day a lady, who was a friend of his, showed him a handkerchief made of very precious material. A blot of indelible ink had fallen upon it, and the lady was lamenting to Ruskin that the very valuable handkerchief was ruined beyond repair.

Ruskin asked if he might have it. The lady said that of course he could have it, but she could not see why he should want the ruined piece of material. Some days later Ruskin brought the handkerchief back, and on it, beginning from the blot, and making the blot the centre of the whole matter, Ruskin had drawn the most intricate and beautiful pattern and design.

God has a way of taking the most unlikely things, and of somehow fitting them into his purposes and using them for his plans. In everything God works for good (Rom. 8:28).

God can make pain and sickness work for good.

Robert Leighton, the Scots divine, after a serious illness, said, "I have learned more of God since I came to this bed than in all my life before."

It was out of the thorn in his flesh that Paul discovered the all-sufficient grace of God (2 Cor. 12:7–9).

Many a man has discovered God in illness in a way in which he never discovered him in health.

God can make sorrow work for good.

God can make even sin work for good. It is in sin that a man finds the real wonder of the grace and the forgiveness of God.

God, in his providence, is still able to fit all things into his pattern and to work all things together for good.

FOLLOW ME!   April 17

Garibaldi, the liberator of Italy, after the siege of Rome in 1849 issued the following proclamation: "Soldiers, all our efforts against superior forces have been unavailing. I have nothing to offer you but hunger and thirst, hardship and death; but I call on all who love their country to join with me."

They joined in their hundreds.

When Jesus invited men to follow him, what he offered them was a job to do. "Come," he said, "follow me, and I will make you fishers of men." (Matt. 4:19). He did not keep them with him; he sent them out, and sent them out with the clear warning that there was trouble ahead (Matt. 10:5–42). His last words to them were, "Go! Preach!" (Matt. 28:19). What he left them was a task, the task of being witnesses for him and to him (Acts 1: 8).

Repeatedly Jesus spoke to men just as much about what they could do for him as about what he could do for them. He appealed to men to come to him, not only for what they could get, but also for what they could give.

In the present situation there are things for which we might well appeal to men to take their stand with Jesus Christ and with his Church.

Men are needed today to preserve the moral standards by which society is held together.

Men are needed today to preserve the standards of liberty and of freedom which cost so much to achieve.

There is today a danger to the very principles of democracy. There are possible situations today in which the very organisations and institutions which were founded to maintain the liberty of the individual can be used to destroy that liberty. No democracy can exist without the Christian conception of man.

We have a right to say today, "Come and stand with us for the standards without which freedom and liberty cannot survive."

Paul was quite certainly not a handsome man. In the third-century work called the "Acts of Paul and Thecla", there is a description of Paul which is so unflattering that it must be genuine: "A man of little stature, thin-haired upon the head, crooked in the legs, of good state of body, with eyebrows joining and nose somewhat hooked." Certainly, from the point of handsome looks, no one would have looked twice at this man Paul.

Still further, strangely enough, it seems that Paul was not even a very good speaker, and that he was certainly no orator. The Corinthians said of him that "his bodily presence is weak, and his speech of no account" (2 Cor. 10:10).

Paul was not alone in this. One of the most crowd-drawing preachers Scotland has ever seen was Thomas Chalmers; and they said of him that, when he preached, he never lifted his head from his manuscript, that he actually followed the line he was reading with his finger as he read, and that he read in a broad Fifeshire accent innocent of any elocutionary attraction.

Paul apparently had none of the gifts—and yet there can have been few preachers in history who were more effective. Where did this effectiveness come from?

Paul's effectiveness came from one thing. It came from an unanswerable experience of Jesus Christ.

Polish and elegance can often leave a congregation quite cold; experience and sincerity can never fail to move men.

You can never bring to anyone else an experience which you have not had yourself.

In any illness there are certain steps which must be gone through before a cure is possible.

There must be diagnosis by the doctor.
The doctor must be able to put his finger on the spot and to say that this and this is wrong. The most alarming illnesses and the most difficult to deal with are the illnesses in which no one can quite discover what is wrong. You cannot even begin to treat an illness until you find out what is wrong.

There must be acceptance by the patient.
The patient must accept the verdict and the diagnosis of the doctor. If he completely refuses to believe that there is anything wrong, and if he persists in going on as if nothing was wrong, then he cannot be cured.

There must come next the prescribed treatment by the doctor.
The sole purpose of the diagnosis of the trouble is that the treatment which will work a cure must be prescribed.

There must follow acceptance on the part of the patient.

If the patient does not accept the treatment, if he refuses to have the operation, if he pours the bottle of medicine down the drain and throws the box of pills out of the window, if he totally disregards the diet prescribed, then he cannot hope for a cure.

A man is not only a body; a man is also a soul, a spirit, a mind. And the state of a man's mind and soul and spirit can be such as to hinder the prescribed cure or even to make it totally ineffective. The spirit, the mind, must be right before the body can be cured.

For a complete cure two things are necessary: the best medical treatment, willingly accepted, and the most intense prayer, faithfully offered.

When that happens, then the spirit is in a condition for the body to be cured. For then the grace of God co-ordinates with the skill of man, that skill which God himself has given.

THE GREAT MAN   April 20

One of the greatest castles in England is Arundel Castle, and one of the greatest of all the English aristocracy is the Duke of Norfolk to whom that castle belongs.

Once a certain Duke of Norfolk happened to be at the railway station, when a little Irish girl arrived off the train with a very heavy bag. She had come to be a maidservant at the castle.

The castle is about a mile from the station and the little Irish girl was trying to persuade a porter to carry her heavy bag to the castle, for which she offered him a shilling, all the money that she had. The porter contemptuously refused. The Duke stepped forward, shabby as usual in appearance. He offered to carry her bag to the castle, took it and walked beside her along the road to the castle, talking to her.

At the end of the journey, he gratefully accepted the shilling she offered him, never allowing her to know who he was; and it was only the next day, when she met her employer, that the little Irish girl knew that the Duke of Norfolk had carried her bag from the station to the castle and that she had tipped him a shilling!

A very wonderful story of a true nobleman that tells us a good many things about this kind of man!

It is never safe to judge a man by externals.
A great man is always a thoughtful man.
There is grace in taking as well as giving.
The truly great man does not think of his place or his prestige.
It is only little people who think how great they are.

It is only unimportant people who think how important they are. There is nothing in this world which is a surer sign of a small mind than the complaint that one did not get one's place; and there is no motive in this world that is more wrong than the desire for prestige.

In the last analysis, to the truly great man, no act of service can possibly be humiliating.

No task, if it is going to help anyone else, can possibly be beneath his dignity.

It is enough surely for the disciple that he should be as his Lord. The man who "fixes his eye upon Jesus" sees that loving service is the loveliest thing in the world.

LEARNING, LIGHT, LAUGHTER   April 21

One morning, I was coming across from our main University buildings in Glasgow to the Divinity Hall, Trinity College, with four other members of our staff in my car. We reached Trinity College, and as we were getting out of the car one of my passengers began to laugh. "Just look what you've got lying on your back window ledge," he said. And lying on the back window ledge there was a copy of Karl Barth's commentary on Philippians, a copy of the A.A. Roadbook of England and Wales—and two comics called "Judy" and "Bunty", which my daughter Jane had left in the car. The combination of Barth, the A.A., "Judy" and "Bunty" amused my friend.

But there is not much wrong with that combination, because it seems to me to represent three basic needs in life.

There was something to learn.

There was Karl Barth's excellent book on the letter to the Philippians.

By far the most astonishing thing about the Bible is that the longer you study it the more interesting it becomes.

I entered Trinity College as a student in 1929, which means that the study of the Bible, and in particular of the New Testament, has been the main activity of my life for thirty-three years, and I still find that there are so many things about it to know and to learn, and so many things of absorbing interest of which I have touched only the fringes, and so many things which I have not yet studied at all. There is a certain limitless quality about Scripture.

There was something to guide me.

There was the A.A. Roadbook to enable me to find the way from place to place in parts of the country which are strange to me. We need something to guide us.

We have been given things to guide us. We have God's Book; we have the example and the counsel and sometimes the warning and the rebuke of those whom we respect and admire; we have the fellowship of the Church; we have the traditions into which we have entered; and we have the voice of conscience speaking inside us.

There was something to give me laughter.

There was Jane's "comics". The man who can do without relaxation has still to be born.

Learning, light, and laughter—a well proportioned and an efficient life needs all three.

There are three reasons why people yawn.

They yawn because they are tired and therefore sleepy.

When you come to think of it, this must be one of the sleepiest generations in history. On any train or bus or even tube journey you will see people asleep, or at least with their heads nodding. You see people asleep in church— although that's no new thing—and, what is more surprising, you even see them asleep in a cinema!

Sleep is a very wonderful thing. I know that it is a mistranslation, but it is an inspired mistranslation, when the Bible says, "He giveth his beloved sleep." Sleep in itself, apart from any drugs and medicines, is the best of all cures. Not to be able to sleep is the worst of all afflictions.

We yawn because we are tired, because we are hungry, and because we are bored.

How to stop yawning? I think of three great statements and promises and claims of Jesus Christ.

Jesus said (as the N.E.B. so beautifully translates it): "Come to me all those whose work is hard, whose load is heavy; and I will give you relief" (Matt. 11:28).

When he was an old man of nearly eighty, in spite of his travelling and his writing and his preaching and his organising, John Wesley said that he had not known what it was to be tired for years.

Jesus is the rest-giver to the tired.

Jesus said: "I am the bread of life; he that comes to me shall not hunger, and he who belives in me shall never thirst" (John 6:35).

There is a hunger of the body and the soul. Jesus has the food in the strength of which a man may go for many days (1 Kings 19:8).

Jesus said: "I am come that they may have life. and have it abundantly" (John 10:10).

Jesus offers real Life. In living this life no man can ever be bored.

THE PERSONAL TOUCH   April 23

There are some things that make all the difference to life.

We all like to be treated as persons.

The great danger in any well organised welfare state is that men and women begin to be treated as numbers on a schedule, types of a certain group of some kind or other, entries on a schedule. Everyone knows what a difference it makes when an official treats us as a person, when a doctor seems interested in us as someone with a name and a home and a problem and not as a case. Men and women are individual persons and can only be treated as such.

We all like people to be interested in us.

We all know what a difference it makes to be served by a shop assistant who is really trying to help and not by one of these take-it-or-leave-it-I-couldn't-care-less characters who are behind some counters. Charm is really the attitude of one who obviously cares.

We all like to be remembered.

It is very pleasant to go into a restaurant where the waiter remembers you, or where the waitress smiles at you like a returned friend. It is one of life's grimmest experiences to be introduced to someone, and then to meet him a second time and find that he has not the slightest recollection of ever having seen you before!

We all like to have our likes and dislikes remembered.

I am sadly conscious of how easy it is to do things which, if I stopped to think, I would remember got on the nerves of other people. All this is part of considerateness which is maybe life's greatest family and social virtue.

Jesus never treated two people in the same way. To every single invididual he made the personal approach; everyone to him was different; everyone was a person.

See in Jesus the personal touch.

Go and do likewise.

A WATCH   April 24

How like a good watch a good man is!

A watch counts the hours. So does the wise man.

"So teach us to number our days, that we may apply our hearts unto wisdom." (Psalm 90:12).

In the longest life, time is short. Like the watch, we should count the hours.

A watch keeps time well. The useful man is the punctual man.

An immense amount of time can be wasted in waiting for other people. "Punctuality," as someone has said, "is the politeness of princes." Unpunctuality is discourtesy.

It is bad to waste one's own time; it is worse to waste that of other people.

A good watch is well regulated. It is neither too fast nor too slow. The wise man never hurries and never loiters : he neither dashes nor lingers.
Without haste and without fuss, and yet without procrastination and without delay, he goes about his business.

A watch has a mainspring inside it, and it is the mainspring which keeps it going. The wise man has his strength within.
"The life which I now live is not my life," said Paul, "but the life which Christ lives in me." (Gal. 2: 20). The wise man's secret is the presence and the Spirit of Christ within his heart.

A watch is wound up by someone else. So the life of the good man does not spring from his own strength and his own methods.
His inspiration is Christ. He goes in the strength of the Lord.

A watch, when it is damaged, has to be returned to its maker.
It must be so all through life with us. When life goes wrong, and when we go wrong, then there is nothing to do but to take it back to God so that he may forgive and he may mend us to send us out to work better in the time to come.

A LIFE OF YOUR OWN   April 25

One of the insoluble problems of a man who becomes a public figure is that he no longer belongs to himself, or to his wife, or to his family. He begins to belong to the public; and there is a very real sense in which that has to be so.

A great surgeon cannot refuse to carry out an emergency operation because he happens to have planned a family party.

A great police officer cannot refuse a sudden investigation of a crime because he would like to spend a night at home.

A great statesman cannot refuse a tour of the country when he would much rather be with his family.

A parson cannot refuse a summons to comfort the sorrowing and soothe the troubled and the ill on an evening when he has planned an outing with his wife and children.

The demands of public life are merciless and inexorable on the man who has something which the public needs and demands.

This makes things very difficult for those who are nearest and dearest to him. Sometimes the human relationship collapses under the strain, as for instance in the tragic break-up of the marriage of Dick Sheppard, whose wife, in the end, left him.

Sometimes this relationship can be solved, as it was by Sangster. Soon after his marriage, Sangster said to his wife, "I can't be a good husband and a good minister. I'm going to be a good minister." He never took his wife and family out; he often forgot his wife's birthday unless he was reminded of it; he spent much of his time on preaching and lecturing tours at home and abroad.

As his son writes, "It all depends, of course, what you mean by a 'good husband'. If you mean a man who dries up as his wife washes the pots, or a handyman about the house, or even a man who takes his wife out for an occasional treat, then my father was the worst of all husbands.

"But if a 'good husband' is a man who loves his wife absolutely, expresses that love daily, asks her aid in all he does, and dedicates himself to a cause which he believes is greater than both of them, then my father was as good a husband as a minister."

All talent is a responsibility, and the greater the talent a man has, the less he belongs to himself. Jesus himself said that a man who puts even the dearest relationships of life before him is not worthy of him (Matt. 10:37, 38); but where love is great enough and where love lets itself be known, even this problem can be solved.

NEVERTHELESS   April 26

Howard Williams has said that often the whole of the Christian faith is contained in the word "nevertheless".

It happens when prayer seems to be unavailing.
Studdert Kennedy wrote of Jesus Christ:

> 'E prayed to the Lord, and 'e sweated blood,
> And yet 'e were crucified.

There is a time when all we can say is, "Nevertheless, not my will but thine be done".

It happens when faith seems to be a losing battle.
I have been reading William Purcell's magnificent biography of Studdert Kennedy, *Woodbine Willie*, and that book is full of this.

Studdert Kennedy had his own unorthodox way of putting things and once in his rich Irish brogue he announced from the pulpit to the shocked astonishment of a conventional congregation, "There comes a time in every man's life, when he must wonder what the hell it is all about." He wrote of himself, "Every man, whether Christian or not, must sooner or later stand in the last ditch face to face with the final doubt. I know that last ditch well. I have stood in it many a time; and I know that before I die I shall stand there again—and again." There is a time when there is nothing left to say but, "Nevertheless I do believe."

It happens when events are a complete contradiction of belief.

I turn again to Studdert Kennedy. Just before one of the summer battles on the Somme in 1916 Studdert Kennedy had a communion service. There was present a young corporal in the full glory of his splendid physical manhood. As he gave him the bread and the wine, Studdert Kennedy spoke the well known and well loved words: "The body of our Lord Jesus Christ, which was given for thee, preserve thy body and soul unto everlasting life . . . The Blood of our Lord Jesus Christ, which was shed for thee, preserve thy body and soul unto everlasting life." Three days later, as he wandered the post-battlefield he came on that same young corporal, a mutilated, shattered, dead body in a shell-hole.

How can any man relate the two things? There comes a time when a man can only say, "Nevertheless this will not take my faith away."

SHUT UP (1)   April 27

No man can love God without loving his fellow-men. If he says he does, then he does not know what loving God means. That is why the social gospel is never an addendum to Christianity but always the very centre of Christianity.

Once Henry Scott Holland said: "The more you are interested in the Incarnation, the more you must be concerned about drains."

If you believe that God was sufficiently concerned with humanity to take humanity upon himself, then you must also believe that God is concerned that men and women should have decent conditions to live in.

Bishop Weston of Zanzibar said at the Anglo-Catholic Congress in 1923, "It is folly, it is madness to suppose that you can worship Jesus in the Sacrament when you are sweating him in the bodies and souls of his children."

It is blindness to think that we can meet Christ in the Sacrament if we comfortably forget that he said that what we do and do not do to our fellow-men is done and not done to him.

Here is something that Studdert Kennedy himself saw with vivid intensity. He had no time for those whose religion consisted in making their communion and in long prayers and so forth and so on. It was in fact therein that he saw the failure of the Church. "We have been calling men to services," he said, "when what they wanted was the call to service."

In his book *The Word and the Work*, he said, "Nobody worries about Christ as long as he can be kept shut up in churches. He is quite safe there. But there is always trouble if you try to let him out."

Was there ever a time when Jesus Christ was more thoroughly shut up in the Church than he is today?

The tragedy of today is that there is a tacit kind of agreement, conscious or unconscious, that Christianity is impossible. And this agreement is not among non-Christians, but very often among Christians.

It is clear that Christianity is regarded as impossible in the international world.

A world which has agreed that the only way to keep peace is to possess so-called nuclear deterents has clearly come to the conclusion that Christianity can be written off as an impossibility in the relationship between nation and nation.

It is clear that Christianity is regarded as impossible in the industrial sphere.

It seems impossible for the two sides to sit down at any industrial dispute without each of them being firmly convinced that the one thing that matters is self-interest.

It is clear that Christianity is regarded as impossible in the political sphere.

Any politician who announced that he proposed to judge each issue in terms of soul and conscience and so to cast his vote would quite certainly be told in effect that the party whip was very much more important than his conscience, and that the party line was very much more important than the Christian gospel.

It is even clear—God forgive us—that Christianity is regarded as impossible in the Church.

Before a man, at least in certain quarters, is allowed to preach the gospel or to come to the communion table, the question that is asked is not, "Is he a Christian?" but, "To what denomination does he belong?"

We have come to a stage today when we are content to shut Christ up within the church, and when we quite bluntly regard it as impossible to bring Christianity into the ordinary concerns and affairs of the world. Christianity has become rather an optional extra on the circumference of life than a complete essential, dominating the whole of life. What happens if we let Christ out? That is not the question, for the question for the Christian ought always to be, not, "Is it safe?" but, "Is it right?"

I once visited that amazing parish church in Boston in Lincolnshire, one of the largest parish churches in all England. Boston is still busy, but compared with what it once was it is a little place, for there was a time when Boston was second as a seaport only to London. But still that famous tower, Boston Stump, stretches 275 feet into the sky, a landmark for miles around and a guide to the sailor at sea.

They say of Boston church that it is built in a very special way. They say that there are seven doors to stand for the seven days of the week; twelve pillars in the nave to stand for the twelve months; twenty-four steps to the library to stand for the hours of the day; fifty-two windows to stand for the weeks of the year; sixty steps to the chancel roof to stand for the seconds in a minute; 365 steps to the top of the tower, to stand for the days of the year. So if you know the way that Boston church is built, you cannot look at it without remembering the passing of time.

I have not yet reached the age of decrepitude, but it is worthwhile to stand and think what time has done to me.

There are things on the debit side.

Time certainly takes physical strength away.

There are things which are more of an effort and things which are impossible now.

I find myself forgetting much more readily than I used to.

Names and telephone numbers and the like escape the memory with an ease which they used not to do.

I find that I cannot work as fast as once I did ; things take just a little longer to do.

But I think that because they take longer they are maybe a little better done than once they were.

CREDIT   April 30

Here are some things on the credit side after half a century of life.

I find that I am much more sympathetic than once I was.

You cannot live for over half a century without seeing how easy it is to go wrong, and when someone does make a mistake now, I am much more likely to say with George Whitefield, "There but for the grace of God go I," than I am likely to condemn.

No one can pass the half century without having sorrowed and suffered, and to have sorrowed oneself is to be a little better able to help others who are going through it. The passing years bring sympathy—and that is no small gift.

I find that I am much more tolerant than once I was.

It is not that I am any less sure that certain things are right, and it is not that I am no longer willing to argue as hotly as I can, and even, as Goldsmith said of Dr. Johnson, to try to knock a man down with the butt-end of it, if my pistol misses fire! But I am very much more willing to admit that perhaps I may be wrong, and that there are many more ways to God than the way which I have found.

I think that the years do not make one any less sure that he is right, but they do make him less sure that everybody else is wrong.

I find that I am much more selective in what I undertake to do.

I suppose that sub-consciously one knows that time is not as long as once it was and one must concentrate on the things which really must be done. The years tend to give us a sense of proportion and a better ability to see what is important and what does not really matter.

As the years go on, you come to see time not as an enemy, but rather as a friend. For the odd thing about time is that, when one stands still and reckons up the balance, time gives as much as and probably more than it takes away.

May

As a motorist I have been very fortunate indeed. In twenty-nine years of driving I have only had one accident, and I have never yet been stuck on the road. But once I did run into trouble.

Late at night, when I was on my way home, a fault developed in the electrical system of my car. I knew that sooner or later the car would come to a dead stop and nothing except a tow would move it.

I have been a member of the Automobile Association for as long as I have been driving. I have always paid my subscription; I have always used the handbooks and the route books and all the helps to travelling; but in all those years, I have never had any occasion to call for help from the breakdown service. Then I needed it. I could call on it. I got it.

There is here a remarkably close parallel to what happens in life.

For long enough, life can go on smoothly, with an easy routine in which nothing happens with which we cannot deal. The road is pleasantly level. There may be no relaxation, but there is no effort which is beyond us. There may be no great joys, but there are no great sorrows. There may be no great flashes of vision, but there are no agonising struggles with evil. We can cope.

Then quite suddenly life falls in. There comes a demand for an effort which we know quite well is beyond us. There comes a temptation which we know we cannot struggle against. There comes an illness or a breakdown which lays us low. There comes a sorrow in which the sun sets at midday, and in which life becomes unbearable.

In that moment we turn to God, because, as Lincoln said, there is nowhere else to go. But it will make all the difference in that moment, first, if we know where to go, and second, if through all the years we have kept our contact with God and if we are going not to a stranger but to a familiar friend.

In other words, the better we know God, the easier it is to go to him when we need him so desperately; the more close we have kept our contact with him, the easier it is to find him.

How is this close contact with God to be kept in the routine of every day, when nothing special is happening?

We must listen daily to God.

It is well if, day by day, we go to God's word to see what it has to say to us, for then, when the time of need comes, the promises, which we already know as beautiful words, will suddenly become powerful realities.

We must daily speak to God.

There must be no day without that time of prayer which brings eternity near to time, and which brings God into the human situation.

We must think of God and remember God.

We shall do that best, if, week by week, we worship with his people in his house, and if we make God's day the day when we deliberately think of and remember God.

To come back to my car breakdown and A.A. membership mentioned yesterday it would have been easy to feel that, since nothing had happened for all these years, nothing would ever happen, and so to have said, "It's not worth while keeping up this contact. I'll let it go and not bother about it any more." Had I done that, then things would have been much more difficult when the time of need for help came.

So many people look on the Church as somewhere to go when life has fallen in, when they need comfort, when death enters the family circle.

So many people regard God as someone to be called in in the crisis and in the emergency. Even when things are like that, God's Church and God himself will not fail those who need help.

It is so much easier to find God on the dark day if we have walked every day with him, and to call upon him in trouble when we have been talking to him and listening to him and thinking of him every day and every week.

"Without me," said Jesus, "you can do nothing!" (John 15:5).
There are certain things for which we need and must have God.

We need God to show us what to do.

There are times when it is only God who can give us guidance. We cannot see a step ahead; only God can see the future and what is ultimately to our good.

It is so often so difficult to see things unclouded by our personal wishes and preferences and prejudices; it is so difficult, too, to see things through our own weakness and our own sin. The only way in which things can be seen in their true light is in the light of God. Only in his light do we see the light (Ps. 36:9). Only God can give us guidance as to what to do.

We need the courage to do what is right.

It is seldom that at the moment the right way is the easy way. It is human nature to avoid trouble and to take the easy way. It is only God who can give us the courage to do what is right, for it is one thing to know the right and quite another to do it.

Only God can give us the strength to bring the right thing to its appointed end.

We need the flash of light to show us the way; we need the surge of courage to set us out on the right way. But the really difficult thing is not to begin; it is to continue to the end.

It is only God who can give us power to resist the temptations to take the byways which lead to the far countries of the soul.

It was after the thrill of his baptism that the temptations came to Jesus. It is so often after we have made our decision to do something which is right that there come the temptations which seek to stop us.

If we are walking always in the presence of the living God and always in the companionship of the Risen Christ, then it is possible for us to walk through the world and to keep our garments unspotted by the world, because of the company in which we walk.

THE PASSER BY   May 4

Beside the still figure on the roadway, there knelt three people. One was a friend of the victim of the accident and she was very upset and quite helpless. The second was someone from the crowd who had come forward to offer what assistance he could. The third was a policeman who had taken his coat and made it a pillow for the injured woman and who was rendering first aid. That moment was a picture in miniature of life, for it was a study in reactions to the trouble and the distress of other people.

There was the person who had been the cause of the accident.

I cannot tell whether he was to blame or not, but he was certainly a very worried man.

Saul Kane, in John Masefield's *Everlasting Mercy*, was appalled at "the harm I've done by being me". If we would only think about the consequences of things before we act, we would often have to worry less about the results of things after we have acted.

117

There was the hurrying crowd which never even stopped.

Some of them would be too intent on their own business to have time to stop. There are people who deliberately avert their eyes, because their first instinct is to refuse to get involved in anyone else's troubles.

There was the friend fluttering helplessly.

One of the most heart-breakingly frustrating experiences in life is to see someone in trouble or courting trouble and to know that we cannot do anything about it. But to have to stand helplessly by is one of life's unhappiest experiences.

There was the passer by who went forward to help—one out of so many.

It is a sad commentary on the essential selfishness and self-centredness of human nature that only one was found to help.

There was the gaping crowd.

It is an odd fact of life that there are certain people who get a bigger kick out of hearing bad news about someone else than they do out of hearing good news. There are few lower occupations in this world than gaping curiously at the troubles of someone else.

There was the policeman.

Here was someone whose function was to help and who was equipped to render help. Here was the one whose first instinct would be not to run away from trouble and not to stand and look at trouble, but to run towards it and to do something about it—which is the Christian reaction.

LET GO!   May 5

If ever there was a time when the Church ought to be concentrating on the main thing, that time is today. If the Church is to face a situation in which the choice is Christ or chaos, then the Church needs to concentrate on the all-important things and let the lesser things go.

We must let our labels go.

Liberal, fundamentalist, radical, conservative, the labels which we attach to people in order to divide them into opposing parties, must go. Whatever our approach to it, we are all lovers of the Word of God.

We must let our sectional affiliations go.

Presbyterian, Baptist, Congregationalist, Anglican—the sectional affiliations must go. S.C.M., I.V.F., C.U., S.U.—the sectional loyalties must go. We often seem to be so busy arguing amongst ourselves that we forget that we are all supposed to be fighting against the devil and his angels.

We are not members of any section or party; we are Christians, and unless Christians stand united we cannot resist evil as we ought.

We must let our organisational differences go.

Bishop or Presbyter, even infant or adult baptism, questions of ordination and the validity of each other's orders, we must let them all go.

That the world is becoming increasingly pagan while we pursue our private warfares and theological arguments is the tragedy of the divided body of Christ.

We must let our old quarrels go.

There is a time to remember history and a time to forget history. When history is remembered as an inspiration it is good; when history is remembered as a means of maintaining divisions it is a curse.

We are in a position today when the Church is on the whole an ageing and shrinking community. We are in a situation when the advancing tide of paganism and secularism is running strongly. It is time to let a great many things go and remember the one thing on which there must be concentration—the fact that we stand for Jesus Christ in an increasingly Christless world.

"YOU", GOD   May 6

If I am broadcasting, and often in ordinary church services, I use in prayer "you" and not "thou" in address to God. I often receive a good many letters, not so much complaining or criticising, but sometimes regretting it and sometimes asking why. I would like to set down why I do this.

Jesus himself called God by the name "Abba" (Mark 14:36).

As Paul twice says, it is our Spirit-given privilege to do the same (Rom. 8:15; Gal. 4:6).

This word "Abba" was the word by which a young child called his father within the home circle in Palestine, as *jaba* still is in Arabic today.

In any ordinary context there is only one possible translation of this word. It is the English word "Daddy", precisely and exactly.

To call God by that name in English would sound fantastic and grotesque; but what the word does is to lay down once and for all our relationship to God. That relationship is the relationship of love, confidence, trust and intimacy which exists between a little child and his father.

If that be so—and it is so—it seems a contradiction in terms that we should address this God whom we know so intimately in Elizabethan English which no one has used for three hundred years.

I do not talk to my best friend like that.

God is my best friend.

How can I talk to *him* like that?

The Authorised Version of the Bible does in fact use exactly the same word for address to God and man.

In the Authorised Version both God and man are "thou". There is in fact no differentiation between address to God and address to man.

This is perfectly correct, because in Hebrew and in Greek and in seventeenth-century English the second person singular of the pronoun was in common use. It was in fact in English, as it is in French, the familiar usage to friends.

If, then, we are to follow the example of the Authorised Version, we will use the same pronoun to God as to men, and since in English we no longer use the second person singular pronoun, the pronoun we use *must* be "you".

Religion must always be contemporary.

COURTESY (1)   May 7

More than one attitude can be encountered in evangelism.

There is the evangelist who preaches with an unconscious superiority.

He utters his condemning tirades against the sinner, he dangles the sinner over the pit of hell; his stock in trade is largely threat and denunciation. He speaks from a height downwards; his whole assumption is that he speaks from a position of safety to those who are in peril.

Evangelism like that is far more likely to produce resentment than response.

There is a kind of pugnacious evangelism.

Its attitude is that there is no salvation outside its particular way of thinking, and that any theology which does not think as it thinks is a lie. It is marked by intolerance and by harsh criticism of all those who differ from it. It attempts to bring men to Christ, but it has not itself the spirit of Christ.

The highest and most effective kind of evangelism is marked by the basic quality of sympathy.

It does not stand over the sinner; it sits beside the sinner. It does not draw a distinction between itself and the sinner; it identifies itself with the sinner. It speaks as one hell-deserving sinner to another.

"True evangelism," as someone has said, "is one starving man telling another starving man where he has found bread."

We wonder sometimes why evangelism is not more effective than it is. So long as it speaks from above and so long as its accent is threat and condemnation, so long as it speaks with intolerance and limits the way to God to its way, it is bound to awaken nothing but resistance and resentment.

When it speaks with Christian courtesy, when its accent is sympathy and love, when it sits where the sinner sits, then it wins its victories for Christ.

Dryden once said of Jeremy Collier, "I will not say, 'the zeal of God's house has eaten him up', but I am sure it has devoured some part of his good manners and civility."

A man has a right to his own opinions and he has a right to state them.

I can never forget the vivid statement of Voltaire in speaking to someone with whose views he entirely disagreed: "I hate every word you say, but I would gladly die for your right to say it." Take away the right of liberty of opinion and freedom of speech and the very basis of democracy is gone.

It will be a bad day when Christianity has to defend itself by forcibly silencing those with whom it does not agree.

A man has a right to speak his own opinions, but equally he has a duty to listen to the opinions of others.

Nothing does a man more mental good than to listen to things with which he does not agree. Augustine Birrell once said that every man should be compelled to read the books which present the points of view opposite to his own.

Nothing stimulates the mind like listening to a contradiction of one's own thoughts. Belief never becomes really and truly ours until it has passed through tension and conflict; it has to come to birth in the cut-and-thrust of argument and debate; it has to be confirmed by attack and strengthened by opposition.

There are far too many people, and far too many alleged students and scholars, who refuse to look beyond their own version of the truth. To listen to the other side of the question can be a salutary experience.

TALE-BEARERS   May 9

The image of the Church is not the image of a community where there is nothing but peace and light and love; the image of the Church is that of a community in which more than a little time is spent in squabbling and in argument.

Now the reasons for trouble in a congregation do not vary very much.

There will be trouble because someone has not got his place.

In some way he has been slighted. He should have got a seat on the platform, but he didn't. His name should have appeared somewhere, and it didn't.

A Christian has only one place—Jesus said it—and that is the place of a servant (Mark 10:43, 44). His place is where Jesus's place was—at other people's feet (John 13:14). The minute people start worrying about their place they stop being Christian. If we want to carve out a personal career and to achieve personal prominence, then the sooner we get out of the Church the better.

There will be trouble because someone has not been thanked.

Someone's name has been accidentally omitted from the votes of thanks—and there will be trouble. Someone has given something, or done something, and it has not been noted, and publicly mentioned—and someone goes off in a huff.

There is no place in the Church for those who are in the work for their own sakes. The world is the place for them.

There will be trouble because someone said something about someone else, and that something reached the other person's ears (and it quite certainly did not reach them in the form in which it was said).

Whispering tongues, as Coleridge has it, can poison truth. They can disseminate a lie; they can destroy a friendship: they can murder a character and assassinate a reputation over the teacups; they can sow suspicion and dissension; they can ruin unity and they can break hearts. What crimes are committed by the tale-bearers!

PATIENT GOD   May 10

There is no time when we cannot go to God.

God does not work office hours or have his half day off. God neither slumbers nor sleeps; and he is always listening for his children's voices.

There is nothing too small to take to God.

John Baillie says somewhere, "If a thing is big enough to worry about, it is big enough to pray about." And very often the surest way to see whether or not a thing is big enough to worry about is to take it to God, for in God's presence things have a way of really appearing in their proper proportion.

There is nothing too private to take to God.

We can take to God the things we cannot take to anyone else. We may fear that others might laugh at our dreams and mock at our failures and misunderstand the secret of our thoughts. But God sees the inmost thoughts of a man. He knows them and with him we can share the things which we cannot share with anyone else. And there is nothing in the world like having someone to whom we can really and fully open our hearts.

There is nothing too shameful to take to God.

There are things which we seek to hide from men; there are things which we even seek to hide from ourselves; and often that process of hiding is what drives a man to a nervous collapse and breakdown. But we can tell God the worst as we can tell him the best.

There are in the world good people with hearts like a tideless pool and with blood whose temperature never rises to emotional or passionate boiling-point. There are people so constituted that there are temptations which they never experience and which they therefore can never understand. But the great fact about God is that he knows the human situation because in Jesus Christ he fully entered into it, and therefore he can understand.

Of all things about God maybe his patience is the greatest thing. He loves each one of us, as Augustine said, as if there was only one of us to love.

And love is the secret of patience, both human and divine.

NEVER TOO LATE (1) May 11

Part of my duties in Glasgow University is to teach Hellenistic Greek. Not very many people take the class because it is something of a specialist subject, although a necessity for those who want to read the New Testament in its original language.

A letter came to me from a lady who had been a schoolteacher in one of Glasgow's most famous schools for girls. After a long and honourable career in the teaching world, she had come to the age when she retired. And now she was well over sixty years of age.

The letter said that all her life this lady had wanted to study the New Testament in Greek. Now that she was retired, she said, she had time to do so. So she made a request—would she be allowed to attend the class of Hellen-. istic Greek as a student on the benches?

There was only one answer to that; it would be a pleasure and a privilege to have her. And so, since the beginning of October when the University term began, this lady of over sixty has sat on the benches of a University class-room, listening and taking notes with students a third of her age.

This is a magnificent example.

It is never too late to learn.

Cato lived in the days of the Roman Empire when Greek culture was invading Rome, and at the age of eighty he set himself to learn Greek.

At the age of seventy, Corot, the great painter, said, "If God spares me for another ten years, I think I may learn to paint."

Mozart was never an old man in years, for he died all too young. But when he was famous as one of the great ones even in his own lifetime, he was even then taking lessons in counterpoint and musical theory.

At the age of ninety Sir William Mulock, the Lord Chief Justice of Canada, said, "The best is yet to be, hidden beyond the hills of time."

If you want to stay alive, keep learning. For one of the tragedies of life is that there are so many people who are physically alive, but who are mentally and spiritually dead.

It is never too late to go back to school.

Emile Cammaerts, as John Baillie reminded us, said that the first rule of life with which any young person should start out is never to close the book of life until we have read the last page of it. The Christian is told that he must have the childlike spirit; and one of the great characteristics of childhood is that it is the age for learning.

It would be no bad thing for all of us—it would be something to keep alive the vital interest of life—to learn some new subject every year in life.

It is never too late to make a new beginning.

One of the features of a modern divinity college is the number of older men who come into it. There come men who have been headmasters in schools or who have held high executive and administrative offices in the educational world. There come men who have held high posts in industry, in commerce, in the newspaper world.

Time and again these are the most vivid and vital people in the college. They are beginning a new job when other people are stopping working. Life for them is beginning when life for other people is stopping; and it keeps them young, young in body, young in mind and young in heart.

How different life would be for many people if they saw the end of one career as the beginning of another! They might well see the end of the work which hitherto claimed them as the beginning of the work which they always in their heart of hearts wanted to do.

It is never too late to seek a newer world, in the strength of him who makes all things new.

WELCOME   May 13

I worshipped once, to my great pleasure and profit, in Martyrs' Church, St. Andrews. St. Andrews is a world famous holiday resort, as every golfer knows. During the summer months especially, many visitors find their way into the pews of the St. Andrews churches.

I was a stranger in Martyrs' that day. No sooner had I sat down than I noticed a little white card in the book board in front of me, and I noticed that similar cards were laid out along all the book boards. I took it up and read it, and my heart was strangely warmed for the little card ran:

> We welcome you to our Church and Fellowship
> and extend Christian greetings to you.

I did not feel a stranger any more.

After the service I told one of the office-bearers what a fine idea I thought this was, and how much I personally had appreciated it, and he at once went on to tell me about two other cards which Martyrs' Church uses.

The first is put into the pews on Communion Sundays and it runs:

> The minister, kirk session and congregation of
> Martyrs' Church, St. Andrews, welcome you to the
> fellowship of the Lord's Table.

I know how touched I would have been to find that card in my pew had I happened to come to Martyrs' on a Communion Sunday.

But perhaps the third card is the most original of all. It is a card which the members of Martyrs' Church take with them when they go to other congregations, for instance when they are away on holiday, and it runs:

> As a visitor to this Church, I bring warm
> Christian greetings to all who worship here
> from Martyrs' Church, St. Andrews.

And the members of Martyrs' Church leave that card in the churches in which they happen to worship.

I don't know who first thought of all this, and I certainly don't know how many other churches may do this, but this is a splendid idea. I wish that many more congregations would take it up and practise it.

"SHOW ME . . . !"   May 14

On the basis of what he sees of them, the man outside the Church has come to the conclusion that the claims made for and by Christians are just not true. To him it must seem that Christians are forever offering to others things which they quite certainly do not possess themselves.

Just think of some of the claims which so-called Christianity makes.

It claims that Christianity is the religion of joy, and yet it would be difficult to find a more joyless thing than that which many people produce as Christianity.

It claims that Christianity is the religion of peace, but the majority of Christians are just as worried as anyone else, and the Church spends a lot of its time trembling for the ark.

It claims to be the religion of power, but Christians are not noticeably more able to cope with life, nor are they notably more efficient, than anyone else. It claims to be the religion of service, and yet Christians are just as selfish and comfort-loving as men of the world.

It claims to be the religion of love and forgiveness, and yet it is the truth that there is more strife and squabbling in the Church than in any other institution in this troubled world. The church where there are no feuds and resignations is the exception rather than the rule.

Nietzsche, the German pagan philosopher, said bluntly, "Show me that you are redeemed and then I will believe in your redeemer."

It is not an unfair demand.

Christianity will only become effective when Christians become as Christian as their claims.

A MUST   May 15

There are compelling reasons why church attendance is necessary to keep the Christian life alive, and to fulfil the duties of the Christian life. So it is worth looking again at some familiar reasons for going to church.

There are certain things in life which gain a great part of their value and of their impact from being experienced together.

However well a great orchestra might play, the experience of listening to it would lose something if the listener were the only person in the concert hall.

A football match would lose far more than half its excitement and its thrill, if you were the only person present.

There are many things which can be perfectly well done and experienced alone, but which have an infinitely greater impact and effect when they are done and experienced in the company of others.

Worship is like that. Of course, we can worship alone; and, of course, there are times when we must worship alone. But the fact remains that togetherness is an essential part of worship.

There is a real value in being assured that the Christian faith is not only a personal experience, but the possession of a whole community.

In the earliest days the creed began not, "I believe," but "We believe." There are times when it is a very great comfort to remember that Christian faith and belief depend not on my acceptance of any part of it, not on my ability to understand any part of it, but on the faith of the whole Church.

There is a togetherness without which even worship becomes a colder and an emptier thing; there is a community of faith which does much to buttress the inadequacy of our own personal faith; there is a claim which it would be both folly and ingratitude not to acknowledge.

We need the Church and the Church needs us.

OPPORTUNITY   May 16

Do you look for something to criticise, or do you look for something to praise?

For instance, if in your church the choir puts on an anthem or a cantata or an oratorio, do you jump on the mistakes and the inadequacies that are bound to be there, or do you comment on the parts which were well sung, stressing that a very creditable attempt has been made to sing a piece of great music, even it it did not reach professional standards?

Do you encourage or discourage?

When some course of action is suggested, do you promptly see all the difficulties which make it impossible, or do you see the possibilities which make it well worth trying?

Do you count your blessings or do you count your misfortunes?

Adler the famous psychologist, tells somewhere of two men each of whom lost an arm. At the end of a year one of them was so discouraged that he had decided that life was not worth living with a handicap like that. The other was so triumphant that he went about saying that he really did not know why nature had given us two arms when he could get along perfectly well with one.

Do you thank God for what you have, or do you curse God for what you have lost?

Do you look on a difficult situation as a disaster or an opportunity?

It is worth recalling again that Sir John Reith, the first director of the B.B.C., used to say! "I do not like crises, but I do like the opportunities they provide."

Do you regard a crisis as a time to sit down and wail, or a time to rise up and act?

RIGHTS AND DUTIES   May 17

If Christianity and all that Christianity stands for are removed from this world, then there will be very few privileges to enjoy.

The care of the sick, the aged and the poor began as a Christian undertaking.

There was no such thing as a hospital till Christianity came. Aristotle, in laying down the laws for his ideal state, says, "Let there be a law that no deformed child shall be reared." Varro, in giving rules for farming, advises that any aged slave who is past his work should be thrown out and left to die, just as a broken farm implement is thrown on to the rubbish heap.

If the Christian ethic is removed, all that is good in the welfare state will be removed too. It happened in Germany. Christianity was banished from the state; the gas chamber became the end of the aged; the poor and the sick were used for medical experiments; the Jews were tortured and died by the thousand.

Let those who wish to enjoy the privileges of a Christian country remember that they will not enjoy them long if the country ceases to be Christian.

Freedom of speech and conscience are specifically Christian possessions.

It was the Christian Church which won these things for this and for every other country which possesses them. Take Christianity away and they are lost.

It happened in Russia. Under a Communist régime an opposition party is unthinkable and criticism of the government is suicide. Let those who wish to enjoy Christian freedom remember that they will not enjoy it long if the country ceases to be Christian.

Life is full of people today who want all the privileges and none of the responsibilities, all the rights and none of the duties.

Those who wish to enjoy all the privileges of a Christian civilisation ought to ask themselves if they are doing anything to keep civilisation Christian; and, if they are not, they will have no one but themselves to blame if they wake up some day to find that their privileges are gone.

TRUE MANHOOD   May 18

God is a refiner; man is the metal which must be cleansed; and God's aim is to make man such that he can see his own reflection in him.

What then are the qualities which this true manhood must have?

Our lives are meant to reflect the patience of God.

One of the most obvious of all contrasts is the contrast between the patience of God and the petulance of man. If God had been a man, very certainly he would have taken his hand and wiped the world out of existence long ago. When we find people difficult to deal with, we impatiently break out upon them, or we simply have nothing more to do with them. What a contrast with the divine patience of God, who bears with all the world's sinning and will not cast it off.

Our lives are meant to reflect the divine reliability.

From beginning to end the Bible stresses the truth, the dependability, the steadfastness, the reliability of God. God does not change his mind; God does not make a promise and then go back on it; what God says he means; and what God promises he will do.

Man means to be loyal, but there is a basic weakness in human nature which makes disloyalty a continuous danger. What a contrast between the divine reliability and fidelity of God and the ingrained shiftiness of human nature!

Our lives are meant to reflect the love of God.

There is in God's love a quality of undefeatableness. Shakespeare wrote movingly:

Love is not love
Which alters when it alteration finds . . .

But the human heart finds it very difficult to go on loving when there is no response.

The supreme quality of the love of God is that it has refused in any situation to cease to love. What a contrast between the indestructible love of God and the brittle love of the human heart!

EXPERT

A Christian is a man who ought to be able to do things which other people cannot do.

A Christian is a person who can bear disappointments in a way that other people cannot bear them.

It is very interesting to see how people react when they do not get some position for which they applied and for which they were eager. Some people grow soured and embittered. They spend weeks—some of them the rest of their lives—bewailing the fact that they were so unfortunate, and implying, or even insisting, that they are far better men and women than the person who did get the job.

On the other hand, I know a man who applied for a position, and who might well have expected to get it, and who did not get it, and whose first action was to write a letter of congratulation and blessing to the man who did get it.

The Christian is a man who can bear disappointments, because his heart is cleansed of envy, in a way that is not possible for other men so to do.

A Christian is a person who can bear burdens that other men cannot bear.

That is because he knows that he is not bearing them all by himself. I have always loved the story of Bishop Quayle, the great American bishop. For years he worried himself to death about his church and his clergy and his work and about all the things that had to be done. He used to sit up half the night worrying about all kinds of things. Then one night as he sat worrying he tells us that he heard God's voice as clearly as if it had been someone sitting in the same room, and God was saying, "Quayle, you go to bed, I'll sit up for the rest of the night!" And thereafter there was in Quayle a wonderful serenity, for he had learned to cast his burden on the Lord.

The Christian can shoulder burdens which would overwhelm any other man because he knows that there is no burden which he has to carry alone.

The Christian can bear sorrows in a way that other men cannot bear them.

Life can never be easy; life is full of the things which try men's hearts. It is not so much a question of going on, for a man has to go on whether he likes it or not; it is a question of *the spirit in which a man will go on*. Some may go on in resentment, bitterness, defeated hopelessness, grim despair; but in face of the disappointments, the burdens and the sorrows of life, the Christian can maintain the strength, the serenity, the joy which only Jesus Christ can give.

"Whosoever shall compel thee to go a mile," said Jesus, "go with him twain" (Matt. 5:41). This was the most practical advice in the world, for it is the extras of life which make all the difference in the world.

The extras make all the difference in doing things.

It makes all the difference in the world to a thing whether it is done with a smile or done with a bad grace. There is no reason why efficiency and courtesy should not go hand in hand. And there is no sphere of life—in the home, at business, in study, in our pleasure—when the spirit in which a thing is done does not make all the difference in the world.

The extras make all the difference in giving.

There are so many ways in which a man may give. He may give as if the giving was—as indeed it is to him—a grim duty from which he cannot escape, much as he would like to. He may make it clear that the gift is being unwillingly extracted from him, and that he dislikes parting with it as much as he would dislike parting with a tooth.

It may even happen that a gift, even a much needed gift, may be given in such a way that it becomes an insult. It may be given with a contemptuous superiority, like throwing a bone to a dog. It may be given simply for the pleasure of being thanked, and the receiver well knows that, if he does not express the most flattering thanks, the giver will be very displeased. Or the gift may be given as a joy and a pleasure, which brings even more gladness to him who gives than to him who receives.

There are many cases in life in which a man would be better not to give at all than to give in the way in which he does give.

In this, as in all other things, Jesus is our great example. Every time Jesus gave to men, he gave nothing less than himself. Every time he gave them his help, virtue went out of him. And yet we never find a case where Jesus gave ungraciously and unwillingly. There are many people in this world to whom we hesitate to go if we need anything. We know well that they will either refuse, or that they will give in such a way as to make us wish that we had never asked. But we have only to read the gospel story to see how easy it was to approach Jesus, how no one was ever afraid to ask him for help, how none was met with ungraciousness, and how all went happier away.

All the good is gone out of a deed or a gift when no happiness is given with it. The gift may be important, but the extra—the spirit in which it is given—is more important still.

Dependence and independence have to go hand in hand.
There is no lovelier feeling in this life than to be needed.

E. V. Lucas wrote a very lovely kind of parable. "A mother lost her soldier son. The news came to her in dispatches from the war. He had fallen fighting nobly at the head of his regiment. She was inconsolable. 'O that I might see him again,' she prayed, 'if only for five minutes—but to see him.' An angel answered her prayer. 'For five minutes,' said the angel, 'you will see him.' 'Quick, quick,' said the mother, her tears turned to momentary joy. 'Yes,' said the angel, 'but think a little. He was a grown man. There are thirty years to choose from. How would you like to see him?' And the mother paused and wondered. 'Would you see him,' said the angel, 'as a soldier, dying heroically at his post? Would you see him as he left you to join the transport? Would you see him again as on that day at school when he stepped to the platform to receive the highest honours a boy could have?' The mother's eyes lit up. 'Would you see him,' said the angel, 'as a babe at your breast?' And slowly the mother said, 'No I would have him for five minutes, as he was one day when he ran in from the garden to ask my forgiveness for being naughty. He was so small and so unhappy, and the tears were making streaks down his face through the garden dust. And he flew to my arms with such force that he hurt me.'"

The one thing that the mother wished above all to recapture was the moment when her son had needed her. There is nothing more moving in life than to hear someone say, "I need you; I cannot do without you."

There is a lovely dependence which should be the aim of every parent in connection with his or her child.

There is no more uplifting feeling than to see someone—a child, or a pupil or a student—facing the tasks of life competently, adequately and gallantly, and to know that you had something to do with equipping him for them.

It would be a very wrong thing to aim to keep a child forever tethered to the apron strings, and forever dominated by a father's personality. Our aim must never be to do things for children, but rather to enable them to do things for themselves. Our aim must never be to take a child's decisions for him in every case, but to enable him to take them wisely and bravely for himself.

However lovely dependence is, independence is the aim of the whole process of upbringing and of education.

We must also be dependent forever upon God; and yet, at the same time, we must be able to stand on our own two feet and to meet life as it comes to us.

EXHAUSTION   May 22

For Jesus to bring help and healing to others was a costly thing.

When the woman in the crowd slipped up unseen, and touched the hem of his garment, Jesus stopped because he knew that virtue had gone out of him (Mark 5:30).

Paul Tournier in his book *A Doctor's Casebook* tells of a certain experience. He tells about a doctor in Florence who sometimes used the laying on of hands to assist in healing; but he had to give it up because of its effect on himself. "Thus," he told us, "for example, my patient suffering from angina would find that his angina had suddenly gone; but I myself at once suffered a similar attack."

Tournier goes on, "When I told my wife about this, we were reminded of the fact that we had frequently observed: that we regularly had a quarrel ourselves on the evening of a day in which we had been able to help in the reconciliation of another married couple."

No one can help anyone else without virtue going out of him, and without in the most real sense entering into the other person's actual experience. It is in fact in many cases our greatest fault that we seek always to get and seldom to give.

We do that in friendship.

There is a kind of friendship so-called which has a kind of vampire-like quality. Its one desire is always to be drawing help and comfort and strength from its friend without any reciprocal giving. There is the kind of person who will talk for hours about his own troubles to his friend, but is quite disinterested, if the friend even mentions his. There is the kind of person who will presume largely on the rights of friendship, but who obviously finds it very inconvenient if anything is demanded from him.

We do that with the Church.

The Church has a large number of people who are forever talking about what they expect to get from the Church, and what, alas, they do not get. But they are very unwilling to see that the Church has any demands on them, and that the Church is waiting for something from them. They are very willing to use the Church, but they are very unwilling to be of use to the Church.

We do that with God.

There are many of us who for long stretches of time conveniently forget God—until we need him. We use God as someone from whom to get, and never think of him as someone to whom to give.

There is in life an inevitable exhaustion, which is the price of greatness in all things. No man can seek for a comfortable ease and know what greatness means and gives.

LINGERING   May 23

It is easy in every sphere of life to linger too long in the vestibule.

We can do it in preaching.

It is very necessary to put a subject into its context, and to set it against its historical background, but it is quite possible to say so much by way of introduction that there is no time to deal with the subject proper—especially in a generation which regards twenty minutes as a long time for a sermon.

We can do it in study.

There are many students who never get past the vestibule of any subject. There is a reason for that, of course. To get into the heart of any subject requires work, study, discipline; and it is not every student who is prepared to pay that price. The result is that there are many of them who never get past the fringes of any subject, and who never arrive at the inner treasury. It takes work to get beyond the vestibule of the riches of Scripture.

We can do it in friendship.

It is characteristic of life that we have many acquaintances, but few friends. Friendship too needs effort. It needs the effort to penetrate into the inner sanctuary of the other person's heart; and it needs an effort to reveal our own heart.

The essence of friendship is the giving and the receiving of nothing less than the whole self.

We can do it with Jesus Christ.

In their relationship with Jesus Christ so many people linger in the vestibule. They admire Jesus. Christianity, as Browning put it, has their vote to be true. They would like to be Christians. But Christ demands total surrender; and Christianity means total commitment. And short of that they stop. They keep him in the vestibule.

There was a day when Agrippa said to Paul, "*Almost* thou persuadest me to be a Christian" (Acts 26:28).

There spoke the man who kept Christ in the vestibule.

OLD ENOUGH TO DIE?   May 24

Is anyone old enough to die?

One of the most obvious things about this life is that you cannot measure it in years.

The length of life has little to do with the value of life. Alexander the Great died at thirty-three, but not before he had literally changed the face of the world, and paved the way for the coming of Christianity. Chatterton died at eighteen, Keats at twenty-six, Rupert Brook at twenty-eight, Shelley at thirty, but not before they had left poetry that the centuries will never take away. Schubert died at thirty-one, Mozart at thirty-six, but not before they had given to the world music that time will never silence.

Duration is no measuring rod for life.

In a sense no one is old enough to die, because to die is to meet God, and no one is fit to meet the awful holiness of God.

But in a sense anyone is old enough to die who has learned to walk with Jesus Christ, for he who walks with him has always lived in the presence of God.

There are two wonderful passages of Scripture. One is in 1 John 2:28. John is thinking of the coming of our Lord, and of what will happen then. "Little children," he writes to his people, "abide in him; that, when he shall appear, we may have confidence, and not be ashamed before him at his coming." John is saying that, if we live with Christ, if we abide with him, his coming will be no interruption in life. It will be the most natural thing in the world.

So long as God is a stranger we are never old enough to die. When God becomes a friend, through Jesus Christ, we are old enough to die, whether the call comes for us at morning, at midday or at evening.

INTO SHAPE   May 25

One summer when we were motoring in the north country near Aberdeen, we came on a stone let into a wall in a place called Dinnet. The date of it was 1897, and it had to do with Queen Victoria.

I copied out the inscription on the stone; and here it is:

> Shape thyself for use;
> The stone that may fit in the wall is left not in the way,
> Then may fate thy measure take and say:
> I find thee worthy;
> Do this deed for me.

The stone that is shapeless is useless, and will be cast aside, and left lying useless and unused; the stone that is shaped is useful, and will be fitted into something which will stand, and which men will remember and use. And life is exactly like that.

For everyone in this world, there is a place.

It was Peter who had the vision of each man as a living stone to be built into a spiritual house by God and for God (1 Pet. 2:5). God needs us as stones in the edifice which he is building up.

There is a place which every one of us can fill in this world. And there is something for every man and woman to do in the purpose and the plan of God.

But no stone can fill its place without being shaped to fill it.

The mason's hammer and chisel must mould and form it to fill the place it is designed to occupy. That means that none of us can fill our place in God's plan of things without discipline.

Life is strewn with the wreckage of lives which refused to accept discipline. One of the tragedies of life in so many spheres is the sight of people who had great gifts, and who had great success, and who refused to accept discipline, and who ran to seed, and who ended in tragedy.

Lack of self-discipline has probably ruined more men than any other single cause.

Life from the beginning to the end is seeking to shape us.

Our parents shape us; our teachers shape us; but most of all, in this life, the experiences of life are designed to shape us.

"God," said Paul, "works all things together for good" (Rom. 8:28). Even the things which seem like disasters are meant to do something to us, and for us.

The tragedy of life is when a man refuses to be shaped.

TWO NATURES May 26

Which is the real man? I read in the papers about a criminal who, during his gaol sentence, had tamed a magpie and who had so won over the bird that if was quite fearless. The criminal, or the man who with infinite patience tamed the bird—which is the *real* man?

This question is written into the Bible. Which is the real David? The David who spared Saul's life with infinite magnanimity, who would not drink the water which his mighty men brought from the well which was by the gate, at the jeopardy of their lives, or the David who callously arranged the death of Uriah that he might lustfully possess Bathsheba?

Which is the real Peter? The Peter who denied Christ in the courtyard of the High Priest's house, or the Peter who took his life in his hands for Christ before the Sanhedrin?

Which is the real John? The John who wanted to call down fire from heaven to blast a Samaritan village, or the John who had but one message: "Little children, love one another."

For that matter, which am I? I can work to the point of exhaustion and I can be completely lazy; I can be generous, and I can be mean; I can be kind, and I can be cruel; I can be patient, and I can be impatient.

The Jews said that inside every one of us there are two natures — the *Yetser Hatob*, the good nature, and the *Yetser Hara*, the evil nature. They said that every man had two angels, a good angel on his right hand pulling him up, and a bad angel on his left hand dragging him down.

Socrates said the soul was like a charioteer with the task of driving two horses, one gentle and tame, the other wild and undisciplined. The one was the passions, the other the reason. With almost poignant vividness Paul described the struggle within in Romans chapter 7.

It is a characteristic of human nature that we are a mixture. To the end of the day that remains true. There is only one person who can control the evil side of us and who can make the good supreme, and that is Jesus Christ himself.

In this life we never finally win the victory, but the nearer we live to him, and the more constantly we remember him, the more the good in us is victorious and the evil is defeated. In him alone there is conquest of ourselves.

There is something in most people which responds to the hymns and the psalms which are part of the very heritage of a Christian people.

Often in my student days I went on evening cruises on a summer night down the Firth of Clyde. There would be singing and dancing and fun and games. but again and again the singing would end up with the twenty-third Psalm.

One of the most moving things at great international football matches is the singing of "Abide with Me". There is something in the depth of the human heart which responds to this.

People are not essentially irreligious; they are essentially religious, if only we could get at them.

If people will not come to church, is it not our duty to bring the church to them?

One of our greatest failures in the modern Church is that we have identified the Church with what are "officially" known as the church buildings.

In the letters of Paul there meet us a husband and wife about whom I wish we knew a little more. Their names are Aquila and Priscilla; and twice greetings are sent to or from Aquila and Priscilla and the church that is in their house (Rom. 16:3, 5; 1 Cor. 16:19).

On the one occasion they were in Corinth and on the other they were in Ephesus; but, wherever Aquila and Priscillla were, their house became a church.

The Church is where Christ is: "Ubi Christus" as the Latin tag has it, "ibi ecclesia".

We must rediscover that any place can become a church, if we have the courage and the winsomeness to make it so.

God would have us meet life with the merry heart and the happy face.

To be happy is to do good to ourselves.

The writer of the Proverbs has a saying which the Authorised Version translates: "A merry heart doeth good like a medicine." (Prov. 17:22). But, if we look in the margin, we find another translation: "A merry heart doeth good to a medicine." Moffatt has it: "A glad heart helps and heals." The A.R.S.V. has it: "A cheerful heart is a good medicine."

A medicine will do far more good to a man with a happy heart than it will do to a gloomy and pessimistic soul. A doctor can hardly write in his prescription "To be taken three times a day with a merry heart," but he certainly would, if he could. It is a medical fact that those who laugh most live longest.

A hearty laugh expands the lungs, and is good for any man.

Every time we greet life with a happy human face we are stretching the span of life for ourselves and giving ourselves the best of medicines.

To be happy is to do good to others.

"A happy man," said Robert Louis Stevenson, "is a better thing to find than a five pound note." And, when we come to think of it, he is almost as difficult to find.

There are so many people whose faces are liable to crack, if they allow them to smile. And there are still many congregations who are a little shocked, if they are compelled to smile.

Somehow they cannot connect laughter and the worship of God.

The book of Job tells us that at the foundation of the world: "The morning stars sang together and all the sons of God shouted for joy" (Job 38:7). "Sing unto the Lord, O ye saints of His," says the Psalmist (Ps.30:4).

There are people in whose company the sun begins to shine even on a rainy day; and there are people who can put out the sun even on a midsummer day. There is no one more valuable to meet than the person you leave feeling that life is not such a grim business after all.

... MERRY HEART   May 29

It is worth remembering that we see our own reflection in other people. There is a common saying that we have to take people as we find them, and no doubt that is true. But it is also true that we make people what we find them.

If we find people bleak and unfriendly, all the likelihood is that we are seeing our own reflection in them. If we find people depressing, all the likelihood is that we make them that way.

There is a kind of equal justice in life. Jesus said, "With what measure ye mete, it shall be measured unto you" (Matt. 7:2). It would do us a great deal of good to remember that our criticisms of others are usually nothing other than criticisms of ourselves. If we only had eyes to see it.

So, we have to bring to the world a merry heart and a happy face. But if we have to bring it to others, we must first get it for ourselves. And we can only get it from Jesus Christ. One of the most difficult miracle stories in the New Testament is the story of the turning of the water into wine at the wedding feast at Cana of Galilee (John 2:1-11).

Whatever else that story means, and however we are to take it, one thing is quite certain. It means that whenever and wherever Jesus comes into life there comes into life with him a new exhilaration, which is like turning water into wine.

Grenfell of Labrador once came to John Hopkins University in America looking for a nurse to come back to Labrador to help with the work there.

This is how he put it: "If you want to have the time of your life, come with me and run a hospital next summer for the orphans of the Northland. There will not be a cent of money in it for you, and you will have to pay your own expenses. But I'll guarantee you will feel a love for life you have never before experienced. It's having the time of anyone's life to be in the service of Christ."

There stands the prescription for the merry heart and the happy face!

There is a right and wrong confidence.

There is the confidence of the man who knows that he is prepared and can deal with the situation.

Once someone said to one of these amazing air pilots who fly at such fantastic speeds, "You must take the most frightful risks." His answer was, 'The one thing to be quite sure of in my job is to see to it that you never take any risks." He had everything perfectly prepared in so far as it was humanly possible; he was quite sure of his own ability to cope with any foreseeable situation.

That is not a wrong confidence, that is the confidence of the man who knows what he can do.

There is the confidence of the man who is justly aware of his own gifts.

When Balzac was a lad he told his father that he proposed to give his life to literature and become an author. His father well knew both the risks and the rewards of authorship. "If you become an author," he said, "and if you take literature as your career, you will either be a beggar or a king." "Very well," said the lad. "I will be a king."

It is said that when Admiral Cunningham was a schoolboy and before his career was settled, his father wrote to him saying that there was an opportunity to enter the Navy and asking if he would like to take it. "Certainly I would like to take it," the boy wrote back. "I would like to be an admiral."

There is nothing wrong in a man knowing what he can do, in willingly tackling a big job, in gladly offering himself for some great service, in the confidence that he can do it.

But confidence becomes wrong when it becomes arrogant, conceited and proud.

When a man's confidence makes him his own greatest admirer, then it is wrong. It was said of a certain conceited man, "He claims to be a self-made man, and he has never stopped worshipping his own handiwork."

The self-confidence of pride is always an ugly thing.

DON'T WORRY!   May 31

Things often change completely when you get nearer to them.

A task which looks quite impossible in the distance somehow or other becomes possible when we actually have to face it.

It is an extraordinary thing how in life things which we would have said were impossible become possible when we have got to do them.

It was Edison who said that the only difference between the difficult and the impossible is that the impossible takes a little longer.

Wingate, that strange apocalyptic commander in Burma, once issued a memorable order of the day to his troops which read, "No jungle shall be reported to be impenetrable until it has been penetrated."

It is one of the encouraging things in life that, again and again, that which looks impossible can be done, when it has got to be done.

A problem which looks insoluble in the distance somehow or other finds its solution when it has actually to be faced and solved.

The greatest handicap that many of us have is a kind of innate and instinctive defeatism. Sir John Suckling, the famous Restoration poet, has sound advice for the gloomy and the pessimistic lover who wandered round wan and pale and hopeless:

> Will, when looking well can't move her,
> Looking ill prevail?

The Christian is bound to be an optimist, because he has behind him the grace of God.

A sorrow which looks unbearable in the future somehow or other becomes bearable when it actually happens.

Sometimes, when we hear of what has happened to others, and when we think that it might happen to ourselves, we think that if such a thing should happen to us, life could not possibly go on. But life does go on.

No man knows what he can bear, until he has had to bear it; and no man knows what the help of God can be like until in desperation he calls upon it.

The advice of Jesus is good: "Don't worry about tomorrow; let tomorrow worry about itself; sufficient unto each day is the problem and the task which that day brings" (Matt. 6:34).

June

There is no colour bar in the mind of a child.

This is the proof that the colour bar is an artificial and an unnatural thing; for the child it does not exist, and why should it?

In Trinity College we had a most notable experience. Perhaps the most famous series of preaching lectures in the world is the Warrack Lectures. To the Scottish Colleges on the Warrack foundation there are brought the princes of preachers to give our students help and guidance and instruction in that which will be the business of their lives.

A. J. Gossip, Henry Sloane Coffin, James Stewart, Reinhold Niebuhr, Emil Brünner, and many other great ones have given these lectures. That year the lecturer was the late D. T. Niles, that great ecumenical church leader from Ceylon.

It was the first time in history that the Warrack Lectures had been given by one whose skin was not white.

That was epoch-making in church life. A man from Ceylon had come across the ocean to teach the students of Scotland how to preach. In D. T. Niles the younger churches, the people whose skin is coloured, had arrived to teach the people who once had taught them. We will not soon forget D. T. Niles in Glasgow.

There can be no Christianity where there is a colour bar.

There is no colour bar with God. He is colour-blind. I do not for a moment say that this simple statement solves all problems, like the problem of inter-marriage and the like. There are many practical problems which will still have to be wisely and understandingly and slowly worked out. But one thing is certain, that the colour bar and the Christian Church cannot go together.

It was the world which God so loved, and within the Church it is the world which is the family of God.

141

Barrie, in *The Little White Bird*, talks of the moment when a mother tucks up her child for the night, and when she looks down into the child's eyes with an unspoken question in her own: "Have I done well today, my child?" It would do some of us good sometimes to think a little less of what we want from our children, and a little more of what they want from us.

The child needs guidance.

In his autobiography, G. K. Chesterton told of his father. In his childhood Chesterton had a cherished possession—a toy theatre with characters made of cardboard cut-outs and a stage and a curtain and all accessories. One of the characters was a man with a golden key.

Chesterton tells us that he had long since forgotten for what the man with the golden key stood but that the man with the golden key was always associated in his mind with his father because his father unlocked the door for him to so many things.

Chesterton must have had a wonderful father; but every father and every parent should be a guide.

The child needs friendship.

It is strange and tragic that often parents are the last people to whom a child will turn with his troubles. He will talk more easily to a well-loved teacher, or doctor, or scoutmaster, or some other relation.

One of the most important, and one of the hardest tasks of the parent, is to establish a relationship with the child in which the child will be able to speak of hopes and fears, triumphs and failures, successes and mistakes.

There are few things in this world which can do so much psychological harm as a nagging question in the child's mind which cannot be asked. It will be ultimately buried in the subconscious and there it will do as much harm as some poisonous thing lodged in the body and festering there.

The child needs love.

The greatest of all human needs is the need to be needed, the need to feel that one matters to someone. The deepest of all human desires is the desire for security, the desire to feel safe in a circle from which fear is shut out.

There is nothing that the child needs more than simply to know that he is loved. And that is why the poorest of homes with love is better than the most efficient of institutions in which individual love is almost impossible.

If we want to hear the right things, we have got to be attuned to the right wave-lengths.

If we wish to hear ourselves correctly, our wave-length must be honesty.

There are in this world comparatively few people who are honest with themselves. For instance, there are very few people who are honest with their own faults and feelings. They can see the faults of others, but to their own they are quite blind. I had a minister friend who used to have a favourite illustration of this. Sometimes you see a snapshot photograph of a group of people, and it makes them look like a gang of criminals or a collection of mourners at a funeral!

There is a widespread tendency when we look at such a photograph, to say, or at least to think, that it is quite a good likeness of everyone else, but that it is not a bit like ourselves! We are quite prepared to believe that the rest do look like that—but not us! We need honesty in our dealings with ourselves.

If we wish to hear others correctly, our wave-length must be sympathy.

It is a curious feature of conversation—I find myself at it continuously—that we can hardly wait for the other person to finish telling of his experience or his misfortune or his sorrow because we want to break in and tell of our experience, which is so much more interesting, and our misfortune or sorrow which is so much worse. In this world there are perhaps fifty good talkers for every one good listener. The most useful person in the world is a listener to whom you can pour out your heart.

The reason for our failure is simply lack of sympathy. We are really so concerned with ourselves, and our own feelings and our own affairs, that we have neither the time nor the desire to listen to anyone else.

We need sympathy in our dealings with others.

If we wish to hear God correctly, our wave-length must be humility.

The basic mistake that so many people make in regard to prayer is that they think of prayer far too much in terms of talking to God, and far too little in terms of listening to God. Prayer ought to be an activity in which we do not so much tell God as God tells us.

When we are on the right wave-length—and not till then—we will hear the right things from ourselves, from our fellow-men, and from God.

BRIDGE-BUILDERS   June 4

A very distinguished teacher and theologian was recalling his experiences in chaplaincy service in the army in the days of the war. Very often, he said, in the army, the padre was referred to quite simply as the man of God. He went on to say that when you looked back and sorted out your memories and impressions, you could see that in their padre the men looked for three outstanding qualities.

They looked for a man who knew them and was interested in them as persons.

Paul Tournier in *A Doctor's Casebook* speaks of what he calls the modern "massification" of society. The tendency nowadays is for the individual to be lost in the mass. It is so easy for the individual to cease in any sense to be an individual and to become a number on a form, an entry on a file, a specimen pigeon-holed in some neat classification. Paul Tournier says that the doctor's great danger is that he ceases to think of a man as a person, and begins to think of him as a gall-bladder or a lung case.

We live in an age when people tend to be numbers, entries, specimens. The basic human need is to be treated as a person. Treatment as a person is one of the basic things that anyone has a right to look for in a church.

A man may be a mere number in the world. To God he is a person with a name, and, in the Church of God, each person must be a person.

They looked for a man who knew their position and who knew what they were going through.

They would not have any use for a man who had no knowledge and no understanding of their problems, their experiences, their temptations.

Ezekiel brought the message of God to those who were in captivity; he need not himself have shared that captivity, but what he says is worth repeating: 'Then I came to them of the captivity at Tel-abib, that dwelt by the river of Chebar, and I sat where they sat." (Ezek. 3:15). "I sat where they sat"—that is the secret of being able to bring any help to men. That is what God did in Jesus Christ.

They felt that the padre should be a man who could speak a word for them to God and who could speak a word to them from God.

He must be a man who could somehow take their prayers and their needs and their requests to God; and he must be a man who could somehow bring to them from God a message to meet their condition.

That, indeed, is the greatest task of all. To fulfil it a man has to live close to men and close to God. He has to be the *pontifex*, the priest, the bridge-builder between God and men.

It was about the work of the ministry in particular that we were thinking and speaking, but surely these things must be the work, not only of the ministry, but of every Christian, to his fellow-men.

LOVELINESS   June 5

A. J. Gossip used to love to tell a story about Mungo Park, the great explorer. He had been journeying for days and miles in the wilds of China, in the most desolate surroundings. Then quite suddenly he saw on the ground at his feet a little blue flower. And, as he saw it, he said gently, "God has been here!"

This is exactly how Jesus felt.

There is always loveliness to see. Again to quote A. J. Gossip—Gossip used to say of the pessimism of Thomas Hardy that, if Hardy looked at a field, green with grass, and many-coloured with the wild flowers, all that he saw was the muck-heap in the corner. There is always loveliness—a glimpse of the sky and the clouds, or the stars and the vault of heaven, even in the city streets; the wonder and the concentration in the eyes of a child; two young people walking together, lost in their own world of happiness, with no eyes for anything or anyone but each other; a kind thing done to us, a word of praise or thanks spoken when we least expect it; a friendship and a personal relationship in which is the wonder of beauty.

Even when the world is at its worst, and when life is at its worst, there is still beauty left, and we should never forget it. It is not that to look at the beauty and to think about the beauty is an escape from reality—far from it. Any such glimpse of beauty should move us to three things.

It should move us to the memory of God, the awareness that this is God's world, and that not even the sin and the thoughtlessness and the selfishness of man can entirely obliterate the beauty of God.

It should move us to gratitude, and to the realisation that there is always something left for which we ought to give thanks.

It should move us to resolution and to action, so that, as far as we can, we may increase the beauty and remove the ugliness that is within this world.

CERTAINTY   June 6

Certainty is the most valuable thing in the world.

Certainty is the way of effective appeal to others.

Paul quotes the Psalmist: "I believed, and therefore have I spoken; we also believe, and therefore speak," (Ps. 116:10; 2 Cor. 4:13). Oddly enough, Spurgeon had a great admiration for the preaching of Martineau, the great Unitarian. Someone once asked Spurgeon why he admired Martineau so much, saying, "You don't believe what he preaches." "No," said Spurgeon, "but he does!"

The one note which all men will recognise in anyone who preaches or speaks is the sincerity of real belief.

Certainty is the way to effective strength.

The man who clearly knows where he is going, and who has no doubt that he is right, is the man with real strength. One strong man who is sure of himself will carry a whole committee with him. The man to whom others will listen, and the man who will get things done, is the man who obviously knows what he is talking about.

Certainty is the way to peace.

Someone once used the phrase "wandering in a horrible no-man's-land of indecision". No man can be at peace when he is torn in two directions at the same time. The first essential of peace is a mind made up.

Certainty is the way to comfort.

In *A Window in Thrums* Barrie tells the story of Jess, whose brilliant son, Joey, was killed when the cart ran over him. Joey was going to be a minister, and his first sermon was to have been on the teaxt: "Thou God seest me." Jess is telling about it twenty years after. "Aye, but that day he was coffined, for all the minister prayed, I found it hard to say, 'Thou God seest me.' It's the text I like best noo . . . I turn't it up often in the Bible . . . But juist when I come to 'Thou God seest me,' I let the Book lie in my lap, for aince a body's sure o' that, they're sure o' all."

For Jess—as it must be for everyone—certainty was the way to comfort and to peace.

THE LISTENERS   June 7

There is somebody listening every time we speak. And surely that is a very good reason for being very careful how we speak.

When we speak an ugly, unclean, impure word, someone hears it—and it sticks in someone's mind.

Old Thomas Fuller once said sadly, "Almost twenty years ago I heard a profane jest, and still remember it. How many pious passages of a far later date have I forgotten!" The profane jest had stuck. We can see this happen. It can happen that, to our shocked surprise, a child will suddenly utter an ugly word that he had overheard in the street, and which he was not supposed to hear. We speak a word. That word goes out. "Three things come not back, the spoken word, the spent arrow, and the lost opportunity."

Next time we are about to say something which it is not fitting to say, let us remember that we do not know who may be listening.

When we speak a fine and a true word, when we speak a word for Jesus Christ, someone hears it.

The classic example of that is what happened to John Bunyan. One day in Bedford he heard three or four poor women talking, as they sat at a door in the sun. At that time he himself was "a brisk talker" and had a surface veneer of religion. "They were far above, out of my reach; their talk was about new birth, the work of God on their hearts," and "of their own Righteousness, as filthy and insufficient to do them any good. And methought they spake, as if joy did make them speak; they spoke with such pleasantness of Scripture language." And Bunyan's heart began to shake. It was because he heard the talk of three or four poor women, sitting at the door in the sun, that Bunyan found, not half the way, but the whole way of God.

When we say a fine thing, rebuke an evil thing, commend a good thing, someone is listening; and that very word of ours may be the thing which turns the scale of their hearts, which saves them from temptation, which sets them on the way to God, which lodges in their hearts and, maybe many days or years afterwards, is the memory which saves their souls.

We know that one is listening—and that one is Jesus Christ.

He is the hearer of every word we speak. Jesus himself said, "I say unto you, That every idle word that men shall speak, they shall give account thereof in the day of judgment. For by thy words thou shalt be justified, and by words thou shalt be condemned." (Matt. 12:35–37).

June 8

What we put into a child's mind and a child's life when he is young is there for good.

That is what Ignatius Loyola meant when he made his famous dictum, "Give me a child for the first seven years of his life and I care not who has him afterwards."

From his earliest days we should teach the child to have regard for truth.

Boswell tells of a breakfast table discussion with Johnson in the Thrale household. Johnson was insisting on a strict attention to the truth, even in the slightest detail, an attention which he himself meticulously practised. "Accustom your children," he said, "constantly to this; if a thing happened at one window, and they, when relating it, say that it happened at another, do not let it pass, but instantly check them. You do not know where deviation from the truth will end."

Boswell agreed that once you allow variations into any narrative you do not know where they will end. Mrs. Thrale objected to what she considered an undue fussiness, "Little variations in narrative," she insisted, "must happen a thousand times a day, if one is not perpetually watching."

Dr. Johnson thundered, "Well, Madam, you ought to be perpetually watching. It is more from carelessness about truth than from intentional lying that there is so much falsehood in the world."

Dr. Johnson was right. From the very beginning, teach the child an unvarying respect for truth.

From the earliest days we should teach the child the meaning of Christian love, Christian consideration and Christian courtesy.

Too often the child is treated to the sight of his parents arguing and bickering and criticising and differing with each other. He may well unconsciously absorb the idea that married life consists of a continual jangling argument.

So often we seem to reserve the right to treat our loved ones with a discourtesy which we would never use to strangers. We must see to it that the child is brought up to have the conviction that the atmosphere of the home is Christian courtesy and Christian love.

From the earliest days teach the child the habit of worship on God's day.

I think that it was Dick Sheppard who used to declare what was to happen to the child who was brought up to regard Sunday as the day on which Daddy stayed in bed until lunch time.

There is nothing stronger in this world than the force of habit; and one of the greatest defences of church-going is to make it a habit.

Day in, day out we are inserting into the child's mind things which will never come out. See to it that the right things, and the fine things, and the noble things, are inserted there.

THE DEAD SPEAK   June 9

In the great eleventh chapter, the writer of the Letter to the Hebrews says of Abel, "He being dead yet speaketh" (Heb. 11:4). That is true of many another.

For many of us it is true that, though our parents are dead, they still speak.

For many of us it is true to this day that, many years after their death, our parents are still the greatest influence in our lives. Unconsciously it may be, we still apply to life and its decisions the standards and the principles they taught us. Unconsciously it may be, we still seek their approval in the things we do. God grant unto us to pass on to our children the heritage our parents passed on to us.

Many a teacher, being dead, yet speaks.

That is obviously true of a University teacher, who may deeply impress his students with his own thought, and who may even found a school of teaching which will last long after he is gone. But it is also true that the humblest teacher in the humblest school lives on in his or her pupils. A good teacher is always immortal in someone's life.

Many a time a friend, being dead, yet speaks.

The influence of a great friendship is not terminated by death. When Charles Kingsley was asked the secret of the winsome purity of his own life, his answer was, thinking of F. D. Maurice, "I had a friend."

The influence of a great friend is something which overpasses death.

Many a preacher, being dead, yet speaks.

No preacher ever knows what he is doing, nor does he ever know where his word is going, or how far it is reaching. But many, although they may never have told him so, owe their lives to the faithful preaching of some faithful preacher and man of God of whom the world at large has never heard, and many in the hour of temptation remember the words they heard.

Every man leaves something of himself in the world. Every man being dead yet speaketh. God grant that when we leave this world we shall leave something which is still speaking for Jesus Christ.

THE RIGHT STUFF   June 10

There is more than one lesson here:

Don't judge anyone until you know him personally.

One of the most dangerous things in life is our way of classifying people.

To some people all Roman Catholics are outside the pale. To some people all fundamentalists are impossible people. To some people all liberals are heretics on the way to eternal punishment.

We must remember that persons are persons and not just units in some scheme of classification that we have formulated for ourselves out of our own prejudice.

To Jesus every human being was a person. Matthew wasn't just a tax-gatherer; he was Matthew. Mary Magdalene was not just a sinner; she was Mary. Simon the Pharisee was not just a Pharisee; he was Simon.

So long as we simply classify people without knowing them, there are going to be a lot of people we don't like; but once we stop classifying people and get to know them personally, there are a lot of people we can't help liking.

How many young people get into trouble for the simple reason that they have nothing to do? "It's Sunday," said two lads, "and we've nothing to do." It is all very well to say, "Let them come to church and to the Youth Fellowship, and so on." But I wonder if this is a fair question. The Church caters more than adequately for what you might call the "discussion group" type of young person who likes to argue and who has some gift of being able to speak, but does the Church cater at all adequately for the lad who doesn't much care for discussion groups but who loves tinkering with the family car? It is not perhaps just faintly true that in the Church Youth Fellowship we are far more at home with the budding theologian and the embryo politician than we are with the lad for whom motor bikes are a kind of religion?

If Christianity believes anything, it believes that all kinds of gifts can be dedicated to God, but it does seem that the Church finds it a bit difficult to find ways of dedicating gifts which lie in the hands rather than in the tongue.

NO EASY WAY (I)   June 11

One of the delusions which most people have is that the great men do things easily. People talk about inspiration as if inspiration was something which enabled people to do things without any effort at all. But all the evidence is that the precise opposite is the truth.

149

A fact which I had **forgotten**, and which I have just rediscovered, turned my thoughts to this again. The fact is this. We think of Byron and Tennyson as two of the great masters of the techniques of verse-making; and yet both of them habitually used rhyming dictionaries!

Their rhyming words seem to come with a complete inevitability; they seem to fall into place naturally and effortlessly; but time and time again they were the result of laboriously studying a rhyming dictionary to find a word which would rhyme.

You might think that a lyric poet above all would sing as a bird sings, with no effort and with instinctive ease. But W. B. Yeats, the great Irish poet, tells of his debt to Lady Gregory in a time of indolence after an illness: "I asked her to send me to work every day at 11, and at some other hour to my letters, rating me with idleness, if need be, and I doubt if I could have done much with my life but for her firmness and her care." It may seem odd to think of a lyric poet being sent to his desk at 11 a.m., but that was the way in which the poet's work was done.

Balzac, the master of the short story, speaks of himself as "plying the pick for dear life like an entombed miner". Not much sound of effortless ease there. Flaubert, that master of French style, speaks of himself as 'sick, irritated, the prey a thousand times a day of cruel pain", but, "continuing my labour like a true working-man, who, with sleeves turned up, in the sweat of his brow, beats away at his anvil, whether it rain or blow, hail or thunder."

Clearly the work which men look on as inspired was the result of the labour of the sweat of the brow and the struggle of the mind.

NO EASY WAY (2)   June 12

It is characteristic of all of us that we want an easy way to success in life and in living.

A man came to James Agate, who in his lifetime was probably the most distinguished of all dramatic critics, and asked him for the secret of how to become a dramatic critic. James Agate's reply was that he must study the works of about thirty great dramatists to see what great drama is, before he dared to become a critic at all. The man objected that he would be at least forty before he had got through the list. Agate's reply was, "You must be at least forty before your opinions have any value."

No man can reach the greatness without the toil. The truth is that toil is the coin which pays for everything.

It is a lesson we need to learn.

We need to learn it in the social and the economic sphere.

It is impossible to build up a stable society and a stable system without some kind of sacrifice.

We are today living in a society where most people do no less than claim the right to be cushioned and insulated against all effort and all sacrifice. The aim is for more pay for shorter hours. Whenever the cost of living goes up, the cry is that wages, pay and salary should go up with it.

The odd thing today is that people claim a right not so much to a living as to luxury. But the fact remains that no stable system of life or society can ever be built in any civilisation where the element of sacrifice has been completey eliminated.

To aim at luxury as a right is to end in disaster as a result.

We need to learn it in the religious and spiritual sphere.

We cannot live the Christain life unless we work at it. Paul would have been the first to agree that the faith which does not issue in works is not faith at all. Paul would have been the first to insist that, if grace is the greatest gift in the world, grace is also the greatest responsibility in the world.

"The Kingdom of Heaven," said James Denney, "is not for the well-meaning but for the desperate." It is maybe time that we began to learn the lesson that there is only one way that a man can go without an effort—and that is down-hill.

The way to the stars is steep.

USE THAT DISASTER! June 13

Any situation is what you make it. The very same situation can be a disaster or a blessing.

A certain schoolmaster in his autobiography tells of a thing which he always remembered. In a practice football match one of the younger boys fell awkwardly and heavily and broke his arm. It was his right arm.

When he was waiting for the ambulance to take him to hospital, he asked for some paper and a pencil. They asked him, "What on earth do you want paper and a pencil for just now?" He answered, "Well, since my right arm is broken, I thought that I had better start practising writing with my left hand at once."

A broken arm wasn't going to get him down!

One of the things in this world which we do well to remember is that every situation is an opportunity.

One of the great missionary stories is the story of Mary Reed. In India she was haunted and oppressed by the fate of the lepers, for in those days nothing was done for them.

She herself took ill with an illness which no one could diagnose. A visit to a hill station made no difference. She was sent home, and still no one could place her trouble. She had a numbness in one of her fingers and a stubbornly unhealable spot on her face.

At last a doctor realised what was the matter with her. She had contracted leprosy herself.

She was told the news. What was her reaction? Her reaction was to go down on her knees and to thank God that he had made her a leper, for now she could spend her life with the lepers for whom her heart was sore.

Mary Reed went back to India and for many years, herself a leper, she worked among the lepers and was the means of bringing health and hope to them. She thanked God for what looked like a disaster, for in it she saw a boundless opportunity.

Things will happen to us—things may have already happened to us—which look like disaster. Let us remember that nothing is a disaster unless we make it so, and everything is an opportunity if we believe in the God who is working all things together for good.

WRONG DIRECTIONS   June 14

We so often try to get our destination in life by going in precisely the wrong direction!

Is it not the case that we may well be taking the wrong direction on the road to happiness?

There never was an age which put its trust so much in material things. We think we will be happy if we get more pay, if we get a new television set, if we at last acquire a car or a house of our own, if we manage this year to have an expensive holiday abroad, or something like that. And yet a man has signally failed to learn the lesson of life, if he does not see that it is not in the power of things to bring happiness to anyone.

You will remember the old story of the king who was dying of melancholy. The doctors tried every cure; and then it was suggested that the king's melancholy could be cured, if he managed to procure and to wear the shirt of a perfectly happy man. So a search was made throughout his realm for a perfectly happy man.

At last they found such a man. He was a tramp on the road, bronzed, care-free, utterly happy. They offered him any price he cared to name for his shirt —only to find that the happy tramp did not possess a shirt to his back!

The way to happiness is in a right relationship with oneself and with one's fellow-men—and we will never get that from things, and we will never get it apart from Jesus Christ.

Is it not possible that we may be taking the wrong direction on the road to satisfaction?

We are living in a time when the general opinion seems to be that the less work a man does the happier he will be. We want shorter hours; we want to put a brake on work and effort; we want to take things easily.

Surely the lesson of life is that the way to satisfaction is through hard work, and not through dodging work. The discontent, the unrest which is abroad today, may well be due to nothing other than the boredom and the loss of self-respect which are bound to enter into life when a man is putting far less than his best and his whole effort into the work that he has to do. The way to satisfaction is not by easier but by harder work.

The word conversion literally means a turning round about. To be converted means to alter the whole directions of life; it means that we were going in one direction, and we make a right-about turn and start off in the other direction. What are the two directions?

The wrong direction is when we are facing ourselves; the right direction is when we are facing God.

EXTERNALS June 15

It is just as wrong to judge anything by externals as it is to judge a book by its cover.

It is wrong to judge a man by externals.
A man may look an insignificant character, and yet be a great man.

William Wilberforce, who was responsible for the freeing of the slaves throughout the British Empire, was weak in health, insignificantly small in body, and without any external attractions.

Boswell heard him speak, and after that experience Boswell said, "I saw what seemed to be a shrimp mount upon the table; but, as I listened, he grew and grew until the shrimp became a whale."

It is always wrong to judge a man by his personal appearance, by his clothes, by his physical stature. These are but the external accidents beneath which there lies the real man.

It is wrong to judge a church by externals.
A stately building, a noble liturgy, do not make a church. It must always be remembered that in the New Testament itself the word "church" never means a building, but always means a company of men and women who have given their hearts and lives to Jesus Christ.

That is not to say that we must not strive to give to God the best that the hand and the mind of man can contrive, but it is to say that, many and many a time there is a more vital church in some "tin tabernacle" than in some magnificent cathedral.

In the Sermon on the Mount Jesus most penetratingly puts externals in their proper place. It is not enough, he says, not to murder; we must never even feel anger in the heart. It is not enough not to commit adultery; the unclean desire must never even enter our heart. This is the test by which we are all judged and by which we all fail.

Few of us have hit a fellow-man; but what Jesus says is that we must never even have the wish to strike.

Few of us have committed adultery; but Jesus says that no unclean desire must ever enter the heart.

The demand of Jesus is that not only outward conduct, but also innermost thoughts, must stand the scrutiny of God. Only he can enable us to meet his own demand.

CHILDREN   June 16

What is it about a child that appeals?

There is the child's trust.

A child is not suspicious; a child instinctively trusts other people. A child still thinks the world is full of friends. And trust begets trust, just as suspicion begets suspicion.

There is the child's enjoyment.

To a child even the simple things are wonderful. The tragedy of the advancing years is the loss of wonder, the coming of boredom, the time when we grow deadeningly used to things. It is so easy to bring pleasure to a child, and to make a child's face light up. It is not that the wonder passes from the world, for there is wonder in the creation of God and the love of God for him who has eyes to see. It would be a good prayer: "God, keep me from losing my sense of wonder."

There is the child's appreciation.

As we grow older, we begin to take so many things for granted; but the child still so obviously appreciates any attention that is given to him or her. Maybe people in hotels and restaurants grow weary of guests who accept perfect service without ever a word or a look of appreciation, or even with a churlish complaint, and maybe that is why they are fascinated by a child who so obviously appreciates it all.

It is a bad day when we forget to be grateful to men and to God for all that they do for us, and when we forget to express that gratitude.

There is a child's innocence.

A child is still good. I know very well how "bad" a child can be in the parental sense of the word! But beyond it all and behind it all there is the still unsoiled innocence of the child. We see in the child that which we have lost, and that which still haunts us, and that which we yearn to be.

And it is in Christ that we grown-up children can by his grace and power regain the lost goodness and the lost loveliness of life.

"I can't help you, I can't do anything for you, unless you let me."

That is so often what a parent has to say to a child.

A parent knows the way of life, because he has walked it before. He knows the dangers and the perils and the pitfalls and the temptations. He would like above all things to help his child, but so often the child takes his own way and follows his own counsel, and the parent is left wistfully saying, "I can't help you, unless you let me."

That is so often what the teacher has to say to the pupil.

There are things that the teacher would like to do for the pupil; there is teaching and guidance and instruction which the teacher would like to give. The teacher knows at least sometimes that out of some pupil he could make a real scholar. But the pupil will not accept advice, will not concentrate will not study, will not apply himself as he could. And the teacher is left regretfully saying, "I can't help you, unless you let me."

Sometimes that is what a doctor has to say to a patient.

The doctor in his knowledge knows that, if the patient is to be cured, certain treatment must be given, a certain discipline must be accepted, certain things must be done, and certain other things avoided or maybe a certain operation is necessary. But the patient refuses to take the prescribed medicine, fails to keep to the correct diet, will not undergo the required treatment. And all that the doctor in the end can say is, "I can't help you, unless you let me."

That is what God must always be saying.

It may be that the greatest mystery of all is the mystery of the freedom of the will. God cannot, however, force his will upon us. God cannot force his guidance upon us. God cannot compel us to accept his way, his love, his grace. So again and again God is saying to his self-willed children, "I cannot help you, unless you let me."

As Jesus came into Jerusalem in the last week of his life, he looked down on the city and said, "How often would I have gathered thy children together, even as a hen gathereth her chickens under her wings—and ye would not!" (Matt. 23:37).

The first necessity of Christianity is submission, and unless we make that submission, God is left saying in sorrow, "I cannot help you, unless you let me."

The Book of Revelation, quoting Jeremiah, speaks of God who searches "the reins and the heart" (Rev.12:23; Jer. 11:20). Now, although it may seem odd to us, in Hebrew psychology the seat of the emotions is in the lower viscera, in the reins, that is the kidneys and the bowels (Phil. 2:1), while the seat of the thoughts is in the heart.

So what this phrase means is that God scrutinises both the inmost desires and the inmost thoughts of a man. A man must bring both his emotions and his intellect to God.

If we use only our intellect, our religion can become dry and arid and a philosophy rather than a religion; if we use only our emotions, our religion can become a frothy kind of thing with no depth in it.

Now it seems to me that that very seldom happens. It is the tragedy that the technical scholar and theologian is very seldom an evangelist; and the evangelist is very seldom a scholar. And this division is fatal.

When my thoughts were on this, I happened to be reading the magnificent volume in memory of A. S. Peake, edited by John T. Wilkinson, which has been newly published. Peake was one of the greatest influences on the Church of this land. He was a scholar; he knew and accepted all that wise criticism has to say of the Bible; he was in that sense a modernist. He laboured to be a theological middleman, and to transmit this knowledge to the ordinary person. If Britain largely escaped the bitter fundamentalist conflict of America, it was largely due to Peake.

But, to use a colloquial expression, How did Peake "get away with it"? Why was he listened to without resentment, at least by a large majority of people? H. G. Meacham gives the reason: he speaks of the combination in Peake of "intellectual eminence and unwavering loyalty to the evangelical faith". "Suspicion dissolved before his passionte devotion to Christ."

If Christianity is to capture the people of this land, the theologian must become an evangelist, and the evangelist must become a scholar, and intellect and emotion must go hand in hand.

BE KIND!   June 19

Donald Baillie has a sermon on the text: "What is that to thee? Follow thou me." (John 21:22). He talks about the things which we should never mind, but just keep on following Christ. He writes, "Never mind your perplexities, but follow Christ."

Baillie does not belittle the real and haunting doubts that come at some time to every man. He goes on to say, "Of course, you have to face your doubts and perplexities quite honestly and quite frankly and try to think them out and get light on them. But the great and salutary and reassuring lesson is this: that it is not just thinking it all out that light comes, and you don't have to wait until you have thought it all out (or you would have to wait for ever). You can go on bravely in the path of duty and purity and love. That must be right —you are sure enough of that. So much of Christ is plain to you, and so far you can follow him with your eyes wide open. And that is how further light comes. He that does the truth cometh to the light."

There are many things about which we may not be sure, and there are not a few things about which we may never be sure. But we do know that "kindness in another's troubles and courage in one's own" is always part of the Christian way, and we can get on with that.

I am aware of the contempt with which the theologians regard a religion which, as they put it, consists of "being kind to granny and the cat". But the man who has translated the kindness of God into the life of men is not far from the Kingdom.

In an old scrapbook I came across these lines:

> The wise men ask, "What language did Christ speak?"
> They cavil, argue, search and little prove.
> O sages, leave your Syriac and your Greek!
> Each heart contains the knowledge that you seek;
> Christ spoke the universal language—love.

At the end of the day, I would take my chance with the man who was no theologian, but who was kind.

THE LONG VIEW (1) June 20

Lord Northcliffe was gifted with very long sight. It was said of him that he could read the prices of articles in shop windows while he was sitting in a taxi-cab driving down the middle of the road. But by far the most of his time was spent reading books and newspapers.

At one time he was threatened with blindness. A London oculist took the view that only an operation could save Northcliffe's sight. Northcliffe was unwilling to undergo an operation, and sought another opinion. He went to a German eye specialist. The verdict of the specialist was that Northcliffe was suffering from extreme weariness of the optic nerve. And the cure was that Northcliffe must at least for a time give up looking at things close at hand, and look at things in the distance and far away.

The cure for Northcliffe was to stop peering at the things which were close at hand, and to look at the things that were far away. There is much sound truth in that.

In every action we would do well to look at the future of our own lives.

Many a thing may seem very unpleasant at the moment, but it will bring much regret in the years to come. We would be saved from many an error, and we would overcome many a temptation, if we stopped to think how the thing would look, not at the moment, but in another month or another year or even at the end of life.

Many a thing only requires its true proportion and its true significance when we learn to take the long view of it.

We would do well sometimes to think not only of the future as it affects ourselves, but also as it affects other people.

Anthony Collett tells how he was building a country cottage, and how he was planning to lay out the garden of it. In charge of operations in the garden there was an old man. Anthony Collett had given him instructions to plant apple trees and walnut trees in certain places. But the old man came to him and said, "You did tell me to plant apple trees there; but I have put the walnut trees here, and the apples trees there, for I did think that when you and me were gone, those walnuts would shade them apples."

The old man was thinking how the garden would look years after he and Anthony Collett were gone.

THE LONG VIEW (2)   June 21

It is sometimes good for us to remember that the consequences of the things we do will continue to operate long after we are dead and gone.

A certain American sociologist made an examination of the descendants of a certain drunken reprobate, whom he called Martin Kalikak, who married a woman as bad as himself. This investigation was made in 1920; Martin Kalikak lived about 1770. In the 150 years, Martin Kalikak's descendants totalled 480. Of these, 143 were feeble-minded; 36 were illegitimate; 24 were alcoholics; 3 were epileptics; 82 died in infancy; and 3 were executed for capital crimes. It is easy to see what an unstoppable stream of evil Martin Kalikak unloosed upon this world.

It is for a good man to remember that he leaves a legacy to generations still unborn. He can pass down a taint which will endure from generation to generation; and he can pass down something fine which will be a constant inspiration. It is no bad thing for a man to have his eye on generations still to come.

We would do well sometimes to look beyond them into eternity.

It is only then that we see life in its true perspective.

Once, after a fretful, peevish day, Dr. Johnson sadly said, "Is this the kind of life to which eternity is promised?" It we were creatures only of time there are many things that we might do. If life stopped with this world, there might be many things that we would allow ourselves.

We are not only creatures of time, but we are creatures of eternity also; and what we are in time will decide what we will be in eternity.

There is every reason in life for sometimes looking into the distance.

IDENTIFICATION (1)   June 22

One of the commonest activities is the attempt to find classifications into which we can divide people. The fundamental difference between one kind of person and another can be seen in a person's attitude to other people. By and large, that attitude may be one of two things—it may be identification and it may be detachment.

I have recently come across instances of both these attitudes to men.

Clifford Bax writes of George Russell, or A.E. as he was commonly called, "People were not real to A.E. Never once did he show any interest in a man's background, in his hopes, in his troubles. We were shadows, shadows and listeners."

George Russell was quite detached in his attitude to men; to him men were not persons with hearts and emotions and feelings and experiences; to him they were merely an audience to talk to and to impress.

H. G. Wells, who knew her well, said of Beatrice Webb, the famous Fabian socialist, "She saw men as samples moving." To her again people were not persons; they were samples and specimens to be statistically analysed and recorded and entered on schedules.

On the other hand, James Agate wrote of G. K. Chesterton, "Unlike some other thinkers, Chesterton understood his fellow-men; the woes of a jockey were as familiar to him as the worries of a judge . . . Chesterton, more than any man I have ever known, had the common touch. He would give the whole of his attention to a bootblack." Anybody, jockey, judge, bootblack, was to Chesterton a person in whom he was intensely interested and with whose feelings and experiences he was determined to identify himself.

Again, Clifford Bax notes that, in a letter, Keats, the poet, said that "a poet has no personality, is a chameleon, finds that he is the billiard balls, if he watches a game". That is to say, the poet instinctively and because he cannot help it, identifies himself with everyone he sees. He instinctively enters into their experience, even identifies himself with the balls which are knocked about in a game of billiards.

IDENTIFICATION (2)   June 23

John Woolman, the great American Quaker, was a man with an ever passionate desire to enter into the experience of others, that he might be able to understand and, therefore, to help. He made a voyage across the Atlantic in the steerage of an uncomfortable little ship. The atmosphere of the dark, crowded space between the decks was often almost unbearably foul.

Woolman wrote, "Several nights of late I have felt my breathing difficult; and a little after the rising of the second watch which is about midnight, I have got up and stood near an hour with my face near the hatches to get fresh air . . . But I was glad to experience what many thousands of my fellow-creatures often suffer in a greater degree."

He was on a mission to the Indians in which he had to stagger under a great pack like a slave. He staggered on tormented by flies and thirst, suffocated in the airless forest, grilled by the sun. But he was full of joy, "because he had felt in his own body with his five senses what it was to live as a slave".

His one aim was to identify himself with his fellow-men that he might be enabled to help them.

No one can think along this line without his thoughts turning to the greatest self-identification in history, which is the Incarnation of God in Jesus Christ. It would be true to say that the characteristic of all pagan gods was detachment from humanity and from the sorrows and the woes and the ills of humanity; while the characteristics of the God whom we love and adore and in whom we believe in his self-identification with the sorrows and the pain of men.

The pagan gods were the gods who refused to share the afflictions of men. Our God is the God who is afflicted in all our afflictions.

So, then, for the Christian, duty becomes clear. We believe in a God, not of detachment, but of identification; and there falls on us the duty, not of comfortably detaching ourselves from men, but of identifying ourselves with their sorrows and their pains.

For us the glory and the privilege of life lies in bearing the sorrows of others on our hearts.

NUISANCES   June 24

The men who have done most for the world have been nuisances.

They called Socrates the gadfly (we mentioned this earlier), because he stung men out of their contented, sleepy lethargies.

Antisthenes, the great Cynic philosopher, used to say that truth is like the light to sore eyes, and he who never hurts anyone, never helps anyone either.

A man from Corinth once said of the Athenians, who were the explorers of the world and of the mind, "You Athenians never rest yourselves, and you will never let anyone else rest either."

Jesus likened the Kingdom to leaven, and when leaven is put into the dough, it makes the dough bubble and seethe and erupt (Matt. 13:33).

The Thessalonians characterised the Christians as those who were turning the world upside down (Acts 17:6).

Two men were once talking about a great satirist who bravely and passionately rebuked the world for its sins and follies and mistakes. "He kicked the world about," said one, "as if it had been his football." "True," said the other, "but he kicked it to the goal." There is a sense in which the man who would help men must be a nuisance.

The way to amendment is never to regard rebuke and criticism as a nuisance but as a blessing.

"Thank you," said our chairman, "for being a nuisance." He who will not listen to criticism can never hope to see, or to overcome his faults, And he who does not wish to be disturbed can never bear the presence of Jesus.

The great question is: What if a man does not want to? What if he is well content to stay the way he is? What if his one aim is simply to keep things as they are, and not to be bothered? What if he does not wish to be changed and remade?

For such a man the Christian way is impossible, and for such a man Jesus Christ is only a nuisance to be avoided, and if possible, to be eliminated.

The man who would help the world must run the risk of being a nuisance; and the man who would be helped must have the grace and the humility to accept criticism, never to resent rebuke, and so, by seeing his faults in the light of Christ, and by conquering them in the grace of Christ, he will rise to higher things.

A NAME   June 25

There is always something about a great name.

John Chrysostom has a most interesting tract on the right way to bring up children. He writes: "Let us afford our children from the first an incentive to goodness from the name that we give them. Let none of us hasten to call his children after his forebears, his father and mother and grandsire and great-grandsire, but rather after the righteous—martyrs, bishops, apostles. Let one be called Peter, another John, another bear the name of one of the saints." "Let the names of the saints," says Chrysostom, "enter our homes through the naming of our children."

It is Chrysostom's idea that the child should be given a great name; that he should be repeatedly told the story of the great bearer of the name; and that thus he should be moved to make himself like the great owner of the name which he bears.

There is always a thrill in that which gives us contact, however remote, with greatness.

Not long ago I was preaching in a London church. I had not brought my own pulpit robe with me from Scotland, and the church officer was providing me with one. "Would you like to wear this one?" he said, "It belonged to John Kelman, and it has his name upon it."

I do not know how John Kelman's pulpit gown got to that vestry; but as I slipped it on I felt around me and about me the spirit of a prince of preachers.

And there is one name which everyone of us possesses—and that is the name Christian.

It is something to belong to a team with a great name, to a school or college with a great name. The very name brings inspiration and obligations to nobility and greatness.

It cannot be otherwise with the name Christian. It stood for mutual love and fellowship such as the heathen world did not possess. "See how these Christians love one another," said the heathen.

L   161

It stood for an inflexible loyalty which to the rest of the world was incomprehensible.

The name Christian stood for a stubborn courage and an unbreakable loyalty to Christ.

COMPELLED

You will always get a mob of parents at a prize giving or at school sports. And, if they were honest, they would tell you that they have really come to see only one figure walk on to the platform to receive the book or the certificate. They have come to see only one figure flash past in the race. They will politely applaud the others. But it is only one—their one—that they came to see. And if you think that that is silly, you are not a parent! Anything our own children do or achieve has a hundred times the thrill that something someone else's child has done possesses.

Thomas Campbell was a famous poet; his father was a simple soul who seldom read a book in his life. His famous son used to send him the volumes of his poems as they emerged from the press. One day someone came upon the old man standing with one of his famous son's volumes in his hand. He was looking at it and saying, "To think that our Tom made that!" It was Tom's book, and Tom's father was thrilled.

Has it ever struck you that God is like that—about you? God is our Father, and we are his children; and all the time God looks down and God watches what we do. It is not that he is watching like a policemen, or a vigilant schoolmaster, or like some snooper out to catch us out, and ready to pounce on us. He is watching as a parent watches his child, and when we do well, it makes him glad, and when we do badly, it makes him sad.

It is surely the most tremendous responsibility in human life that we, being such as we are, can bring joy or sorrow to God.

On one occasion someone came on R. L. Stevenson turning over the pages of a volume of press cuttings about his own books. "Well," said the friend jestingly, "is fame all that it's cracked up to be?" "Yes," said Stevenson seriously "when I see my mother's face."

His mother's joy in his success was dearer to him than all the fame with others.

As Augustine said long ago, "God loves each one of us as if there was only one of us to love." And, therefore, each one of us has it in us to bring pride or grief, joy or sorrow to God.

That is, indeed, something to live for.

IF . . . (1)

What would happen, if Jesus came again? Suppose Jesus were to be born into our town and our community today, what would happen to him?

There is no doubt that, by some, he would be crucified again.

There is a famous story of an almost savage saying of Thomas Carlyle. One evening he was at a small literary gathering. There was present a gushing, sentimental lady who was inveighing against the Jews for what they had done to Jesus. She insisted on how terrible and how wicked these people had been. She was so sorry, she said, that Jesus had not appeared in her time, for she at least would have delighted to honour him and to welcome him. "How delighted," she said, "we would have been to throw open our doors to him, and to listen to his divine precepts. Don't you think so, Mr. Carlyle?"

Carlyle answered, "No, Madam, I don't. I think that, had he come fashionably dressed with plenty of money and preaching doctrines palatable to the higher orders, I might have had the honour of receiving from you a card of invitation on the back of which would be written 'To meet our Saviour'. But, if he had come uttering his sublime precepts, and denouncing the Pharisees, and associating with publicans and the lower orders, as he did, you would have treated him much as the Jews did, and have cried out 'Take him to Newgate and hang him'."

The terrible truth is that anyone who does not wish to be disturbed necessarily wishes to eliminate Jesus Christ.

Dr. Johnson, that most bluntly honest of men, was once asked by a lady why it was that, for all his scholarship and eminence and fame, he was but seldom invited to the tables of the great. "I do not know any cause," said the great blunt doctor, "unless it is that lords and ladies do not always like to hear the truth, which, thank God, I am in the habit of speaking."

A distaste for truth is not confined to lords and ladies; and, because Jesus Christ spoke the truth, there are many who would eagerly crucify him, if he came again.

IF . . . (2)   June 28

When Jesus did enter this world, there was no room for him to be born in the inn.

Of all attitudes to Jesus Christ, that is the commonest. There are so many who do not hate him, and who do not even dislike him, but in whose life there is simply no room for him. To them he is simply an irrelevance who does not matter.

A certain artist, Sigismund Goetze, had a picture hung in the Royal Academy of 1904, entitled "Despised and Rejected of Men". He showed Christ on the steps of St. Paul's Cathedral. And the crowd are blind to his presence.

One man almost brushes against him as he passes buried in his sporting newspaper.

A scientist is too busy with his test-tube to see Christ.

A couple bent on pleasure hurry into a taxi with never a look for Christ.

A dignitary of the Church, sleek, self-satisfied, with an air of piety, passes by oblivious of Christ.

A non-conformist parson passes by so engaged in theological arguments and polemics that he does not even see Christ.

A mob orator harangues the crowd on the rights of men, with never a look for the great Brother of all men.

Only a nurse glimpses Christ and passes on.

That is the commonest situation in life. If Jesus Christ came again, there are many who would not bother to crucify him; he would not seem sufficiently important for that.

There would be some few who would still welcome and adore.

There would be some few who were still waiting for the consolation of Israel; and they would receive him—but they would be few. "He came unto his own and his own received him not" (John 1:11).

We think what would happen if Christ came again. Some would crucify him; some would disregard him; some few would welcome him.

When we examine ourselves, what would *we* do?

One of the great characteristic facts of life is that by and large we make men what we expect them to be. If we treat a man as if we expected him to be an unpleasant character, he will very likely be an unpleasant character; and if we treat a man as if we expected him to act like a man of honour, we will probably find him a man of honour.

Suspicion begets suspicion; and a low view of man produces low men.

It is those who expect the best from men who get the best from men. The schoolboy said of Thomas Arnold the great Headmaster of Rugby, "A fellow can't tell Arnold a lie, because he always believes what you say."

Arnold's belief in the honour of his boys laid an obligation of honour on the boys.

One of the most famous character sketches ever written was the sketch of the beloved captain written by Donald Hankey in the 1914–18 war. The captain came to the platoon; he picked out the awkward ones, not to bully and to criticise them, but to help them. He clearly believed that they could become good soldiers. "His confidence was infectious. He looked at them, and they looked at him, and the men pulled themselves together and determined to do their best. Their best surprised themselves."

Men talked about his smile. "It meant something. It meant that we were his men, and he was proud of us, and sure that we were going to do jolly well—better than any other of the platoons. And it made us determine that we would."

There is no more uplifting feeling in this world than the certainty that someone believes in us.

God believes in us; he believes in us so much that he sent his son to die for us. Jesus Christ believed in men; he gave them commandments and challenges of staggering height—and he believed that men through him could rise to them.

No Christian can shut his eyes to the sin of the world, but, if the Christian is to be like God and like Jesus Christ, he will expect the best from men— and all the chances are that he will get it.

OURSELVES   June 30

It is by no means easy to meet oneself and to know oneself.

There is a very real sense in which no one knows himself.

It is, for instance, true that most people receive a shock when they hear their own voice, when they hear themselves speaking on the tape of a recording machine, or when they hear themselves in a recorded broadcast.

A photograph does not really show us ourselves, for it shows us ourselves in an absolutely static position, a position in which in life we never are. Even to look in a mirror does not show us ourselves as we are, for the very simple reason that in a mirror-image we see ourselves the wrong way round, for in a mirror right becomes left and left becomes right.

It is very hard to know any man as he really is; and perhaps it is hardest of all for a man to know himself as he really is.

It is very easy to have a quite mistaken notion of ourselves.

A man may be just plain conceited, and he may think of himself as being much more charming and witty and clever than he really is. He may think himself charming when he is really smarming; he may think himself witty when he is merely irritating; he may think himself clever when he is really only smart and slick and worldly wise.

We can look at ourselves through a golden haze of self-idolisation; we can look at ourselves through a black cloud of self-criticism; or, perhaps commonest of all, we can quite unconsciously be afraid to take an honest look at ourselves at all, subconsciously preferring delusion to reality.

We ought to be profoundly grateful to those who help us to know ourselves and to see ourselves as we are.

July

I remember going to a translation panel in Oxford without a very essential part of my luggage. I went without an English Bible!

I went into the town to get a Bible, and very naturally, since I am well equipped with Bibles at home, I did not want to buy an expensive one.

Then I happened on what must be very nearly the Bible bargain of all time —the Fontana edition of the Revised Standard Version, magnificently printed and even in its paper covers beautifully bound, and all for some forty pence. I had not known that this edition existed until I saw it then; and it seemed to me the cheapest price for the best book that I had ever seen.

This set me thinking.

We do not realise how fortunate we are. Of course, in the early days, books were copied by hand. There was, in the fourth century A.D., when the great manuscripts were being copied, a standard rate of pay for scribes. Books for copying were divided into what were called *stichoi*. A *stichos* (the singular form of the word) is not a line. It was originally the length on an average of a hexametre length of poetry—the line in which Homer wrote—and it was counted as sixteen syllables. So books were classed as having so many *stichoi*, and, of course, however you recopied them and arranged them on the page, the number of *stichoi* remained constant.

Now there is a sixth-century New Testament manuscript called the "Codex Claromontanus" which gives the number of *stichoi* in each New Testament book. Further, there is an edict of Diocletian published early in the fourth century which fixes the prices for all sorts of things; and amongst other things if fixes the rates for the pay of scribes; and the pay is twenty to twenty-five denarii per hundred *stichoi*. A denarius was about four pence; so we may say that the rate was approximately one hundred pence per hundred *stichoi*.

Now in Matthew there are 2,600 *stichoi*, in Mark 1,600, in Luke 2,900 and in John 2,000. That is to say, in the four Gospels there are 9,100 *stichoi*, which is to say that at that time a copy of the four Gospels would cost ninety-one pounds. If you work it out on the same basis, a copy of the letters of Paul would cost more than fifty pounds! And now you can buy the whole Bible for less than fifty pence.

THE BOOK OF BOOKS (2)   July 2

When Wycliffe published the Bible in English for the first time at the end of the fourteenth century, it was, of course, before printing was invented. The Bible still had to be copied by hand. Later, George Foxe was to say, "Some gave five marks (equal to about forty pounds in modern money), some more, some less for a book. Some gave a load of hay for a few chapters of St. James or St. Paul in English." Again, remember the price at which we can buy the word of God.

When the Great Bible was published in 1540, Bishop Bonner placed the six copies in convenient places in St. Paul's Cathedral; and such was the eagerness to read them, and to hear them read aloud, that services were rendered impossible and the traffic disrupted and the crowds so great that Bonner had to threaten to take the Bibles away if the eager disorder did not cease.

What a difference today! I have heard the production manager of the British and Foreign Bible Society quote with gusto four lines of doggerel which were current when the Bible was even cheaper than it is today:

> Holy Bible, Book Divine,
> Leather-bound at one and nine;
> Satan trembles when he sees
> Bibles sold as cheap as these!

When George Foxe had spoken of the eagerness of the people to read the Wycliffe Bible and of their sacrifices to pay for one, he went on, "To see their travails, their earnest seekings, their burning zeal, their readings, their watchings, their sweet assemblies . . . may make us now in these days of free profession to blush for shame." It was 1563 when Foxe wrote that, and if it was true for him, it is still truer today.

Professor James S. Stewart has pleaded for the might of the Bible to be unleashed throughout the land. When there are Bibles like the Fontana Revised Standard Version available for all, we are left without excuse.

DEBT TO LIFE (1)   July 3

By the time he was thirty, three worlds lay open to Albert Schweitzer for the conquering; and it was then that he embarked upon a course of six years of medical training which was to be the prelude to his life-work in his hospital in Lambarene.

By that time he was a Doctor of Philosophy, and a brilliant academic career was his for the taking. By that time he had studied the organ under Charles Marie Widor in Paris, and, young as he was, he was the foremost authority on the music of Bach.

By that time he was a Doctor of Theology and he was already Principal of the Theological College at Strasbourg, with an attractive residence, a good stipend, and the prospect of an honourable and brilliant career as a theological teacher and thinker.

It was then that he took the road that ended in Lambarene.

It was not a sudden decision: it was a decision that went back to a summer morning, full of happiness and beauty, at Gunsbach nine years before. On that morning, as Schweitzer tells, "There came to me as I awoke the thought that I must not accept this happiness as a matter of course, but must give something in return for it."

Certain things stand out in the life of Schweitzer. One is this.

Schweitzer had a sense of responsibility.

He did not think, "What do the world and life owe me?" He thought, "What do I owe the world and life?"

We are living today in an age which demands its privileges; which in fact, takes its privileges as rights. People today think a great deal about what the world, the country, the state, and life owe them. Life owes them, as they see it, an education for nothing when they are young, a job when they are older, housing better than they are willing to pay for, help to bring up their children, care and attention when they are ill or old or out of work.

Make no mistake, these are the things which the state does owe its citizens, and these are the things which life should bring to every man. But what of the reverse process? The debt cannot be all on the one side. We cannot go on and on taking and taking out of the common store without putting anything back into it.

It is time we thought of what we owe life as well as of what life owes us.

DEBT TO LIFE (2)   July 4

Schweitzer knew his debt to life, and he equipped himself to pay it.

No man becomes a Doctor of Philosophy, a Doctor of Theology, a Doctor of Medicine and the foremost authority on the music of Bach without the discipline of work and of study: to achieve all that he must have toiled terribly. But, being equipped like that, just think of the contribution that he was able to bring to life.

We have become today very largely a people who are looking for an easy way. There are students who want the easiest possible course, with the easiest possible entrance, and the easiest possible examinations and the least possible demands. There are any number of people who want the largest possible rewards for the least possible expenditure of physical and mental energy and toil.

It is obvious that the less work that we are willing to do, and the less discipline we are willing to accept, the less contribution we can make to life. An ill-equipped teacher will make a bad teacher; an ill-equipped doctor will make little contribution to medicine; an ill-equipped student will bring to the ministry of the Church far less than he might have brought; an ill-equipped craftsman will contribute little to the general good.

To equip oneself as well as one possibly can is not simply a matter of academic duty or academic ambition or even of academic discipline. It is the duty we owe to God, to man and to the Church.

Schweitzer knew the meaning of adventure.

"In the many verbal duels I had to fight," he said, "as a weary opponent with people who passed for Christians, it moved me strangely to see them so far from perceiving that the love preached by Jesus may sweep a man into a new course of life."

It may indeed!

DRIFTING (1)   July 5

James Moffatt in his book *The Day Before Yesterday*, has a chapter on fables; and in it he relates one of Tolstoi's fables:

> It was as if I had suddenly found myself sitting in a boat which had been pushed off from an unknown shore, as if I had been shown the direction of the opposite shore, and given a pair of oars and left alone. I ply the oars, I row ahead; but the further I go, the stronger the current becomes carrying me out of my course.
>
> I meet other people afloat, also carried away by the current; some have thrown their oars away, a few are struggling against the stream, but most of them glide with it.
>
> The further I go, the more I watch the long line of boats floating down the current, and I forget the course pointed out to me as my own. From every side cheery voices shout to me that there can be no other direction. I believe them; as men drift down the stream or glide with the current, I let myself drift along with them, until at last I hear the roar of the rapids. Already I can see their boats broken up, and I know I myself must perish.
>
> Then I come to myself.
>
> Before me I can see nothing but destruction; I am hurrying fast towards it. What must I do?
>
> Looking back, I notice a number of boats now struggling to make headway against the current; and then I remember all about the opposite shore, the

course, and the oars. I begin at once to row hard upstream to reach the opposite side.

The shore is God; the current is tradition; the oars are free will, given that I may gain union with God.

Here is a fable which tells how a man awoke to the duty and the danger of life.

It tells of the danger of drifting with the stream.

It is always easier to go with the crowd than to battle your way against it. It is always easier to conform than to be a non-conformist.

It is always easier to accept the standards of the society in which we may happen to be than it is to stand for a set of standards which are quite different.

It is always easier to pursue a policy of drift and of inaction. And yet it is perfectly obvious that there can be no greatness in that direction. "Do not be conformed to the world," says Paul, "but be transformed by the renewal of your mind" (Rom. 12:2).

"Stop saying 'Amen' to what the world says," said Robert Louis Stevenson, "and keep your soul alive."

Drift means disaster.

But there is more.

DRIFTING (2)   July 6

Tolstoi's fable also tells of the glory and the necessity of free will. The Stoics almost mercilessly insisted that virtue can be won by the effort of the mind. A man, they said, learns to walk by walking, to run by running, to read by reading, to write by writing. Just so we learn virtue by being virtuous.

When a boy is learning to wrestle and when he is thrown, the gymnastic master simply says to him, "Get up and wrestle again until you are strong."

You have but to will a thing and it has happened, the reform has been made; as, on the other hand, you have but to drop into a doze and all is lost. For it is within you that both destruction and deliverance lie.

Such is the Stoic insistence on the all-importance of effort. We have to take up the oars and row against the stream, even when hands are blistered and chest bursting with the grim struggle. There is at least a sense in which it is true that we have never really discovered the lengths to which grimly determined will power can go.

But there is another side to this. We have the classic picture of the defeated struggle of the will in Romans chapter 7. "I do not understand my own actions. For I do not do what I want, but I do the very thing I hate ... I can will what is right, but I cannot do it. For I do not do the good I want, but the evil I do not want is what I do". (Rom. 7:15–19). The trouble with the human situation is that the canker is in fact in the will.

It is just there that Christ comes in; and the dynamic of Jesus Christ gives a man power to be what by himself he could never be, and to do what by himself he could never do. As we are, the whole problem of life is that our wills are not free, they are in chains; and it is the power of Christ which alone can make them free.

To drift is to die; we must set the mind to the struggle of the right way; but only in the strength of Christ will we have the strength to take it and to keep it.

IT'S NOT WORTH . . . (1)   July 7

I sometimes feel that the most dangerous phrases in our vocabulary are the phrases which begin: "It's not worth . . ." I can think of several of them which can do infinite harm.

The other day I found myself well behind with my work. I had to go out to an engagement. I had half an hour before I needed to leave my desk, and I had a definite job which ought to have been done. But I found myself saying to myself, "I've only got half an hour; *it's not worth starting*."

Often we find ourselves with a small amount of time; and often we know that there is something which ought to be done; and often we say, "It's not worth beginning with so little time available."

It is a dangerous phrase, because it means that the half hour is wasted—and wasted half hours soon mount up to a considerable amount of time. If we work a five-day week and waste half an hour each day that is two and a half hours. Over a year that is one hundred and thirty hours; and one hundred and thirty hours is not much short of a week— a whole week's time and work wasted and gone.

J. E. McFadyen, my old teacher, used often to tell with great delight how he learned Italian during the tram run from Pollokshields in Glasgow, where he lived, to the college where he taught. I suppose the tram run took about half an hour in the mornings, and in that time he learned a new language, by using the half hours each day.

There is a lot that can be done in half an hour.

It is always worth starting.

Sometimes we say, "*It's not worth trying*." It may be that we think that the job is too big for us; it may be that we think that the resources which we bring to it are too small to be in any way effective. We know we ought to try, but we salve our conscience by saying, "It's not worth trying."

Robert Louis Stevenson was a sick man and he knew that he had not very long to live. Sometimes he used to say: "If you can't finish your folio, at least get started on your page."

IT'S NOT WORTH . . . (2)   July 8

Sometimes we say, "*It's not worth bothering about*."

In some ways this is the most dangerous saying of all. We may know that there is some quite little thing wrong; we may know that some quite little mistake has been made. In either case at the moment it is quite easy to put it right. But we let it go. "It's not worth bothering about."

That is the way in which real trouble can grow and in which a really unmendable situation can arise. That is why a man can lose his health for ever, and perhaps his life. The continual lament of doctors is that people will not come to them in time, when they feel the first little symptom of something wrong. They say, "It's not worth bothering about," and by the time they decide to do something about it, so often there is nothing that can be done.

There are many things which can be cured and mended, if they are dealt with in time. You may say, for example—and it is a parable of life—about a small fault in a motor car, "It's not worth bothering about," but the small fault will become a major breakdown and perhaps in the middle of a wilderness with the nearest garage miles away.

If something is wrong, we should bother about it at once.

Sometimes we say, "*It's not worth the trouble.*" It may be that a job is not quite right and that something remains to be done. It may be that something is just short of perfection. It may be that someone suggests a way in which something can be improved. All such things take time and effort, and we are apt to say, "It's not worth the trouble."

Life would be very much better if people would stop consenting to push things through somehow, and would take that extra trouble and go that extra mile to make them just exactly right. It is always worth the trouble to get something as perfectly done as we can do it.

When we catch ourselves saying, "It's not worth . . ." let us beware.

That way trouble and danger lie.

NEW TRANSLATIONS (1)   July 9

There has never been a time when there has been such a flood of new translations of the New Testament as there has been in the past generation. The number of these new translations has puzzled some people.

There are some people who ask, "Why new translations at all? Why cannot we rest content with the Authorised Version?"

There are some people for whom the Authorised Version is the Bible, and who come near to resenting any attempt to change it.

There are some who would rather have the familiar cadences of the Authorised Version than any of the new translations.

Why then are the new translations necessary?

There is more than one answer to that question.

The Authorised Version emerged in 1611. The basis of the Greek text from which its translation was made was the text of Erasmus, whose first edition was published in 1516.

Now obviously, the older a Greek manuscript of the New Testament is, the more likely it is to be correct. Every time a manuscript was copied, new errors crept in; the nearer a manuscript is to the original writing, the less chance there is for error, and the more likely it is to be accurate.

The earliest manuscript Erasmus used for the Gospels belonged to the fifteenth century; the earliest he had for Acts and for the Pauline letters was from the twelfth to the fourteenth century; the earliest manuscript he had for the Revelation belonged to the twelfth century, and it actually broke off at Revelation 22:15. The last verses of Revelation Erasmus supplied himself in Greek by translating the Latin of the Vulgate back into Greek.

This is the Greek text from which the Authorised Version was made. No manuscript was used earlier than the twelfth century.

As the years went on, far older manuscripts were discovered. In the nineteenth century, Tischendorf discovered "Codex Sinaiticus", and "Codex Vaticanus" became available, and both of these manuscripts date back to the fourth century. In the present century, in 1931 the Chester Beatty manuscripts were discovered and they date back in some cases to the early part of the third century. As recently as 1958, the Bodmer manuscripts were discovered and they date as far back as A.D. 200 or thereby.

This means that we now possess manuscripts of the New Testament which are one thousand years older than anything from which the Authorised Version was made, one thousand years nearer the originals, and which are therefore very much more accurate. The materials which we possess from which to make a translation are incomparably superior to anything that was available when the Authorised Version was produced.

NEW TRANSLATIONS (2)   July 10

The language of the Authorised Version is inevitably the language of 1611, and is therefore archaic. So we need new translations.

In Acts 28:13 the A.V. has: "From there we fetched a compass, and came to Rhegium." The phrase "fetched a compass" is now quite out of date. The R.S.V. has: "From there we made a circuit," and the N.E.B.: "we sailed round".

Acts 21:15 is even more misleading in the Authorised Version: "After those days we took up our carriages, and went up to Jerusalem." Here "carriages" is used in the sense of "that which we had to carry". The N.E.B. correctly has: "At the end of our stay we packed our baggage and took the road up to Jerusalem."

When the New Testament was first written in the original Greek, it spoke to men in the ordinary everyday language that they used to each other daily. The English of 1611 cannot be like that to us. The Bible ought to speak to men in their own contemporary language; that is the way it originally spoke; and only a modern translation can make it so speak again.

We now know much more about the kind of language people spoke in New Testament times than the Authorised Version translators ever could know.

There has been discovered a host of documents such as private letters and accounts and legal documents and income tax returns and census papers and minutes of meetings.

Seventy-five years ago dictionaries used to lay it down that out of the New Testament's 2,829 different words about 550 occurred nowhere else than in the New Testament. More than 500 of these words have turned up in the documents which have come to light, and now we are much better equipped to define their meaning.

Today we have aids to the translation of the New Testament which did not exist in 1611; and to refuse to use them is to despoil ourselves of a new knowledge which can make the Bible more meaningful than ever.

Neglect of knowledge is always a sin.

LOYALTY   July 11

"I am not ashamed of the gospel of Christ," Paul said (Rom. 1:16). And, wherever we are, we ought to be unshakeably loyal to Jesus.

Are we loyal to Jesus in public?

I wonder how many church members, professing Christians, say grace before meat in a restaurant?

Perhaps this is quite a small thing; but it is a symbol. Do we in our public life boldly and willingly witness to the fact that we are Christian; or do we perhaps almost unconsciously, play it down a little, in case we appear to be different?

Are we loyal to Jesus in social life?

Years ago now, that great Irish churchman and scholar, J. P. Mahaffy, made a famous statement. When asked if he was a Christian, his answer was, "Yes! But not offensively so."

What Mahaffy meant was that he never allowed the fact that he was a Christian to interfere with his enjoyment of the pleasantries of social life. Is it the case that sometimes to avoid social embarrassment we are liable rather to hide the fact that we are Christian than to witness to it?

Are we loyal to Jesus in our working life?

Every now and again we see in the newspapers reports of men who belong usually to some small and quite obscure sect who refuse absolutely to conform to certain accepted practices no matter what the pressure brought to bear upon them may be. It sometimes, even often, happens that they lose their jobs, because their refusal to conform can sometimes be the cause of industrial trouble.

I do not say that we need agree with them, but I do say that I for one cannot help admiring them.

175

Do we conform to the world's standards to avoid trouble? Or do we inflexibly hold to the standards of Jesus Christ, whatever the consequences may be?

No one can answer that question except our own conscience, but even the best of us may well pray Robert Louis Stevenson's prayer that through all the chances and the changes of life, down even to the gates of death, God may keep us true to ourselves, true to our loved ones, and true to himself.

AUTHORITY   July 12

Where, for the Christian, does authority lie?

Does the authority for the Christian lie in conscience?

There are those who have held that conscience is instinctive, inherent and innate.

Epictetus used to say that no one is born with a knowledge of music or geometry, but everyone is born knowing the difference between right and wrong.

But there is no solution here. Conscience is a variable thing. The conscience of a child is not the conscience of a mature man. The conscience of a civilised man is not the conscience of a primitive man.

A man may so silence, stifle and blunt his conscience that it ceases to operate as sensitively as it should operate. Anything so variable and so much the product of circumstances as conscience cannot be the final authority.

Does the authority of the Christian lie in the Church?

It does for the Roman Catholic. But the Church has been guilty of the cruelty of a Spanish Inquisition, of the unspiritual commercialism of a traffic in indulgences, of Pharisaic discipline, of rank obscurantism, and often of the total inability to make any precise pronouncement on the very things on which the ordinary man desires guidance, as, for instance, on the issues of peace and war. The Church on earth is far too human an institution to have any kind of infallibility attached to it.

Does the authority of the Christian lie in the Bible?

The trouble about the Bible is that no sooner have we quoted one text on one side than it is so often possible to quote another text on the other side. We could find authority in the Bible for destroying our enemies and for forgiving our enemies, depending on which part of it we use. We could find authority for arguing that there is no life after death and for arguing that life after death is the very centre of Christian belief, depending on whether we choose to quote the Old or the New Testament.

No man alive accepts every word of the Bible as authoritative. He is bound to select, and he uses some other principle to guide his selection.

There is no such thing as a final authority which can be externally imposed on any man. It is God's method that man is compelled to use his own mind, his own heart and his own judgment. And for the Christian there is only one authority, and that authority is Jesus Christ interpreted by the Holy Spirit.

To know Christ is to have the authority to which all things can be submitted for judgment and decision.

WHENCE? WHERE? HOW? (1)   July 13

Where do I come from? Where am I going? How do I get there?
These are the three basic and essential and universal questions in life.

Where do I come from?
There is more than one answer to that question. A man comes from an act of intercourse between a man and a woman, who are his father and mother, and therefore, humanly speaking, a man may be the product of a great and pure love, or of a moment's uncontrolled passion.

It can be argued that a man comes from purely material things. Fosdick quoted the chemical analysis of an ordinary man. In such a man there is enough fat to make seven bars of soap; enough iron to make a medium-sized nail; enough lime to whitewash a henhouse; enough sugar to fill a sugar-sifter; enough magnesium for a does of magnesia; enough potassium to explode a toy cannon; enough phosphorus to tip 2,200 matches; and a very little sulphur. That then is, in one sense, the origin of man.

But if you ask Christian theology and the Christian thinkers where man comes from, their answer is very different. The Christian answer would be that every man comes from the mind of God; every man is a thought of God; every man is a child of God for whom God has a special task and a special destiny in the world.

Life, as the Christian sees it, is no chance production; life is not a kind of amalgam of chemical elements; life essentially comes from God.

WHENCE? WHERE? HOW? (2)   July 14

Where am I going?
There is more than one answer to that question. There are some at least who would say that we are going nowhere. They would say that we are destined for death and that there is nothing beyond. There are those who would say that the end is nothingness, obliteration, disintegration, extinction.

The Christian answer is very different. The Christian answer is that, just as a man comes from God, so a man goes to God. It is precisely for that reason that this present life matters so much to the Christian.

If life was really going nowhere, if this life was all there was to it, then it would not matter how we used this life. It would in fact be the best and most sensible policy to do what we liked with it, because in the real sense of the term it would not ultimately matter what we did with it.

If life is a thought of the mind of God, then quite inevitably life involves judgment, for a man will necessarily give account of how he fulfilled or did not fulfil the intention of God. The Christian belief is quite simply that because life came from God it must also go back to God—and that is precisely what gives it its significance.

How do I get there?

In the Bible the Christian has the map and the route-book of the good life to show him the way to his goal.

But a map may be difficult to read and to understand and to follow, and there is an even better way to make sure that on a journey we do not lose the way, and that is to get for ourselves a guide who knows the way and who can guide us on the way.

That is what the Christian has in Jesus Christ.

If we are Christians, we believe that we came from God and we go to God and that Jesus Christ is the guide upon the way.

JESUS HAD TO . . . (1)   July 15

D. L. Moody was never afraid to say bluntly and directly what he felt; he was a man who pulled no punches. Once a man did his best to disrupt one of his meetings with interruptions and heckling and every kind of discourtesy. At the end of the meeting he came up to Moody and offered to shake hands with him. Moody looked at him. "I suppose," he said, "if Jesus Christ could eat the Last Supper with a Judas Iscariot, I ought to shake hands with you."

Behind that statement there lies a great truth, the truth that, no matter what we are called on to suffer and to bear and to endure and to accept, Jesus had it worse.

Jesus had to accept insult, and he had to accept slander.

They called him a gluttonous man and a drunkard; they said that he was the friend of tax-collectors and sinners and they implied that he was like the company that he kept.

Sometimes we feel insulted and slandered. Whatever is said about us, let us remember that they said still worse about Jesus—and he was the sinless One.

Jesus had to accept the failure of friendship.

If ever a man was let down by his friends, Jesus was. In the hour of his deepest and bitterest need, in the hour when loyalty would have been infinitely valuable, they all forsook him and fled.

Sometimes our friends fail us; sometimes they are disloyal to us; sometimes they break their promise and their pledge. Often it is hurting, but it is not really the end of all things.

When that happens to us, let us remember that it happened to Jesus and that one of his friends was the traitor who delivered him to death. No matter what has happened to us, worse happened to Jesus—and Jesus was the one, who, having loved his own, loved them to the end.

In his case the supreme loyalty was answered by the supreme disloyalty.

JESUS HAD TO . . . (2) July 16

Jesus had to accept ingratitude and thanklessness.

When Jesus was on trial for his life, when Jesus was led out to die, when Jesus was crucified, where were all the hundreds and the thousands whom he had fed and healed and whom he had saved from death? There was apparently no voice raised on his behalf and no one prepared to stand by him in that hour.

Sometimes we think that people are thankless; sometimes we think that we live in a world in which nothing but the cynical conclusion that it is impossible to expect gratitude must be true. There was no one who gave as much to men as Jesus did, yet, in his hour of need, there was not a single person to speak for him or to stand by him.

Jesus had misunderstanding to accept.

It is quite clear that throughout his ministry his disciples never really understood what he was saying. They never ceased to be selfishly ambitious. They never ceased to be jealous of each other. They never grasped the fact that he must die. His teaching about the Resurrection never ever began to penetrate their minds.

Sometimes we think that we are misunderstood. Sometimes we feel that we have a message and that people simply refuse to take it in. Let us remember that there was never anyone so misunderstood as Jesus was, and yet he never grew bitter and never despaired.

Jesus had undeserved suffering to bear.

No man ever deserved suffering less, and no man ever experienced suffering more terrible. He had done nothing but love people; he had lived a life of moral and spiritual perfection; and yet he came to the end in the agony of the Cross.

There is nothing that we have to experience which Jesus has not already experienced. And it is because he went through it himself that he is able to help others who are going through it.

DILETTANTES July 17

I had to do a journey of more than four hundred miles by car in one day. Four hundred miles is a long way—far too long a way—to drive a car in one day, and naturally I was in a hurry. During that long drive, I could not help noticing that I was held up by two kinds of people.

I was held up by heavy lorries. The lorries could not possibly go any faster and their drivers are the most courteous drivers on the road. These drivers were making the best speed they could.

But there were also the people who are really a nuisance. They are of two kinds.

There is the man who drives a steady thirty miles an hour, who would claim to be the safest driver on the road. Even worse, there are the people who are obviously out for pleasure. They drift along slowly, totally relaxed, gazing around.

There is a parable of the Church and its member here.

We have those who are not very good church members, but who are honestly doing their best. Sometimes we think it would be nice to have a kind of standard of church membership and to insist that all should conform to it. But clearly we can't do that.

To them we owe sympathy and help and encouragement, not criticism and irritation.

But we have the other kind of church member. We have the kind who are very slow and very safe, quite unadventurous, who won't be hurried, whose battle-cry is, "We never did that here." They hold things up because they refuse to move any faster. And they can come near to breaking a minister's heart.

Worst of all, we have the members like the drifting drivers out for pleasure. We might call them dilettante Christians. They drift comfortably along, continuously holding up those who want to get the Church somewhere. For them religion is a saunter and not a pilgrimage, a drift and not a drive.

It is the stragglers who hold up the traffic on the roads, and who, with their dilettante Christianity, hold up the Church.

THE CHURCH   July 18

The first duty of the Church is to build people, not buildings.

The word church never means a building anywhere in the Bible. If you said to an early Christian, "What a lovely church," and you were referring to a building, he would not know what you were talking about. To him "the church" was a body of men and women and children who had given their hearts to Jesus Christ.

This means that when we build churches today, they should be the best that today can build in its own idiom and its own style.

The Church has an odd habit of stopping at certain periods. Its liturgical language stopped five hundred years ago in Elizabethan English. Its architecture stopped even before that. Even the robes that preachers wear are an anachronism and belong really to the travelling monks and friars of past centuries.

This means that church building must be functional; it must be such that the work of the Church can be adequately done in it.

There are two things we must aim at—reality and "contemporariness". So long as the Church continues to live in the past in liturgy and architecture, so long people will regard it as an archaic survival and not a living power.

LIFE AND DEATH (1)   July 19

There is a certain impermanence in life.

"The world is a bridge," says the unwritten saying of Jesus. "The wise man will pass over it, but will not build his house upon it." Man is all his life a resident alien and a pilgrim in the world.

Away back in A.D. 627, the wise men of the ancient kingdom of Northumbria were meeting to discuss whether or not they would accept the new faith of Christianity which Edwin their king had already accepted. And an aged counsellor drew the famous picture of life: "So seems the life of man, O king, as a sparrow's flight through the hall when you are sitting at meat in wintertide, with the warm fire lighted on the hearth, but the icy rainstorm outside. The sparrow flies in at the one door, and tarries for a moment in the light and the heat of the hearth-fire, and then, flying from the other, vanishes into the wintry darkness whence it came. So tarries for a moment the life of man in our sight; but what is before it, what after it, we know not."

There is a pessimism there that is far from Christian belief, for we know that we come from God and we go to God. But there is the essential truth that life is only a moment in God's eternities. Life is not a settled possession; no man has a prescriptive right to life; life is basically and essentially an impermanent moment of time in the midst of eternity.

If then there is this rhythm of life and death, there is also a rhythm of sorrow and joy.

We have only to look at a great daily newspaper. It will have prominently displayed in it the notices of the births, the deaths, and the marriages, and behind these notices there will be in each case human sorrow and human joy.

Sorrow is the price of love. If we could banish love and if we could teach ourselves never to care for any human being, then there would be no such thing as sorrow. But, being as we are, with human hearts and human affections we live in this rhythm of sorrow and of joy.

No man can live in any real sense of the term and escape either of them.

If there is this rhythm of life and of death, and of sorrow and of joy, it must be true that whatever is happening, life must go on.

We cannot stop the world and get off; we cannot opt out of life. There is therefore in life the need for acceptance of life as it is, and the necessity to go on.

Resentment, bitterness, the refusal to accept things as they are can cause nothing but a frustrated beating of the head against the bars of life.

Alistair Maclean—not the famous novelist, but the famous preacher—tells of an incident.

Up in the Scottish Highlands a little group of people were talking about heroism; they were saying that everybody had sooner or later to practise some kind of heroism. A young man turned to an old woman; she looked so ordinary and so serene; he did not know that life had been for her a series of tragic things. "And what kind of heroism do you practise?" he said with an obvious air of thinking that he did not believe that there could be any kind of heroism in a life like hers. "I?" she said. "I practise the heroism of going on."

There is always need for the heroism which takes life as it is and goes on with it.

A man must therefore always be ready to lay life down.

In life there is not only impermanence, but there is also uncertainty. No man knows the day or the hour when the last call will sound for him, coming at morning, at midday or at evening. And therefore, if he is wise, he will have life so ordered, and peace with God so made, that he can at any time answer serenely to his name.

A wedding and a funeral, and between them an ordinary week—that is life. That is life's rhythm. Just because of that a man does well to remember that he is not a resident on earth but a pilgrim of eternity.

DETOURS   July 21

It is often wisest in life to get to your destination by way of a detour. It is specially so when we are working with people. Some people go ramstam, like a bull at a gate, at anything that they undertake—and it can be a big mistake.

This is the way that trouble often arises in churches. It is often quite obvious that something needs to be done; but in churches there is almost always a kind of inertia which likes to stick to the old ways. Well, then, if a leader wishes something done, or if he wishes a change to be made, time and time again his best course is not direct and violent action. It is to sow an idea in the minds of his people, and to wait with patience until that idea germinates and blossoms—and then in the end people will come to think that they thought of the idea themselves! And they will accept it eagerly, when they would have opposed it if it had been pushed down their throats.

The detour of patience will often get a leader his own way when direct action will simply put what he wants further away than ever.

London taxi-drivers, I have been told, have to pass a very strict police examination to make sure that they know the shortest way between any two points in the city. One candidate had studied the maps until he knew them by heart In the examination he was asked the quickest way from one place to another. He gave it according to the map. He was failed, because the route he indicated was the quickest all right, but it would have involved driving the taxi down a lengthy flight of steps and through a lane too narrow for a bicycle!

What we ought to look for in life is not the quickest and the shortest way but the best way. And the best way to get things done very often involves the patience necessary to make a detour and to follow a diversion. The best qualification for leadership is a very rare combination of qualities. It is enthusiasm plus patience.

The man who has both of these will certainly get things done, and done with good will.

HISTORY (I)   July 22

One of the most famous remarks ever made was Henry Ford's dictum that "History is bunk". But Henry Ford went on to add something to that dictum. He went on to say that the history which really matters is not the history that is past and done with, but the history which in our day and generation we are consciously engaged in making.

We may place beside Henry Ford's dictum the saying of Oliver Cromwell. When he was arranging for the education of his son Richard, he said, "I would have him learn a little history."

Here are two points of view about history. Which is the right one? As so often happens in cases like this, they are both right, for history has its uses *and* abuses.

History can lead to pessimism or it can lead to optimism.

It can be quoted as a proof of all the things that cannot be done, and it can be quoted as a proof of all the things that can be done.

Take, for instance, the dictum that we cannot change human nature. We can point at war, at graft, at racketeering, at victimisation, at prostitution, and we can say, "You will never get rid of these things, because you can't change human nature."

On the other hand, a missionary tells how he presided over a communion service in central Africa. At that communion service the members of two African tribes sat in perfect love and harmony. Less than a generation before it had been the custom for the young warriors of these tribes, as they came to manhood, to go out and to blood their spears in each other's blood, to steal each other's women, to burn each other's houses, and to destroy each other's crops. They had done it for centuries. It was engraved into tribal ritual and custom—and yet the power of Jesus Christ had brought ancestral enemies together in fellowship around the table of love.

History justifies a glorious optimism in the power of the Christ who can do things like that.

History can teach hope and history can teach despair; it all depends how you look at it.

HISTORY (2)   July 23

History can lead to cynicism or to faith.

Take for instance, two contrasting verdicts on history. One student of history has said that history is the record of the sins, the follies and the mistakes of men. On the other hand, J. A. Froude, the historian, said that history is a voice sounding across the centuries that in the end it is well for the righteous and ill for the wicked.

The one man sees in history nothing but the human race staggering from error to error; the other sees in history the action of the justice and the providence of God. This much is true, that there is a moral order in the world, and the man or the nation which breaks that moral order comes in the end to disaster. *Magna est veritas et praevalebit*, runs the Latin tag; great is the truth and in the end it will prevail; and, even though sometimes the triumph took the long way round, that triumph has always in the end appeared.

History can be a soporific or a stimulus.

A great past can be one of two things. It can be a very great handicap. It often happens that at some time certain methods produced in a church or in a community are a very great success. And so often the tendency is to think that the methods which were successful in one generation will be equally successful in another. Kipling once gave as his advice to authors: "Never try to repeat a success."

It is almost axiomatic that that which was successful in one generation is not likely to be successful in the next. And so we come to the other side of history. The great function of a great history is not to give people something from the past to copy, but to inspire them to find something which will act in the present.

Pessimism or optimism, cynicism or faith, soporific or stimulus—history can bring them all.

It is for us to make the choice.

I once spent a thrilling and a fascinating week at a Summer School for Christian Education. What has struck me most about that school is that it has been a quite unconscious demonstration of almost complete ecumenicity.

There were at it Anglicans, Methodists, Baptists, Congregationalists, Presbyterians, Roman Catholics, and a Jewish girl.

There were there people from England, Scotland, Ireland, Wales, and Israel. Usually it was only by chance that I found out the denominational affiliation of each person.

Here was unity founded on three things.

It was founded on a common love for scholarship.

The basis of the school was Bible Study. Here is the very basis of unity. No matter who we are and what we are, we can sit down before the Bible together, and we can ask what this book says to us, when it is interpreted with all that modern scholarship can bring to it.

In this sphere today we have a most hopeful situation. In the last ten or fifteen years there has been a notable blurring of the lines between the fundamentalist and critical scholar, between the conservative and the liberal position. People who even a dozen years ago would not have read each other's books and would not have listened to each other's words, appreciate more than they ever did what each has to offer the other. In the world of scholarship there is a coming together which is wonderful.

It was founded on a common love of worship.

It was founded on devotion as well as on scholarship. It was not that the demand to worship was obtrusive or regimented; it was simply that its atmosphere dominated all the fellowship of more than a hundred people. Night and morning we prayed together, and the whole tone of the school was set by that prayer.

Again, in this sphere today we have a most hopeful situation. Again, in the last twenty years or so there has been a notable blurring of the lines between what we might call the liturgist and the advocate of what is usually called free prayer. The people who need pugnaciously to insist on free prayer are coming to see the beauty and the use of liturgy and order, and the liturgist is coming to see the value of an element of spontaneity added to the fixed forms. In the sphere of worship people of opposite traditions are stretching out hands to each other in a very wonderful way, in the new discovery that each has something to offer the other.

That Summer School I mentioned yesterday was founded on personal relations.
For me the most interesting part was when we talked late and argued late,

and when mind sharpened mind as iron sharpens iron. Here again there is a notable blurring of differences. There is a new willingness for Roman Catholic to talk with Protestant and for Jew to talk with Gentile. There is a new willingness at least to try to understand each other a little better.

Scholarship, prayer, human relationships brought us together; but we knew, however, there was a limit. The Sacrament was never celebrated.

What then keeps us apart? I think we could call the separating force ecclesiasticism. And in ecclesiasticism I see four things:

Ecclesiasticism is worshipping systems more than worshipping Jesus Christ.
Ecclesiasticism is limiting the operation of the grace of God.
Ecclesiasticism is making the tradition of the past more determinative than the need of the present.
Ecclesiasticism is holding an exclusive rather than an inclusive view of the Church.

Today there is more hope than ever there was of real unity. It is the ordinary members of the Church who can make that hope a reality, and who can provide the leadership which the ecclesiastical hierarchies have failed to supply.

WHEN IT IS DANGEROUS TO THINK   July 26

Often when we say, "I'll think about it," all that we really mean is that we don't want to decide.

There is a famous story of how in a moment of crisis in the history of Greece, Agesilaus, the Spartan king, assembled his men and prepared to go into action. He sent word to another of the Greek rulers asking him to come to help in the hour of their country's peril. The other king replied that he would consider it. Agesilaus sent back the answer: "Tell him that while he is considering it we will march."

We ought to be very careful that, when we say, "I'll think about it," we in fact mean precisely the opposite, and that we are not simply evading a decision that we ought to make.

Another way of putting this is that when we say, "I'll think about it," we are often simply postponing something that we ought to do.

Sometimes, perhaps unconsciously, we labour under the delusion that, if we talk about a thing for long enough, in some mysterious way we will find that it has happened. No one is going to deny the usefulness of thinking about things and of discussing them, but perhaps we should remember oftener than we do that thought and talk are in the last analysis no substitutes for action. There comes a time when talking and thinking must become doing, and when the phrase, "I'll think about it," ought to be left behind.

It is all too true that often, if we go on saying, "I'll think about it," the thing will so often not be done at all.

It is often this way with some generous impulse. Someone's need moves us to pity and compassion; we would like to help; but we stop to think about it and the fine moment is gone.

There is a time when it is no doubt wise to say, "I'll think about it," but there are still more times when we ought to say, "Don't bother thinking about it! Do it!"

RELIGION (1)   July 27

A correspondent from Canada, who is one of the few surviving people who actually heard Henry Drummond preach and teach, sent me, in a letter, a story about Moody and Drummond.

Moody and Drummond were very different and yet for many years they worked hand in hand. Moody was very conservative and was what would now be called fundamentalist in his standpoint. Drummond willingly accepted a modern scientific view of the universe, welcomed developments in biblical scholarship and was much more liberal in his outlook.

Certain of Moody's followers and associates were highly suspicious of Drummond, and were very critical of Moody for accepting Drummond as a helper. They questioned Drummond's orthodoxy and would, if they could, have insisted that Moody should break with him. To those who attacked Drummond's orthodoxy and who questioned his suitability as a partner in evangelical work, Moody answered, "Henry Drummond is a scholar. I am not; I wish I were. But this I know, that I can only hope to spend eternity with Henry Drummond."

As Moody quite clearly saw, the main thing which clearly matters is not theology but personality. Let Henry Drummond's theology be what it might be, D. L. Moody was quite prepared to take his chance in eternity with Henry Drummond as a person.

This saying of Moody's turned my thoughts to an article on Stephen Colwell. Colwell was troubled about the aridity of so much religion of his day, for Colwell was one of the first prophets of the social gospel. In 1851 he published a book entitled *New Themes for the Protestant Clergy: Creed Without Charity, Theology Without Humanity, Protestantism Without Christianity*. That seemed to him an apt description of the official religion of his day.

RELIGION (2)   July 28

Colwell spoke of creeds without charity.

There is a certain type of Christianity so-called which joins together an unimpeachable orthodoxy and an almost complete lovelessness. It is much more concerned with smelling out heresy than it is with helping human need. It carries with it an atmosphere of permanent disapproval. It is incapable of believing that there is any other way to God than its own way. It claims the right to sit in judgment on the faith and the belief of all others. It may possibly blast men with truth; it will certainly never warm them with love.

Colwell spoke of theology without humanity.

A theology which cannot be communicated to an ordinary man is not a valid theology. That may be a hard saying, but salvation is not of the scholars, but of all men. And if a man has discovered a gospel, he has the obligation of communication.

Colwell spoke of Protestantism without Christianity.

This still exists. It will anger some people to say so, but there are few things less Christian than an Orange Walk with its deliberate flaunting of religious intolerance, and on many occasions its deliberate asking for trouble. There are certain Protestants—and not all in that Order—whose Christianity consists in anti-Roman Catholicism.

You can never found a religion on a doctrine of protest, for protest is essentially negative, and religion is essentially positive. As Wesley said when his nephew became a Roman Catholic, "You can be saved in any Church and you can be damned in any Church. What matters is, How is your heart with Christ?"

Colwell's complaint is still valid, Orthodoxy, intellectualism, protestantism in the narrower sense, cannot win men. What does win men is a Henry Drummond in whom others catch a glimpse of the love of Jesus Christ.

NO "ACT OF GOD" (1)   July 29

One whose main task it is to teach does not have to exercise a pastoral ministry in the same sense as a parish minister has to. But I had to go to visit a mother who had lost a daughter in the most tragic circumstances.

The death of the daughter had taken place as a result of an accident which was in any ordinary way impossible. To this day no one knows just how this accident happened, yet happen it did.

Now, when the accident was being investigated, a certain phrase was used by one of the chief investigators, a man with a long experience in such investigations. He said that the accident was so impossible that all that could be said was that it was "an act of God".

It is difficult to imagine a more terrible and a more blasphemous phrase. What kind of God can people believe in when they attribute the accidental death of a girl of twenty-four years of age to an act of God? How can anyone who is left possibly pray to a God who would do a thing like that?

During my own parish ministry I was never able to go into a house where there had been an untimely and a tragic death or sorrow and say, "It is the will of God." When a child or a young person dies too soon, when there is a fatal accident, maybe due to someone's mistake or misjudgment, that is not "an act of God", neither is it the will of God. It is, in fact, the precise opposite of the will of God. It is against the will of God, and God is just as grieved about it as we are.

If a terrible and an incurable disease strikes someone, if a child is run down and killed by a motor car, driven it may be by a reckless or drunken driver, if there is a disaster in the air or at sea or on the railways or on the roads, that is not the will of God. It is exactly and precisely what God did not will. It is due not to God's will, but to some human failure or to some human mistake.

God gave men free will because there could neither be goodness nor love without free will and exactly for that reason the action of men can run right counter to the will of God.

I do not think that anyone can calculate the vast amount of damage that has been done by suggesting that terrible and tragic events in life are the will of God.

NO "ACT OF GOD" (2) July 30

When Jesus was on earth in the body, he healed the sick; he raised to life the little daughter of Jairus and the son of the widow at Nain. Quite clearly, Jesus did not think sickness and illness and untimely death the will of God. Quite clearly, he thought them the reverse of the will of God. They were the very things that he had come to help and to overcome.

What, then, can we say at a time like that?

We can say that God is as grieved as we are, that he is sharing in our sorrow and our grief, that he is afflicted in all our afflictions, that his heart is going out to meet our heart.

We can say that he has it in his power to make it up to those who are taken too soon away, and to those to whom sorrow and suffering has tragically come. If God is justice and if God is love, I am as certain as it is possible to be certain of anything that there is a life to come. And in that life to come God is seeing to it that the life cut off too soon is getting its chance to blossom and flourish and the life involved in tragedy is finding its compensation. The eternal world is redressing the balance of the world of time.

We can say that Christianity has never pretended to explain sorrow and suffering.

It may often be that in any tragedy there is traceable an element of human fault, human mistake, human sin; in any disaster the reason may well lie in human error. Yet even when all such cases are taken into account there remains much that is simply inexplicable.

Christianity offers no cheap and facile explanation. In face of such things we have often to say, "I do not know why this happened." But what Christianity does triumphantly offer is the power to face these things, to bear them, to come through them on your own two feet, and even to transform them so that the tragedy becomes a crown.

In the New Testament we have a supremely wonderful example of someone who was content to remain in the background and that at no small cost to herself. Of all Paul's helpers there was none so near and so close to him as Timothy. "I have no one like him," said Paul (Phil. 2:20). More than once Paul calls Timothy his beloved and faithful child (1 Cor. 4:17; 1 Tim. 1:2; 2 Tim. 1:2). To Paul, Timothy was like a son.

It was at the beginning of the second missionary journey that Paul as it were took Timothy on to his staff. Timothy's mother's name was Eunice (2 Tim. 1:5). It is in Acts 16:1-4 that we read the first connecting of Timothy with Paul. Now from that passage there is every reason to believe that Eunice was a widow. There are Latin manuscripts which in the first verse call the mother of Timothy *vidua*, and there are certain Greek manuscripts which call her *chera*, and both words mean widow. And it may be in verse 3 that we could translate, "For they all knew that his father *had been* a Greek."

Now, if Eunice was a widow, and if Timothy was her only son, and beyond doubt a good son too, it must have been not only a wrench but a very considerable sacrifice to see her son go off adventuring with Paul for Jesus Christ. Surely the home of Eunice must have been an emptier and financially a much poorer place without the young Timothy there. It may well be that in the background of Timothy there stands a mother, Eunice, of whom the Church at large never heard, but to whom the Church owed Timothy.

There are in life very many to this day who are still described in terms of someone else. They are known as someone's husband, someone's wife, someone's brother, someone's sister, someone's son. For the most part they never complain and they never grudge the limelight and the leading place to their more famous friend, relation, or partner. They are content and well content to take the second place.

The world needs such people; the Church cannot do without such people.

True, we can never do without our leaders, but there is many a Timothy who could never have become a leader in the Church unless at home there was a mother or a father or a family who made it possible for them to go out.

When we give thanks for those who were first, let us never forget to be equally thankful for the great and noble army of those who are content to take the second place.

August

A certain man was sitting in his garden suffering agonies with toothache, trying to make up his mind to visit the dentist.

He thought that he would have a cup of tea and a piece of bread and jam. He got the tea and the bread and jam; he took a bite of the bread and jam without noticing that a wasp had settled on it. When he took the bite, the wasp stung him extremely painfully in the gum. He dashed indoors and saw in the mirror that the gum was swollen and inflamed; he treated it and bathed it and gradually the pain subsided; and when the pain of the wasp sting had subsided, he suddenly realised that the pain of the toothache was gone too.

A medical man, commenting on that story, said that it is medically quite common for two pains to cancel each other out. In other words, paradoxically the best way to get rid of one pain is to get another, and then they will eliminate each other.

There you have an excellent example of the Principle of Displacement.

The Principle of Displacement is the title of a sermon by that once justly famous preacher, Percy Ainsworth. He took as his text Isaiah 55:13: "Instead of the thorn shall come up the cypress," (R.S.V.) The A.V. has fir tree for cypress. You wanted to clear a piece of ground; you took out a spiky jagged thorn tree; but you did not leave the ground empty; you put in a gracious cypress instead. You displaced the one with the other.

When a farmer looks at a weedy piece of ground, he tears out the weeds; but he does not then leave the ground empty; he displaces the weeds with a useful crop.

In life the way to get rid of a bad thing is to displace it with a good thing. This is a lesson of the parable of the empty house (Luke 11:24-26). The demon was ejected from the house; the house was swept clean; but it was left empty; and the consequence was that the demon came back with seven demons worse than himself and reoccupied the empty house. To keep the demon out, he should have been displaced by good occupants.

Not emptiness, but displacement must be the principle of life.

DISPLACEMENT (2)   August 2

It is this way with thoughts.

No man ever got rid of evil and unclean thoughts by simply saying, "I will not think of this or that." The more he does that, the more in fact he concentrates his thoughts on the thing of which he does not wish to think. He can only get rid of the evil thought by thinking of something else. He must get a new interest, a new thought. You cannot empty your mind; you must displace one thought with another.

It is this way with disappointment.

A person may be disappointed in some hope. It is not enough simply to accept it; one hope must be displaced by another hope. This is in fact very largely what the psychologists mean by sublimation. When something vital is taken out of a man's life, the way to handle the situation is to displace the lost thing by something else, to give all the thought and energy which would have been given to the lost or unattainable thing to something else, not simply to leave an empty hole in life, but to displace the lost thing with some new interest and activity.

It is this way with sorrow.

The best way, perhaps the only way, to forget one's sorrow is to enter into the sorrow of someone else. To sit alone and to think and to remember and to brood and to resent will quite certainly make things worse. The only way in such a situation is to enter into someone else's tragedy. We will best bear our own sorrow by helping someone else to bear theirs.

We ought to remember the principle of displacement. We will find that there is nothing which so effectively displaces one's own troubles as sharing those of someone else.

GOD   August 3

How do we feel about God? What is our attitude to what God sends?
You can have three attitudes to what happens in life.

You can accept it just because God is bigger than you.

In the last analysis you can't do anything about it anyway, so it is better to accept it and to be done with it.

That was the Stoic point of view. The Stoics believed that everything that happened was according to the will of God. They therefore said that the one thing to learn was to accept everything without complaint. Not to do so was simply to batter your head against the walls of the universe, a painful process which got you precisely nowhere. So the Stoics said epigrammatically, "If you can't get what you want, teach yourself to want what you can get."

You can accept things because God is wiser than we are.

This is better, but it is still not the best. We have all known the kind of people who have a passion for arranging the lives of others. They know best and they genuinely think that you ought to accept their guidance. Now these people are not usually popular, because no one likes being pushed around.

If we could say no more than that God is wiser than we are, there might well be a kind of cold impersonalness in God's dealing with us. We might think of God sitting in a vast superiority arranging people's lives with a kind of intellectual benevolence, meticulously dealing out what is best for us, but regarding us rather as the pieces in a pattern than as persons with hearts that can be touched and feelings that can be hurt.

God has the wisdom to know, and the power to do; he is bigger and wiser than we are. But God also has the love to understand; and so he does not move us around like pieces on a board who cannot say No anyway. He does not arrange things with a distant superiority. He appeals to us; he trusts us; he leaves us free to say No and to go our own way if we want it that way.

But when we realise that at the heart of things there is love, then we can say, not in resignation, but in joy, "Thy will be done."

CLOTHES (1)   August 4

I wonder how many congregations still make it a rule that their elders should at the sacrament of Communion, wear a morning coat, striped trousers and perhaps a white tie?

The answer to that question I simply do not know. It did not meet me in my own ministry in a parish, firstly, because my own congregation was an artisan congregation in which any such regulation would have been impossible to enforce, and, secondly, because the greater part of any ministry lay within the war years, and clothing coupons would have ruled out any such possibility.

It may well be that there are now no congregations which make this a rule, but I think that there are still a fair number in which it is still the understood practice, at least in my native Scotland.

What is to be said for it, and what is to be said against it?

To dress all alike certainly obliterates differences.

The likeness does away with the differences, and therefore does away with any kind of competition—although without being cynical one may well say that any such competition is much more likely to arise among the female membership of the church than among the male membership. Still, there is something to be said for uniformity.

To have a dress which is a uniform is no bad thing.

It does appear to show that a man is on duty, and that he is not ashamed to show that he is on duty. It identifies a man as doing a particular kind of job, and as being the kind of man who is perfectly willing to show that it is so.

It is the sign of respect.

We normally dress carefully if we are going to any social or important function. It could be argued that the same principle should apply to those who go to serve in the house of God.

I do not think that there is really anything else to be said for this custom. To many, these three reasons will seem good enough reasons for observing it.

CLOTHES (2)   August 5

Now we turn to reasons that oppose formal dress on Communion occasions.

Certainly such dress is archaic and anachronistic.

It is seldom or never worn anywhere now except at weddings.

This was not so forty years ago or so. My own father usually wore such clothes every day in life for his work as a bank manager; but now such dress has almost entirely passed from the scene. Even its last survival in shop-walkers in the great and expensive shops hardly survives now!

This may be yet another of the many things which, to the ordinary person, is an image of the Church as an institution which lives in the past.

It could be argued that there is a certain social snobbery in this.

It could be argued that this is a symptom of the fact that perhaps there was a day when the Church did in fact draw its office-bearers from that class of of the community which wore such clothes, from a day when the "laird" was much more likely to be an elder than the ploughman, and the master much more likely to be an elder than the artisan.

If ever there was such a day, then it belongs to the discredit rather than to the credit of the Church, and if any practice seems to suggest it, then the sooner the practice is abandoned the better.

But the great argument against it is quite simple. It is, quite bluntly that of expense.

Are we, in certain congregations, laying it down as a condition of the eldership that a man will be able to buy a certain kind of clothing? And is the

Church losing young men who would make excellent elders but who are buying a house and paying for furniture and meeting the expenses of a young family?

We would do well to remember Pope's famous couplet:

> Worth makes the man, and
>   want of it the fellow;
> The rest is all but leather
>   or prunella.

It is men we need—what they wear within the limits of decent respectability is totally irrelevant.

CONFLICT (1)   August 6

I write this on the Saturday evening following the tragic death of President Kennedy, and like most other people I have a personal sense of loss at the death of this man, whom I never saw in the flesh.

But it is not about that that I write. I write about one of the most significant things that I have seen for a very long time in regard to the place of the Church in modern life and society.

There is an evening newspaper which on a Saturday has a certain amount of space given to the news of the Churches and to articles on religion. *This Saturday evening that page is missing*. The news of the Kennedy assassination has driven it from the paper.

There might be little enough to regret in that, for clearly news of such world-wide significance must have extraordinary space. But—and here is the significance of the situation—in that issue of the paper five columns were given to racing news, five columns were given to news from the entertainment world, one whole page was given to women's topics and a short story, and there was even space for the usual astrological horoscopes and the alleged information that the stars give about our future.

The situation was desolatingly plain—when something had to go, that something was the news of the Churches and the religious articles.

I am enough of a journalist to know that the Church material was probably fixed and maybe even set up in advance, and that it may well have been quite unsuitable for the occasion; but I am also enough of a journalist to know that there would have been no very great problem in getting any fast-working competent writer to rewrite the whole section through the night and so to give the Church's voice on this world disaster.

But apparently no one thought it worthwhile. What the Church had to say simply did not matter.

I have seldom seen anything which, without a word of comment, showed more devastatingly the twilight of the Church.

But why should anyone really be surprised at the newspaper's action, because this is what is happening in the personal life of so many people? If there is a clash of times and engagements, it is so often the Church and the religious meeting which have to go. People will go to church, but if there are visitors on a Sunday, if someone suggests an excursion on the Sunday, it is the Church that goes.

There are very few like a great scholar whom I know. He belonged to a group engaged on fairly important work; it was difficult to get the group, widely scattered, together through the week, and it was suggested that the group should meet and work at week-ends. This man said gently but firmly, "No! I worship on Sunday." And the astonishing thing was that the whole group accepted this as a final verdict and, in fact, did not meet to work on Sunday.

There are so very few now who can really and truly say, "Christ means life to me" (Phil. 1:21). There are so many who, like Lord Melbourne in the nineteenth century, say, "Religion is all right so long as it does not interfere with a man's private life." For so many the claims of Christ are well enough so long as they don't cause any trouble or bother, and if there is any clash of interests, then these claims are conveniently forgotten.

The tragedy is not so much that the action of the newspaper shows how expendable the voice of the Church is; the tragedy really is that the Church is so full of people for whom their religion is only on the circumference of their lives that we, in fact, have no right to expect anything else.

If we are living in the twilight of the Church, there is no one but ourselves who can usher in a change.

ONE STEP (1)   August 8

A well-known bacteriologist tells me about a little assistant that he had. About 300 samples of milk had come into his laboratory for testing; and it was the assistant who had to do the testing. He was sorry for her faced with such a task; so he said to her, "Isn't that far too much for you to do?" "O no," she said. "I'll just do them one at a time!"

Can you think of a better way?

And then my bacteriologist friend went on to quote a Chinese saying to me: "A journey of a thousand miles begins with one single step."

There is sound advice here to anyone who has a great deal of work to do, and who does not know where to start.

When we have a great deal of work to do, the first thing to do is to make a start.
That sounds as if it was hardly worth saying, but it is. When we have a great deal of work to do, one of the greatest of all temptations is to sit and look at it. At a time like that, a kind of lethargy seems to descend on us, and we tend to sit and look at, and think about, all that has to be done. In such a situation, whether it be concerned with writing letters, washing dishes, com-

posing sermons, paying visits, working for examinations, the first rule is to make a start somewhere.

To start is half the battle.

The next rule is to concentrate on the thing we are doing at the moment.

The determination to concentrate on the thing in hand is not altogether common. You find the lad who, when he is a student, spends most of his time thinking about the first charge that he will get; and you get the minister in his first charge thinking about what he will do when he is called to his second charge; and the quite inevitable result is that the student is not a very good student and the minister is not a very good minister.

The only way to do a job well is to do it as if it was the only job in the world. And all the likelihood is that if a man does a job in that way, it will lead to a bigger and a better one without him thinking about it all.

ONE STEP (2)   August 9

Remember that it is steady and consistent even if slow work that gets things done rather than brilliant spasms of work.

It is worth setting down Aesop's old fable of the hare and the tortoise.

A hare one day ridiculed the short feet and slow pace of the tortoise. The latter, laughing, said, "Though you be swift as the wind I will beat you in a race." The hare, deeming his assertion to be simply impossible, assented to the proposal; and they agreed that the fox should choose the course, and fix the goal.

On the day appointed for the race they started together. The tortoise never for a moment stopped, but went on with a slow but steady pace straight to the end of the course. The hare, trusting to his native swiftness, cared little about the race, and lying down by the wayside, fell fast asleep. At last waking up, and moving as fast as he could, he saw that the tortoise had reached the goal, and was comfortably dozing after her fatigue.

As the Preacher had it many centuries ago: "The race is not to the swift, nor the battle to the strong'. (Eccles. 9:11). Steady perseverance will, in the end, achieve far more than spasmodic brilliance.

I suppose that everyone, now and again, becomes overwhelmed with the things with which life confronts them. When that happens, we must not sit and look at things. We must start somewhere. We must not think of the next task, but must concentrate on the one in hand.

We must remember that steady and unremitting effort, and not spasmodic brilliance, is the way to real achievement.

WISER THAN WE THINK   August 10

There are at least some of us who under-rate people very badly indeed.

We often under-rate children.

We quite certainly under-rated our grand-daughter Karen's intelligence on one occasion and we under-rated her ability to take what we thought would be news that she wouldn't like.

Perhaps we sometimes keep from children what they could perfectly well be told. Sometimes we don't even try to explain to children that which they could perfectly well understand. We often brush off a child's question to which we might well give a straight and honest answer. One of the worst faults in our bringing up children and our teaching of children is that we under-rate their intelligence and their power to take things.

There are very many preachers and teachers who completely under-rate their congregation and their audience.

There are very few preachers who make any attempt to pass on to their congregations any of the results of modern scholarship or modern thought; and the main reason for this failure is, bluntly, that they are afraid to do so. So long as they do the thing positively, and so long as they do not deal in destructive negatives, their fears will nearly always be quite unjustified.

Well over a quarter of a million people bought John Robinson's *Honest to God*, and practically no one would buy the normal book of sermons if any publisher would publish one.

People want honesty. They want to be treated as theologically and intellectually adult. They want to know how the case stands and what a man thinks.

I do not wish to tread on dangerous ground, nor do I wish to confound legitimate criticism with conceit, but I am bound to say that this seems to me specially true of broadcast and televised preaching. There is here given to the Church an incalculable weapon of systematic Christian education, and yet so often a preacher spends the precious moments trying to be entertaining rather than informative.

As the writer to the Hebrews saw long ago, there is nothing worse than feeding people with milk when they need strong meat and of making babies out of adult men and women (Heb. 5:12–14).

TEARS August 11

It is extraordinary how mindful the Bible is of the broken-hearted. I turn to only one prophet, to Isaiah. "Comfort, comfort my people, says your God" (Isa. 40:1) "I am he that comforts you." (Isa. 51:12) "The Lord has comforted his people.' (Isa. 52:9).

You remember how the prophet interprets his commission from God—and here none of the newer translations can ever really take the place of the Authorised Version. It is to bind up the broken-hearted; to give beauty for ashes, the oil of joy for mourning, the garment of praise for the spirit of heaviness (Isa. 61:1–3). "As one whom his mother comforts, so will I comfort you", (Isaiah 66:13).

Sunt lacrimae rerum, said Virgil in that phrase at once unforgettable and untranslatable. There are tears of things. And the Bible never forgets the tears of things. And yet it can so often happen that a person can go to a service of the Church and find that the note of comfort is forgotten.

If we are to preach on Sunday, let us remember that there will be those in sorrow there.

But let us remember this. The Bible never forgets the older meaning of the word comfort to which we referred earlier. Frequently the Greek word is *parakalein*, and *parakalein* as we have seen before, does not only mean to comfort; it also means to *encourage*. It is for instance used of soldiers encouraging each other as they go into battle.

It must never be forgotten that the Latin root of the word comfort is *fortis*, which means "brave". The true Christian comfort is no easy and sentimental thing, but something which puts courage into a man when life is threatening to take his courage away.

In any service, there should be that word of comfort that will keep men and women on their feet.

SELF-DISCIPLINE (1)   August 12

I suppose that W. B. Yeats was one of the most musical and the most mystical of modern poets. Anything less "made to order" than Yeats' poetry would be hard to imagine. But he himself, in a scrap of autobiography, gives us a curious glimpse of his work.

He had been ill, and the illness had left him indolent and lethargic and unwilling to work. He had gone to stay with Lady Gregory, and afterwards he said that he owed everything to her. "I asked her," he said, "to send me to my work every day at 11 a.m., and at some other hour to my letters, rating me with idleness, if need be, and I doubt if I should have done much with my life but for her firmness and her care."

It sounds an extremely odd thing that anyone should say to a poet at 11 a.m., "Go to your desk and write poetry," and yet that is precisely what Yeats did, and there is no poet in whom the stream of true poetic inspiration is clearer.

Beverley Nichols, in his first youthful autobiography written at the age of twenty-five, tells of a meeting with Winston Churchill. Beverley Nichols had just written his very successful book, *Prelude*. "How long did it take to write?" asked Churchill. Nichols said that he did not know, that it was done in patches over five months. "Didn't you work at it regularly?" Churchill demanded. Nichols said that he had found regular work impossible, that he had had to wait for the mood. "Nonsense," said Churchill, "you should go to your room every day at 9 o'clock and say, I am going to write for four hours."

Nichols asked what happened if you found you could not write, if you had a headache or indigestion, and so on. Churchill answered, "You've got to get over that. If you sit waiting for inspiration, you will sit waiting till you are an old man. Writing is like any other job, like marching an army, for instance. If you sit down and wait till the weather is fine, you won't get far with your troops. Kick yourself; irritate yourself; but write; it's the only way."

To put it succinctly, Churchill believed that you could produce something very like a work of genius using office hours. He himself proved that it could be done.

SELF-DISCIPLINE (2)   August 13

One of the difficulties of the work of the ministry is that a man has no necessary office hours. There is no one but himself to see that he does his work. But there are certain things that he might well keep before his mind and his conscience.

Is a scholar or preacher going to accept a life in which he has to exercise much less self-discipline than a clerk in an office, a salesman in a shop, a worker in a factory?

These people have to be at their desk, at their counter, at their bench at a certain hour. Why shouldn't he—as we said in an earlier entry?

Does the work of scholarship or the work of the ministry give or imply the right to begin work when we like and to stop when we like? Is the very nature of our calling not such that we ought to have more, and not less, discipline than the people to whom we minister?

What is the scholar or the preacher really thinking about when he is waiting for the mood or waiting for an idea?

Certainly, if we have no method in our preaching, we may well be searching for an idea even late on a Saturday night. But the essence of a teaching ministry is that a man does not preach as the whim or the preference takes him. He preaches his way systematically through the Christian faith and through the Bible.

It is far easier to preach systematically—and it is far better. If a man does not do that, the unfortunate congregation will get all the things the man likes and all the things the man prefers and all the things in which he is interested—and not a total and rounded exposition of the Christian faith.

Does this mean that I must preach on things in which I am not interested, on things which do not attract me, on things which at the moment I know nothing about?

That is precisely what it means. And, if one man's experience is worth anything at all, I think that it is quite certain that the things we thought un-interesting become filled with interest when we work at them, and the books of the Bible we never opened become very arsenals of sermons when we study them, and the things we knew nothing about are very likely the very things we need to know about.

It takes self-discipline to do this, but as Churchill said: "It's the only way."

MIND OVER MATTER   August 14

I once read an article by a journalist called Bertram Jones, on cramp. I suppose that most people at one time or another have experienced that stabbing pain when a muscle knots, often when we are lying in bed. Now it seems that no one quite knows what causes cramp, and it also appears that no one quite knows how to make it better.

Different people have different ways of dealing with cramp, according to Mr. Bertram Jones, and very interesting some of them are.

Dr. Roger Bannister, the first man to run a mile in less than four minutes, claims to have beaten cramp by carrying a small magnet around with him.

A Hampshire housewife takes a bag of corks to bed with her to beat cramp. A London man claims that barrel bungs are best.

Others use a ring of buffalo horn, a crimson thread tied round each toe, the powdered teeth of a sea-horse, the skin of an eel, a hippopotamus tooth. All of them claim that their own special method brings a cure.

When you read things like that, you can almost think that you are back in the days of magic and spells. But all this is just another example of the universal fact that, if you think a thing is going to do you good, it will do you good. And this brings us back to the fact that the cure is in the mind, not in the body.

Now all this adds up to what the Bible calls the necessity of faith. Faith just means that, if you believe that a thing can be done, then it in fact can be done.

It often happens that a student finds some subject difficult to pass in examinations, not because it is difficult, but because he thinks it is difficult. Anyone who has, for instance, worked with choirs knows how a choir will get a mental stagger at a bar or two of music, not because it is really difficult but because they made themselves think that it is difficult.

This all means that life is built on faith. It is the truth that with God all things are possible (Matt. 19:26). To believe that a thing can't be done is the surest way never to be able to do it; to believe that a thing can be done is half way to doing it, for when the mind is convinced, the body will follow.

WRONG EMPHASES (1)   August 15

There is in Khartoum a very famous statue of that great Christian soldier, General Gordon. It shows Gordon mounted on his horse. One day a small boy was taken to see the statue and was told that it was a statue of Gordon. At the end of the day, his father said to him, "Well, you saw Gordon's statue today and that was something worth seeing and remembering." "Yes," said the small boy, "I liked seeing it very much. It's a lovely statue. But tell me, Dad, who is the man on Gordon's back?"

To the small boy the most important thing about the statue was the horse. To him it was not the statue of a man on a horse; it was a statue of a horse with a man on it.

This is an example of getting the emphasis all wrong, and of letting the quite unimportant thing quite overshadow the important thing.

A famous, or notorious, example of that comes from Edmund Gosse's *Father and Son*, his study of his youth and of his relationship with his parents. His father was a zoologist and a writer of books on natural history and he was immersed in his zoology. He was fairly old when he was married, and so was the lady whom he married. Maybe against all their expectations, Edmund the son was born to them. And Edmund tells how the event was described in his father's diary: "E. delivered of a son. Received green swallow from Jamaica."

The arrival of the son and the arrival of the green swallow are set down as if they were equally important. The emphasis had got itself wrong. Edmund Gosse's father was a zoologist as much as he was a father.

Dag Hammarskjöld, the one time secretary of the United Nations, left behind him his diaries, and remarkable selections from them have been published under the title *Markings*. One extract reads like this: "He was a member of the crew of Columbus's caravel—he kept wondering whether he would get back to his home village in time to succeed the old shoemaker before anyone else could grab the job."

Here is the picture of man who, when continents were being discovered, could not see beyond a job in the village shoemaker's shop; when he was involved in the greatest possible events, he could not see beyond his own tiny and petty concerns.

The wrong emphasis can completely break up the rhythm of the melody; the wrong point of view can destroy the correct proportions of the whole.

WRONG EMPHASES (2)   August 16

In a country, the emphasis on a party rather than on the state can spoil everything.

So long as a nation is seen in terms of a series of warring classes, a collection of opposed strata of society, it cannot in the real sense prosper. So long as any party exists to further the interests of one section of the country, whatever that section may be, good government is impossible.

If government is designed solely to retain and maintain the privileges of the privileged, and if government is motivated solely by the assertion of the claims of those who regard themselves as under-privileged, in neither case can it be good government. Good government can only exist when the emphasis is on the whole and not on the part.

In a home, the emphasis on the material rather than the spiritual can spoil every-thing.

When a home begins to assess everything by the amount of money which comes into it, by the number of things which it can buy, by the number of enjoyments which more money can purchase, then it is on the way to trouble. Long ago the wise old Hebrew sage said, "Better is a dinner of herbs where love is than a fatted ox and hatred with it" (Prov 15:17). When those in a home forget that it is love which makes a home—not things—then the home is in danger.

In a Church, the emphasis on self rather than on service can spoil everything.

It so often happens in a church that someone resigns office or refuses to go on with work because he or she did not get his or her place, or things were not done as they should have been done. Anyone who does that has been working for no one else than himself. Anyone who does that hurts the church, hurts the kingdom of God, hurts Jesus Christ—and in the last analysis hurts himself or herself most of all.

In the long run, the real loser is the person who permits himself to act like that.

ON THE ROAD (1)   August 17

Anyone who is interested in railways is bound to know the books of O. S. Nock. In his book *British Steam Railways*, he has a chapter about the early days of railways, when the railways were growing up, and when travel was still an adventure.

In it he tells how, more than a hundred years ago now, there was published a little book of official advice to travellers entitled *Official Guide to the North Western Railway*, solemnly dedicated to The Most Noble The Marquis of Chandos. One section of this little Guide was entitled "Hints Before Starting."

The first three hints were as follows:

"Before commencing a journey the traveller should decide:

1. Whither he is going.
2. By what railway train and when.
3. Whether he will have to change carriages at any point, and where."

Then later on there is this: "The traveller is advised to take as little luggage as possible; and ladies are earnestly entreated not to indulge in more than seven boxes and five small parcels for the longest journey."

There is a good deal of sense in this for travellers in more than railways; there is a good deal of sense for those making the journey of life. You could hardly give a young person beginning on the journey of life better advice than is contained in these rules.

Anyone setting out on the journey of life ought to make up his mind clearly, firmly and early where he is going. He may not get there, but he will at least be trying to get somewhere. The person who does not know where he is going, will literally get nowhere fast.

Broadly speaking, the young person who starts out on the journey of life will have one of two aims—he will start out either to give or to get; either to do all that he can for the world and his fellow-men, or to try to make the world and his fellow-men do all that he can make them do for him.

He will think either of the satisfaction of a job or of the pay for a job. To put it crudely, he will either want a job where he can be of service to his fellow-men, even if the pay is not lavish, or he will want the kind of job which he visualises as finishing up with a Rolls-Royce and an unlimited expenses account.

In making his choice he will do well to remember a thing Dean Inge once said: "The bored people are those who are consuming much but producing little."

ON THE ROAD (2)   August 18

Anyone setting out on life must decide how he is going to get there, what route he is going to take.

Again, people are, broadly speaking, divided into two classes. There are the people who believe that the only way to success lies through hard, faithful and conscientious work, that the gods, as Hesiod said, have placed sweat as the price of all things; and there are those who think that the way to success lies through knowing the right people and exerting the right influence, and making use of others for their own advancement. In the end there is only one way, the way of faithful work, for in the last analysis a man will never hold down for long a job for which he is not fit.

Anyone setting out on a journey has to find out whether he has to change on the way.

To translate this into terms of life, this would mean that a man has to decide whether a job is a stage or an end.

Now this much is true—and it is particularly true of the ministry—a man will never do a job well if he is always thinking of the job to which he is going to move on. He should do every job as if it was the only thing in the world for him, and then—and only then—the next job will come along in its due time.

The advice in the early Railway Guide, mentioned yesterday, was not to carry too much luggage.

This is so in life, too. As Jesus said, "A man's life does not consist in the abundance of his possessions." (Luke 12:15). We travel farthest and fastest when we travel light, and the wise man will always remember that happiness is never to be found in things. He will appreciate his possessions, but he will never see in them the highest values in life.

To decide where we are going, to make up our minds how we propose to get there, to do each job as it comes with our whole heart and strength, and to value possessions but not to value them too much—that is our Guide.

CONVERSION (1)   August 19

George Ingle in his book, *The Lord's Creed*, wrote, "Someone once said that there are three conversions in a man's life—first to Christ, then to the Church, and then back to the world."

This is a very wise and a very true and a very penetrating saying. The first step in conversion is for a man to be convinced of the wonder of Jesus Christ, and to know that Jesus Christ can do for him what he can never hope to do for himself.

The second step in conversion is the conviction that this experience brings both the privilege and the responsibility of becoming a member of the fellowship of people who have had the same experience and who share the same belief.

The third step in conversion is the awareness that we are not converted only for our own sake, that we are not converted to gain the entry only into a society of believers, but that there is laid on the Christian man the obligation to take upon his shoulders and into his heart the sin and the suffering and the sorrow of the world.

From this we can see ways in which an alleged conversion may be incomplete and imperfect.

A conversion is incomplete if it does not leave Jesus Christ in the central place in a man's life.

The shortest possible description of a Christian—a description with which the New Testament would fully agree—is that a Christian is a man who can say, "For me, Jesus Christ is Lord" (Rom. 10:9; Phil. 2:11).

Herbert Butterfield's words about facing the future are good advice: "Hold to Christ, and for the rest be totally uncommitted." Any alleged conversion which does not leave a man totally committed to Jesus Christ is incomplete and imperfect.

CONVERSION (2)   August 20

A conversion is incomplete if it does not leave a man integrated into the Church.

By this we do not mean any particular part of the Church; what we do mean is that conversion must leave a man linked in loving fellowship with his fellow believers.

Conversion is not something between man and Jesus Christ, with no other person involved. True, it may start that way, but it cannot end that way. Conversion is not individualistic. It is in fact the opposite of individualistic.

It joins man to his fellow-men and certainly does not separate him from them.

Now here is sometimes the trouble. There is a certain kind of so-called conversion which separates a man from his fellow-men. It may fill him with a self-righteousness which rejoices in its own superiority to those who have not had a like experience. It may move a man to a Pharisaic self-isolation from all whom he does not regard as Christians. There have in fact been not a few so-called conversions as a result of which a man left the Church to belong to some smaller and holier body. The plain truth is that a man should begin very seriously to examine himself if he finds what he regards as his Christian experience separating him from his fellow-men, or his fellow Christians.

A conversion is incomplete if it does not leave a man with an intense social consciousness, if it does not fill him with a sense of overwhelming responsibility for the world.

The Church must never be in any sense a little huddle of pious people shutting the doors against the world, lost in prayer and praise, connoisseurs of preaching and liturgy, busy mutually congratulating themselves on the excellence of their Christian experience.

Committal to Jesus Christ, integration into the fellowship of the Church, active, caring love for our fellow-men—these are the marks of the threefold conversion that is real conversion.

FRONTIERS (1)   August 21

There had never been a war between the Argentine and Chile, but in 1899 there was a frontier dispute which had highly explosive possibilities. By Easter 1900 the two armies were poised to strike and war seemed inevitable.

During Holy Week, Monsignor Benavente preached in Buenos Aires on Easter Day a sermon which was a passionate appeal for peace. News of the sermon carried to Chile and a bishop in Chile took up the message. Both these bishops set out on a preaching campaign for peace. At first little seemed to be happening and then bit by bit the whole country in both nations was caught up in a great movement for peace. In the end, the two governments were forced by the will of the people to submit the frontier dispute to the arbitration of King Edward VII of Britain.

A treaty was entered into which promised in the future to submit all matters of dispute to arbitration, and then the wonderful thing happened. The guns of the frontier fortresses were now useless and irrelevant. They were taken to the arsenal in Buenos Aires and melted down and out of them there was cast a great bronze figure of Jesus. The right hand is stretched out in blessing; the left holds a cross. It was decided to carry this great statue 13,000 feet up the mountains to the frontier. It was taken by train as far as the railway went; it was then taken on gun carriages drawn by mules; and for the final steep rise to the top of the mountain it was dragged up with ropes by soldiers and sailors. On March 13, 1904, it was at last erected and unveiled, and there it stands.

Beneath it there is written the words: "These mountains themselves shall fall and crumble to dust before the people of Chile and the Argentine Republic forget their solemn covenant sworn at the feet of Christ." On the other side there is inscribed the text: "He is our peace who hath made both one." The text is Ephesians 2:14.

That is surely a tale worth telling and worth remembering.

FRONTIERS (2) August 22

There is no doubt that, in the early days of the faith, the most miraculous thing about Christianity was its astonishingly unifying influence. The ancient world was full of lines of division, the line between Jew and Gentile with its embittered hatred on both sides; the line between Greek and barbarian with the Greek contempt; the line between the slave and the free man with the slave regarded as a thing, no better than a living tool; the line between male and female with the woman also regarded as a thing with no legal rights whatsoever.

Yet Paul can say: "There is neither Jew nor Greek, there is neither slave nor free, there is neither male nor female; for you are all one in Christ Jesus". (Gal. 3:28).

See what Paul has done in that sentence. In the Jewish form of morning prayer, the Jew thanked God that "thou hast not made me a Gentile, a slave or a woman". Paul took that prayer, the prayer of his fathers and once his own prayer, and turned it upside-down.

The differences that the prayer once underlined and thanked God for are obliterated and abolished.

It is true that the Christian church (God forgive her!) has, on occasion, been the author, the begetter, the initiator and the blesser of wars and violence. But slowly, and bit by bit, men are coming to see that war and Christianity are mutually exclusive.

It is true that there are many even yet who are not prepared to accept the full consequences of that principle, but it is the kind of principle which has in it a dynamic power of self-expansion.

Now, as ever, Jesus Christ is the hope of the world, and in the Christ of the Andes we can see the foreshadowing of the day when men will be one in Jesus Christ. And let it be noted that the peace which the Christ of the Andes symbolises came not from governments, but from an upsurge from the common people which compelled two governments to Christian action.

THE NATION August 23

I remember reading in the newspapers an account of something which was the backlash of the bitter election campaign in Smethwick in England. Of that campaign itself I have nothing to say, other than that to fight an election campaign on racial issues had the most perilous possibilities in it. But what I do want to note is that it was reported that certain people in Smethwick who were connected with local government and who were connected with the campaign registered their objections to the fact that a Church of England vicar and certain of his fellow clergymen stated their mind on this matter. A communicant at a certain church is reported to have said, "I want an assurance from him that he will tackle preaching the Gospel and leave politics to us."

If there is one thing that is clear for the Christian, it is that there is no realm in which Jesus Christ is not supreme.

Christianity is not concerned only with a man's soul; it is concerned with a man's body. Christianity is not only concerned with a man's attitude to God; it is just as deeply concerned with his attitude to his fellow-men.

Christianity cares for social justice, for the conditions under which a man is housed, and in which he works, for the welfare of the aged and the sick, for public morality. And the only way to deal with these things is through political channels.

The necessary changes can only be achieved by political means. Charles Péguy writes, "Everything begins in mysticism and ends in politics." That is simply to say that every dream has to be worked out.

Dag Hammarskjöld, the former Secretary-General of the United Nations, wrote in *Markings*: "In our age the road to holiness necessarily passes through the world of action."

It will be a bad day when the Church accepts the invitation to abandon the world, for its function is not to abandon the world but to change the world, and that can only happen when changed men accept the obligation of working for a changed society in every way that is open to them.

FELLOWSHIP AND . . .   August 24

Fellowship is by no means blind. When people are in fellowship together they are certainly not unaware of each other's faults. They can see them quite clearly.

You remember the schoolboy's definition of a friend: "A friend is someone who knows all about you and still likes you."

True friendship and true fellowship can never exist so long as we insist on wearing rose-coloured spectacles. Any kind of friendship or fellowship or love which is based on illusion or on a refusal to see each other's faults is doomed to grave disappointment.

It is always important to remember that, in true fellowship, we take each other exactly as we are.

How then does fellowship overcome consciousness of each other's faults? It does so in two ways. It does so, first, by doing things together. There is no better way to friendship and to fellowship than joint action and activity.

Here is a lesson for the Churches. The Church has no greater handicap than its divisions. It may be that these differences cannot as yet be solved round a conference table, or from a theological or an ecclesiastical point of view, but they can be solved in action together. This in fact is the natural way to solve them.

If you had escaped from a shipwreck in a small boat in the middle of a storm, you certainly would not ask if the man beside you was a Baptist, or a Congregationalist, or a Presbyterian, or an Anglican before you joined him at an oar.

If you had to deal with a raging fire in a house, you quite certainly would not stop to ask to what branch of the Christian Church a man belonged, before you joined him, or allowed him to join you, in an attempt to extinguish the flames or to rescue those trapped in the house.

Today there can be no doubt that we are in a time of crisis. Only something like one in every ten persons goes to church at all in what we might call the domestic scene. In the international scene we are drifting into a situation in which it is not altogether hysterical to say that life itself is threatened. In such a situation, joint action among the Churches is imperative.

If ever there was a time, the time is now, when we should say with Wesley: "Is your heart as my heart? Then give me your hand."

FRIENDSHIP   August 25

The Greeks had a phrase which speaks of "time which wipes all things out", as if the mind of man were a slate and time a sponge which passes across the slate and wipes it clean. There are friendships which vanish with the years; there are people from whom we were once inseparable, with whom nowadays we would even find it difficult to make conversation.

There are people and friendships from which we quite inevitably grow away. But the real friendships are victorious over the years. You may not see a real friend for months and even years at a time, but you can take up the friendship just where you left it off.

Time is the great destroyer but time cannot destroy the link which true friendship has forged.

True friendship is independent of distance.

The proverb has it that absence makes the heart grow fonder. But that is not necessarily true. It can be equally true that absence makes the heart forget. But in true friendship there is something which can triumph over distance and separation.

C. F. Andrews used to have a story of a true friendship. In the 1914–18 war there were two men who were close friends. One was left wounded in no-man's-land between the trenches. His friend waited until darkness came, and then at the peril of his life crawled out to help him. The first words which the wounded man said were, "I knew that you would come."

In all the ups and downs of life, in the chances and the changes, when the light shines and the shadows fall, true friendship remains the same.

The writer of the Proverbs said a wonderful thing:

> There are friends who pretend to be friends,
> But there is a friend who sticks closer than a brother.
>
> (Prov. 18:24, R.S.V.)

How true!

DECISIONS   August 26

This generation is very unwilling to make decisions.

A kind of creeping paralysis can get into a man, when he can't even decide what train to take; or what to choose from the restaurant menu, or even to get up out of his chair and go to bed. A man can get into a state in which even the smallest decision is something to put off and to avoid.

There are certain things which ought to be a matter of decision. Our job in life should be a matter of decision. One of the tragedies and disasters of life is that for the majority of people this is not true. Their job is not what they chose, but what they more or less drifted into because there was nothing else available.

This, of course, is not so true of the professions, but it does tend to be true of the man who cannot enter one of the professions. And this is in large measure the cause of discontent and unrest and even of inefficiency and bad workmanship, for there are few people either settled or efficient in a job in which they are not really interested.

Our acceptance of membership of the Church should be the result of a perfectly definite act of decision. Too often it is no more than a kind of hall-mark of respectability. Too often it is entered upon because a young person has reached a certain age, or because a friend is doing it.

If Church membership is to mean what it ought to mean, it ought to be a deliberate and conscious pledge of loyalty to Jesus Christ, made in such a way that it will be impossible to forget it.

ANDY CAPP   August 27

Any speaker ought to be meticulously careful about his pronunciation.

It is not much to my credit that "handicap" and "Andy Capp" should sound exactly the same, as a little boy found when I was speaking.

I have told before of the child whom I once knew who always, when he was very young, prayed the Lord's Prayer's petition in a form of his own: "Deliver us from eagles," and of the other child who always had it: "Harold be thy name."

More legendary and less historically probable is the change of the line, "Weak and sinful though we be" into "We can sing full though we be."

It is *always* a somewhat daunting experience to hear one's own voice. Those of us who preach and teach are under the simple and basic obligation to pronounce words in a way that cannot be mistaken.

It is significant that this six-year-old was much more interested in Andy Capp than he was in Jesus. His reason for listening was not to hear about Jesus; it was because he thought that somehow this talk was leading up to the personal appearance of Andy Capp.

If the substance of the story is not a fault, then quite clearly the presentation of the story is. Andy Capp is a figure in a strip cartoon. I am bound to admit that I do not like a day when I do not see the unfolding story of George and Gaye Gambol!

Is this to say—personally, I think it is—that the Christian educator ought to seize upon the strip cartoon to get his story across? Perhaps you think it almost, or wholly, blasphemous to teach the story of Jesus in that way. But it may be that the reason why the child is more interested in the character in the cartoon than in Jesus is that we have wrapped up Jesus in so many layers of stained-glass religion that we have taken all the virile, human manhood out of him.

WHAT'S IN A NAME? (1)   August 28

I once heard of a new baby who was to be named Tiffany—if that is the right way to spell it! Here is one of the changes in family customs which have come in my lifetime.

There was a time when the selection of a name was no trouble. You simply called a son after his father, who had been called after his father, and a daughter after her mother, who had been called after her mother.

Names, like the family estate, descended from generation to generation. But nowadays this custom is often abandoned, or, if it is still maintained, the family name is the second or the third name, and the name for general use is something quite different.

There are many ways of choosing a name.

Tiffany, I gather, is one of James Bond's heroines! Chrysostom, in the fifth century, tells of one odd way of choosing a name in his day. The parents would get a number of candles. They would give each candle a name. They would then light all the candles, and the child was given the name which had been attached to the candle that burned longest!

Very often in the Bible a name is the expression of a parent's faith.

Elijah means "Jahweh is my God," and this name was given to the young Elijah when Baal worship was very prevalent, and in giving it to their child the parents asserted their faith. The Puritans did this in a way that reduced the whole thing to the ridiculous. So Macaulay tells of the man called Tribulation Wholesome and another called Zeal-of-the-Lord Busy.

The most notorious example of this is the name that the Fleet Street leather-worker, himself called Praise-God Barebones, gave to his son. He called him If-Christ-had-not-died-for-thee-thou-wouldst-have-been-damned Barebones. A name which was, unfortunately, regularly shortened to Damned Barebones.

Perhaps the most unfortunate way of naming a child is to give the child, usually a girl, a name that is at the moment very popular. We have girls named in this way called Marina and Marlene and Marilyn. The unfortunate thing about that is that with a little mental arithmetic it is no trouble to guess the age of the person involved!

WHAT'S IN A NAME? (2)   August 29

Nowadays one of the commonest ways of naming a child is just to give the child a name you happen to like. My two grand-daughters are called Jill and Karen, for no particular reason other than that their parents liked the names, although these two have other names which retain the family traditions.

I have often thought that it would be a good idea to delay naming a child finally until you could see how the child turned out! There is not much point in giving a name like Lynette to a chunky little tomboy! It is unfortunate to saddle a small, self-effacing, diffident little boy with the name Hector, greatest of the Trojans, or to call a young tough Lancelot or Gareth! There would be something to be said for waiting for a name to fit.

Chrysostom, who did not like the candle method one little bit, was all for giving a child one of the great saints' names and then telling the child the story of the name so that he would become like the saint after whom he was called. I once knew a girl called Elizabeth Margaret, who was thrilled when she discovered that she bore the names of the most famous queens of Scotland and England. It is quite something to be able to tell a child to be true to his name.

There have been some names too sacred to use, and some too terrible. In New Testament times Jesus was a very common name. It is the Greek form of the name Joshua, but it is easy to understand how both Jews and Christians ceased to use it. Just so, Judas was a common name, but in Christian circles it became very rare.

It is good to know the meaning of your name—Margaret, the pearl; Katherine, the pure one; Jane, the grace of God; Peter, the rock; Andrew, the courageous one; Alexander, the defender; Irene, peace. It is good to have a name to live up to.

And **we** have a name which we all share—the name Christian. Christ's man, Christ's woman, Christ's boy, Christ's girl, the name of the person who has been with Jesus and who is on Jesus's side.

EXTRAVAGANCE   August 30

I once heard of a man who, on his birthday, always made a point of giving other people presents. It was a good idea.

A gift is a way of expressing love and of expressing gratitude. It is a good thing that there are such things as birthdays and Christmases because it reminds us of the duty of telling people that we are grateful to them and that we love them.

I am not one of those people who inveigh against the so-called commercialism of Christmas time and who think that such days as Mothers' Day are just a ramp of the shop-keepers. Anything that reminds us to show our love and gratitude is more than worthwhile. Quite a lot of people who complain about these days just can't be bothered giving a present and really have rather a guilty conscience about it.

You see, the greatest value of these gifts lay precisely in the fact that they were in one sense useless.

The value of a present lies in the fact that it is an extra—and—dare I say it?— the more extravagant it is the better. That is what Jesus felt.

Surely John told us the loveliest story in the Gospels when he told us about the woman who anointed Jesus' feet with the perfume (John 12:1–8). The perfume could have been sold for three hundred silver pieces—about fifteen pounds in modern money—a colossal sum. A denarius, one of these silver pieces—about four pence—was a working man's wage for a day. That phial of perfume cost almost a year's wages.

There were extremely sensible people there who were horrified at the extravagance and who thought that the perfume should have been sold and the proceeds given to the poor.

No one loved the poor more than Jesus did—but he didn't think that. It was the very extravagance of the gift, the very fact that it was fantastically generous and reckless, that went straight to his heart. And he promised that all the world would know about the lovely thing that this woman had done.

FRIENDS   August 31

Jesus had this desire for human company. He chose the Twelve that they might be with him (Mark 3:14), and even in Gethsemane he wanted the chosen three to share his vigil, not that they could do anything, but just that they might be there (Mark 14:32–41).

I told my wife what I was going to say about the value of someone just being there, and she said, "The one thing that I can't stand is someone sitting there doing nothing when I am working as hard as I can." There are two sides to this matter! My wife was right. There are times when it would be the very reverse of friendship to sit there doing nothing. To see a person rushed and over-worked and harassed, and to do nothing about it is certainly not the act of a friend.

Then I began to see that the very essence of real friendship is to know when it is necessary just to be there and when it is necessary to do something.

There is a famous passage in Ecclesiastes (3:1–8) about different kinds of times. There is a time to weep, and a time to laugh, a time to keep and a time to cast away. The preacher did not include in the list a time to act and a time not to act; the nearest he got to it was that there is a time to keep silence and a time to speak, and the real essence of friendship is to know which is which.

Mary of Bethany had this sensitive awareness. She knew that there was a time when the only thing to do was to sit in silence at Jesus' feet and just to be with him with no action at all (Luke 10:38–42), but she also knew that there was a time to take the ointment and to anoint his feet, and so publicly to act so that all might see the devotion of her love (John 12:1–8).

There are times when true friendship demands action, and when just to be there and to do nothing would not be an act of friendship at all. There are times when true friendship demands simply the support of the silent presence of someone who is there.

He is indeed a wise friend who knows which time is which, who knows when to act and who knows when just to be there.

September

DELEGATE   September 1

I am sure that no one is indispensable, and that no one should try to be.

David Shepherd tells in his charming book, *Parson's Pitch*, about a rector who paid a return visit to his old congregation. A lady met him and said, "Oh, rector, the church has gone splendidly since you left!" And, you know, that was just about the greatest compliment she could have paid a man's ministry.

Often a man has what is regarded as a highly successful and even a great ministry. And when he retires, or when he leaves to go to another charge, the whole life of the congregation almost collapses.

Attendances dwindle; the life of the congregation sags; life has gone out of the place. Now, in the real sense that was a bad ministry.

It was a ministry which made the life of the church dependent on one man.

Any person should pray to God that his congregation will go on even better and better when he leaves it. And it won't if he tries to make himself indispensable.

No congregation should ever be dependent on one man. And a ministry after which there is a sag and a collapse is essentially a failure.

This leads to a second conviction. I am sure that no man should ever try to do everything himself.

I am bound to admit that this has been my own failure. I have always been bad at delegating work. And my good doctor has now taught me that work must be delegated.

Not to delegate work is to pass a vote of no confidence in one's staff and one's helpers. It may well be to cheat and rob someone else of the opportunity to do work that he ought to be made to do, and perhaps very much wishes to do. When anything becomes a one-man show, it is on the way to failure. Any wise leader and any faithful parson must learn to delegate work. He must see that his duty is not to do all the work himself, but to train others to do it with him.

Here we are very near to the heart of the failure of the Church. The failure of a church may well be due to the fact that it has come to be centred far too much round one man, the minister or the parson, and that we have all delegated far too little work to the laymen and the laywomen whom we should have been training to do it.

MISTRANSLATIONS (1)   September 2

The more you hear about the Bible, the more you are certain that it is a very wonderful book.

One of the extraordinary things about the Bible is that a man can take the wrong meaning out of it and still get himself something of infinite value for life.

Some time ago I received a letter from a person who has lived a hard life and who has still a great faith. It finished with thanksgiving and with a quotation from the Authorised Version of Psalm 139:13: "Thou hast possessed my reins."

Now I think that the writer of that letter took "reins" in the sense of the reins which guide a horse, and that he took it to mean that God had guided him all through life. And he was profoundly and devoutly thankful for the loving guidance of God which he found within this text.

But in point of fact that is not the meaning of this text at all. True, any ordinary twentieth-century person would almost certainly take the word reins in that sense, for it is the only sense of the word that he knows, but the word here literally means the kidneys; and the meaning of the text is that God knows a man because God has formed even his inmost and his most secret parts. The R.S.V. has: "Thou didst form my inward parts." Moffatt has: "Thou didst form my being." Goodspeed has: "Thou didst create my vitals."

The wonder of the matter is that here a man was feeding his heart on what is really a mistranslation, and even when the Bible was mistranslated it still spoke truth to the heart of a simple and a believing man.

This is true, but remember this is no argument for the neglect of scholarship and for mistranslation.

No one would deny that the Bible speaks directly to simple faith, but to simple faith there must be added that truth and accuracy which scholarship can fully give; and then when scholarship and devotion go hand in hand the Bible really and truly speaks.

MISTRANSLATIONS (2)   September 3

There is one Authorised Version mistranslation which Westcott once called "The most disastrous in idea and influence".

This is the notorious mistranslation in John 10:16. The Authorised Version runs: "Other sheep I have, which are not of this fold: them also I must bring, and they shall hear my voice; and there shall be one fold, and one shepherd."

In the English of the Authorised Version, the word "fold" occurs twice in that translation, but the words are quite different words in the Greek. In the first case the Greek word is *aule*, which is correctly translated "fold"; in the second case the Greek word is *poimne*, which means "flock", not "fold".

Any modern translation—Moffatt, R.S.V., Goodspeed—will show that the last part of the verse should read: "There will be one flock, one shepherd."

The seriousness of the mistranslation of *poimne* by the word "fold" is that this is the text which the Roman Catholics use to prove that there is only one Church, and that outside that Church there is no salvation. But Jesus said nothing like that. He said that there was one flock, which is a very different thing, for a flock could be distributed throughout many folds and still remain the same flock and the flock of the one owner.

There is nothing in this text which proves that there can be only one Church; there is everything in it to prove that there may be many Churches but there is only one flock of Christ which is distributed throughout all the Churches.

How did this mistranslation arise? It arose because the New Testament was first translated not directly from the Greek but from the Latin Vulgate, and for some quite unknown reason Jerome, when he made the Vulgate, translated both *aule* and *poimne* by the same Latin word (*ovile*) which does not mean a fold.

In this case a whole mistaken doctrine of the Church was founded on what is demonstrably a mistranslation.

It comes to this. There are times when simple people can get help for mind and heart out of even that which is a mistranslation; but there are still more times when a mistranslation can end by being the structure of false and misleading and erroneous doctrine.

TIRED?   September 4

A thing to be worth giving must cost something. That which is done slickly and easily will have very little effect. It will sound slick and it will sound easy; it may gain admiration, but it will not move and penetrate the heart.

I do not envy the man who is not nervous before he preaches or conducts the public worship of God. I am quite sure that no musician, no actor, no preacher will ever give anything worthwhile unless he is tensed and strung up before he begins.

This is not a case of lack of faith; this is not a case of not committing oneself and one's message to God. It is simply that no man can ever rise to any heights without a humble sense of the greatness of the occasion, and what greater occasion can there be than to enter into the holy place in the company of the people of God?

Even when a thing seems easily done, there is always behind it an intensity of effort and of preparation.

This is true of any walk of life. The typist's fingers fly over the keys with fascinating speed and accuracy and it all looks so easy, but behind it there are years of training. Even if preaching or speaking looks easy, even if the preacher or the speaker seems to have the gift of communication and the magic of words, behind it there is the preparation and the practice which alone make perfect.

Nothing in this world is effective without toil.

But there is one reason above all why the conduct of public worship is exhausting. Its aim is to help people, and to help people we must be identified with them and involved in their pains and their problems and their heartbreaks.

When Jesus helped the woman with the issue of blood, he knew that power had gone out of him (Mark 5:30). He felt the strength drain out of him.

In order to help, there must be a total involvement with and identification with the sufferer. Even so, Matthew quotes the prophetic word about Jesus: "He took our infirmities and bore our diseases". (Matt. 8:17; Isa. 53:4).

To help others was for Jesus a costly thing. It cannot be otherwise for us.

GOLDEN MOMENTS (1)   September 5

We had just come out of morning prayers in the wonderful chapel with the pulpit from which John Knox once preached. It was a beautiful July morning, with a sky of cloudless blue and a sun of summer heat shining on the green of the lawns and the colours of the flower beds. As I walked along the cloisters to the lecture room for the morning lecture, a lady turned to me and said, "If we could only stop the clock now!" It was a golden summer morning and she would have liked time to stop just there. And I suppose that all of us have had times and moments when we would have liked time to stand still and things to remain for ever just as they were.

But even the golden moment would lose its charm, if it was indefinitely extended, because the interest of life lies not in sameness but in contrast.

It is hunger which gives food its taste. It is thirst which makes cool clear water taste like nectar.

It is tiredness which makes sleep a boon.

It is toil which makes rest the thing which the body and the mind long for.

It is loneliness which gives friendship its value.

It is the rain which gives the sunshine its joy.

It is the dark of the night which gives the dawn its glory.

It is parting which makes reuniting a happy thing.

As Spenser had it in the "Faerie Queene":

> Sleep after toil, port after stormy seas,
> Ease after war, death after life does greatly please.

It is the contrast between the dark and the light which gives life both its pathos and its glory. And even the golden moment, if it was extended for ever, would in the end have a sameness which would turn it into a weariness, just as the dweller in the land where the sun always shines in the end longs for the rain.

GOLDEN MOMENTS (2)   September 6

It is its very kaleidoscopic quality which makes life what it is. As Shelley had it in the famous simile:

> Life, like a dome of many coloured glass,
> Stains the white radiance of Eternity.

If life consisted of only one kind of experience, then it would lose the very quality which makes it life. It is just because life is interwoven of sorrow and of joy, of gladness and of grief, of laughter and of tears, of silence and of song, that it is as it is. It is the many-coloured texture of life which creates the fulness of life.

A life which had no experience of tears would lose something of infinite value, for, as has been well said, "all sunshine makes a desert". A life which never had a problem, a faith which never had a doubt, an existence which never knew anything but luxury and comfort, would all be sadly lacking in something of infinite value.

However golden the moment, it is only golden when it is part of the ever-changing kaleidoscope of life, and when it is a moment and not a permanent condition.

However much we want to, we cannot stop the clock at any one moment.

Life has to go on, and the moment has to pass. But the moment does not entirely pass; it becomes part of the store of memory.

The golden moment can be stored in the memory, and when life is bleakly grim we can go back to it and find sunshine and strength for the dark days. Life can neither stand still nor go back; the golden moment cannot be caught and held and transfixed, and it would not be good for us, if it could.

But it can be stored in the memory and for ever possessed, and every man in his darkest day can go back to his Bethel and meet God again.

R.I.   September 7

I have never liked the title "Religious Instruction".

I should much prefer the title "Biblical Studies", or the good, old-fashioned title, "Divinity."

The trouble about the title "Religious Instruction" is that it cannot be called the duty of the school to instruct in religion. There are too many "kinds" of religion. The teacher of Religious Instruction might well bring a brand of religion which is all against the child's home or church tradition. Ultra-evangelicalism, narrow conservatism, conscious or unconscious indoctrination with the views of the teacher—"propaganda" religious instruction can do a great deal of harm.

There ought to be objective study of the Bible, as of any other great book, and objective study of the Christian belief and the Christian ethic and the Christian Church.

I know that a teacher of the Bible or of theology cannot keep individual faith out of it, but the study of the Bible and of the Faith should be sufficiently objective to be a placing of the facts before the child. That is why at least some of us would be happier with another name for it.

It is time that responsible people stopped talking nonsense about this. It is declared that you cannot examine on religion. True, but you can examine on the content and the meaning and the formation of the Bible and of the Creed.

I once pleaded for this at a gathering of teachers. After I had finished, a very distinguished headmaster rose and declared heatedly that he for one would never "beat the Bible" into schoolchildren. I wonder if he "beat" English and Mathematics and French and History and Latin into his pupils. If he did, he should be dismissed instantly.

The day of "beating" any subject into any pupil is long past. It is perfectly possible to examine in Biblical Studies, and it is perfectly possible to teach that subject with as sound educational techniques as any other subject.

It has often been said that no man who has not read the Bible is properly educated. Let us provide the chance to read it under the academic discipline which will show its true worth.

THE LORD'S DAY (1)   September 8

The use of the Lord's Day is still a living issue. I would like to do no more than state one or two facts from which discussion must start, and ask one or two questions which must be answered.

First, then, as to the facts.

The Sabbath and the Lord's Day are different days.

The Sabbath is Saturday and the Lord's Day is Sunday; the Sabbath is the last day of the week and the Lord's Day is the first day of the week. It is therefore clear that the Christian does not observe the Sabbath, and that terms such as "Sabbath school" are both wrong and misleading.

The Sabbath and the Lord's Day commemorate different events.

The Sabbath commemorates the rest of God after the six days of creation; the Lord's Day commemorates the rising of Jesus from the dead.

The two days therefore have different objects.

The object of the Sabbath is to perpetuate that rest, that cessation from work, which ended the work of creation. It will therefore be very properly a day when human work also stops.

The object of the Lord's Day is to perpetuate the experience of the Resurrection.

The first reference to the Lord's Day is in Revelation 1:10.

By the early second century, at least in Asia Minor, the observance of the Lord's Day was universal in the Christian Church, and Ignatius could speak of Christians as no longer "sabbatising" but keeping the Lord's Day.

Now for some questions.

If the Sabbath and the Lord's Day are different days, is the fourth commandment binding on the Christian at all in its Old Testament form? Are we to assume that it is simply taken over and made to apply to the Lord's Day? If so, how much of it is binding? Does, "Six days you shall labour" (Exod. 20:9) forbid a five-day week just as much as the command to rest forbids work on the Sabbath? What is the relationship between the Christian and this commandment, a commandment which is written entirely in the light of the Creation story and which naturally knows nothing of the Resurrection story?

In any event, suppose I do accept the fourth commandment injunction to the cessation of all secular activity and the summons of the Lord's Day to think of the Resurrection, how far am I justified in seeking to impose all this upon the whole community? Is this something which a Christian voluntarily accepts, if it is to be accepted, or is it something which is accepted by the Christian but imposed upon the non-Christian?

THE LORD'S DAY (2)   September 9

Now for some positive feelings about the Lord's Day—not without their questions.

Since the Lord's Day demands that I remember God and Jesus and his Resurrection, it will naturally and inevitably be the day of worship.

But must I "go to church" to worship? Is the only way to worship to attend a church service?

The Lord's Day should surely be a family day; it may be the one day of the week when the whole family can meet and eat together.

When I moved from the work of a parish to the work of a university, Sunday became to me the day when I was able to lunch with my family, the only day. The Sunday midday meal is not a joke. It comes near to being a sacrament.

The Lord's Day should be a day of rest.

I believe that it is a fact that the leaders of the French Revolution abolished the Sunday and then found that they had to bring it back simply for the health of the nation.

The old rhyme has it : "A Sunday well spent brings a week of content."

Someone once said that he visualised the days of the week as the carriages of a railway train, and Sunday was the engine which pulled them along. The Lord's Day should be the day which recreates and revives and inspires us for the work of the week.

How all this is to be worked out I do not know, but it seems to me that these are at least some of the facts and some of the questions and some of the principles involved.

This is not meant to answer questions but to start us thinking and talking.

SALVATION (1)   September 10

The Christian assertion is that God cares; and the Christian proof of that is that God sent his Son Jesus Christ into the world to live and to die for men. The Christian believes that God is and that God cares.

We might say that the Christian believes that God is both mind and love. But the Christian assertion goes one step further. The Christian believes that God is not only love, but that he is also holiness.

If then God is holy, he cannot look with indifference at sin and disobedience to his law. Therefore, there enters into life the necessity for repentance.

Repentance is very liable to be misunderstood. Repentance involves three things. It involves the realisation that we have done and been wrong. It involves sorrow that we have done and been wrong. Now it is here that, for some people at least, repentance stops; and, if it stops here, it is not repentance at all in the Christian sense of the term. For repentance involves not only realisation and sorrow; it also involves reformation; it involves the amendments of life to match the realisation and the sorrow. It involves fruits meet for repentance, as the Bible puts it. Repentance means sorrow for sin and new goodness.

For the Christian the whole matter centres in Jesus Christ.

It is in Jesus Christ that we see what God is like; it is through him that we see what sin is like and that we are moved to repentance; it is through him that we know that sin is forgiven; and it is in him that we find the picture of the new life that we must live and the strength to live it.

The process of salvation begins, continues and ends in Jesus Christ.

Billy Graham tells how in an American university he and his team had been answering questions for two hours. At the end of the session one of the students said to him, "All right, tell me what you want me to do. What do I do to find God?"

In answer Billy Graham laid down what you might call four steps on the way to salvation.

"First," he said, "you must be willing to admit that God is, that he exists.

"Second, you must accept the fact that he loves you in spite of your sins, failures, and rebellion. This is why he gave his Son to die on the Cross for you.

"Third, you must be willing to repent of your sin. Repentance means that you confess your transgression of moral law and that you are willing to give up your sin.

"Fourth, you must receive Jesus Christ as your own Lord and Saviour."

It would be difficult to find a better summary of the way of salvation.

You must believe that God is.

There is no more convincing proof that there is a God than the nature of the world. As a great scientist has said, "No astronomer can be an atheist." There is in the world a perfect order. The sun observes its time; the tides do not vary; the planets never leave their courses; the same combination of the elements will always produce the same result.

The old analogy is that if you find a watch, you are bound to deduce the existence of a watchmaker. Wherever there is order, there is bound to be mind. If you find a world which is a perfect order and harmony, then you are bound to assume a world-maker. In that sense, reason insists that God exists.

But that does not take you very far. Such an argument does not really prove that God exists; it proves that he existed. The watchmaker who made the watch may be dead long ago. Neither does it prove that God still cares for the world, or that he has anything more to do with it. A watchmaker in Switzerland might make a watch, export it to Britain, and never see or think about it again.

The Christian assertion is not only that God is, but also that God cares.

I have come across a very remarkable and interesting document. It is the outline for the training of Salvation Army officers, put together by Mrs. General Booth in 1884, and contained in the fourth volume of the *History of the Salvation Army.*

The notable thing about this document is that, although it is eighty years old and although it was produced by those, and for those, who had little or no academic training, it still offers a scheme for the training of the ministry which it would be difficult to improve.

The training of the Salvation Army officer had six aims in it.

First, we begin with the heart.

If the heart is not right, the service cannot be right, therefore, the heart comes first. The first essential for the ministry is a heart which has responded in love to the love of God in Jesus Christ.

Second, we try to train the head.

The Salvation Army planners saw quite clearly that the officer must in his knowledge be in advance of those whom he seeks to teach. Knowledge is not everything, but in the modern ministry a man must face many audiences and fulfil many duties, and he will not, for instance, carry out his duty very effectively, if he has to talk to a sixth form in a school in which the pupils are better educated than he is himself. An academic training is an essential, for youth especially will only listen to those whom it can respect.

Third, we teach them how to appeal to the consciences of the people.

The Salvation Army officer is taught to present a God who is love, but also a God of justice and of judgment. The preacher has to learn to tell men, not what they want to hear, but what they need to hear; not to lull them comfortably to sleep with an easy gospel, but to stab them broad awake with a Gospel which condemns that sin for which it brings the remedy.

Fourth, we teach them how to inspire hope in the most hopeless.

The Salvation Army has always gloriously walked in the footsteps of that Jesus who was the friend of outcasts and of sinners.

A certain Captain John Lyons began the work of the Salvation Army in Ceylon in 1888. One of the first things he did was to inaugurate a series of "Thieves' Dinners", to which all the thieves in Colombo were invited—and mightily successful they were. There is little use in a preacher awakening in people the conviction of sin unless he can go on to follow it with the hope of salvation.

TRAINING (2)   September 13

To continue with Mrs. Booth's Salvation Army principles of training:

Fifth, we try to show them how to exhibit the Saviour as a full and sufficient sacrifice for sin.

This salvation is seen, not only in terms of forgiveness for past sin, but also in terms of strength in the future to conquer sin and to overcome temptation. The message is liberation from the past and victory for the future.

Sixth, we teach them how to utilise the trophies they may be permitted to win.

By this Mrs. Booth meant that it was the task of the Salvation Army officer to turn every converted man into a converter of others. The Salvation Army saw conversion and mission as two halves of the same experience, and was quite sure that the man who had really received Jesus Christ will be consumed with the desire to share him with others.

Continually integrated with this teaching was practical training in the methods which the Army uses. "They are led out into actual combat with the ignorance, sins and woes of the people; in open air marches and meetings, house to house visitation, *War Cry* selling, slum visiting, the hunting up of drunkards and harlots, the children's work, and in any kind of guerilla warfare which at the moment may present itself." The Army's curriculum insists on learning by doing as well as on learning by studying.

It was in 1884 that this scheme was first drawn up by Mrs. General Booth. To this day it would be difficult to better it. It has in it the essence of a training religious, intellectual, theological and practical, and those who legislate for the training of the ministry today might still do worse than study it.

TOO BUSY (1)   September 14

Often we are too busy talking to listen.

Really good talkers may be scarce, but really good listeners are very much scarcer. We are usually much more eager to tell people what we think and what we have done than we are to listen to what they think and what they have done. Most people don't really want a dialogue. What they want is a monologue, with a few polite murmurs of respectful agreement just to keep the thing going.

We even take this talkativeness into prayer with us. We forget so often that prayer means listening at least as much as it means talking, and we are too busy telling God what we want him to do, and what he really ought to do, to listen to what he wants us to do. It is just as important to learn to listen and to keep silence as it is to talk.

Often we are too busy earning a living to live.

We live in a society in which there are so many things to buy, and things to buy cost money. And so you get a man working so much overtime, or doing so many money-earning small jobs that he has hardly time to know his family. Or you get the woman going out to work and—not always, but certainly sometimes—neglecting the children God gave her and the home of which she ought to be the centre. They are so busy earning a living that they forget how to live.

In the Old Testament story there was the man who was enjoined to look after a prisoner captured in the battle. He did this and that and the prisoner escaped; and when he was called to account he could only make the lame excuse: "As your servant was busy here and there he was gone." (1 Kings, 20:40)

Be careful you are not too busy to have time for the things which matter.

TOO BUSY (2)   September 15

Life is full of occasions when we are too busy to remember the most important things of all.

Often we are too busy arguing together to pray together.
The *odium theologicum*, the hatred of theologians for each other, is notorious. There are few spheres of life in which there is such violent argument as there is in theology. There are even certain theologians who will attack a man's character because they do not agree with his opinions.

What is true of theology is true of the Church in general. There are few committees and few meetings where argument can be so intense as in Church courts and committees. In a sense this is a good thing, but quite certainly it is a dangerous thing; and it would save many a fellowship from disaster if, when tempers were heated and voices were raised and argument had turned to dispute, we were to say, "Let's stop arguing together now, and let's pray together."

It wouldn't, and it shouldn't, stop the argument, but the argument would then be the argument of brothers and not of enemies.

Often we are too busy planning to think.
It is very easy to get into a state of mind when we think that action as such is the most important thing in life.

There are some people whose principle of life is, "Do something". It doesn't really matter what it is, so long as we do something. Such an attitude is rather like hailing a taxi and saying to the driver, "Drive like fury," and when he says, "Where?" saying "It doesn't matter where, so long as you drive like fury."

Of course it is true that too much deliberation paralyses action; but it would save a lot of trouble and it would make action much more effective if we really thought before we acted.

Time spent in thinking is never time wasted.

THE UNSEEN CLOUD   September 16

I have always remembered the thrill I had in preaching in the University Chapel in St. Andrews and in being told that the very pulpit in which I was to stand had been the pulpit of John Knox. As every day in my own classroom I step on to the rostrum, I remember the men who went before me in that

New Testament classroom—A. B. Bruce, James Denney, W. M. Macgregor, G. H. C. Macgregor—what a company!

Now when this kind of thing happens it has two effects.

It makes one very humble.

It gives one a feeling of complete astonishment that one should be walking in such a company. There is nothing like the memory of the unseen cloud to keep us humble.

Do we never sometimes stop to think of the great souls who were within this Church of ours, the saints, the martyrs and the prophets who were part of it, who maybe worshipped in our very town and buildings? Do we never think of the succession in which the humblest Christian walks? And do we never think of how unworthy we are of all that has gone before? To remember the unseen cloud is to be humbled to the dust.

But to remember the unseen cloud is to be more than humbled.

It is equally to be challenged. We have entered into the labours of other men; we must so labour that other men may enter into ours. The generations are each like links in a chain, and we must surely see to it that ours is not the weak link.

Memory is always a challenge. Am I lessening or am I enhancing the tradition which has come down to me? Do I bring joy or sorrow to the unseen cloud as they look down? When I meet them on the other side of death, will I have to meet their eyes with pride or with shame?

No man lives to himself, and no man dies to himself, and no man can honourably forget those who have given him what he has and in whose footsteps he walks.

If I am humbled and if I am challenged by the memory of the unseen cloud, then still another thing emerges.

I can only be true to them, I can only not fail them, I can only walk in their company if I in my life have the same daily and hourly dependence on Jesus Christ that they had.

The generations rise and pass away in the unending panorama of the years, but Jesus Christ is the same yesterday, today and for ever (Heb. 13:8).

His arm is not shortened, and his power is not grown less.

His presence is still with us as it was with them, mighty to help and mighty to save.

IN THE BACKGROUND   September 17

The more I think of life, the more I am impressed with our complete dependence on other people who do their jobs without ever being heard of.

If my car goes wrong, I shout for help. I could not do my work for a day without my hearing aid. When it goes wrong, there is someone there to mend it in a matter of hours. It takes so many people in the background to enable any of us to go on doing our work. And the trouble is that we so often take them completely for granted.

You have only to think of so simple a thing as how we get to work in the morning. How different it would be if there was no wife or mother to get us out of bed in time, to get a breakfast cooked and on to the table, and to see us out of the door in time to catch our train or bus! We seldom think of the man who drives the bus or the train, or of the policeman who directs the traffic as directly serving us. In fact, we seldom remember that the bus or the train has a driver!

I am quite sure that, far oftener than we do, we should stop to think how we are all bound up together in the bundle of life; that we should stop every now and again to remember our utter dependence on other people; that sometimes we should stop to look at our own work and to see in it, whatever it is, not something by which we earn a wage, but something which is contributing to keeping the world going, and something in which we must, therefore take a pride.

We ought at least sometimes not only to thank God for our work, and not only to thank him for health and strength and knowledge and skill to do it; we ought also to thank him for the great number of ordinary people doing ordinary jobs, for they are the most important people of all. Without them no one would ever be able to get any work done at all.

Thank God for the men—and women—in the background.

KIND   September 18

In regard to people, the Christian life should be characterised by what the Bible, in the Authorised Version, calls "charity".

Maybe the best modern equivalent of "charity" is kindness. The Christian should be kind in his judgments: kind in his speech; and kind in his actions. It is characteristic of the world to think the worst, and put the worst construction and interpretation on any action.

It is characteristic of the world to say the cruel and the cutting thing; it is characteristic of the world to be so taken up with self that it has little time for kindness to others. But the judgments, the words, and the deeds of the Christian are kind.

In regard to self, the Christian life should be characterised by humility.

There are few things so common in this life as conceit, and there are few of us who are not fairly well pleased with ourselves. Humility really means the extinction of self. It is only when self is extinguished that a man can learn, for the first condition of learning is the admission of our own ignorance. Above all, it is only when self is extinguished that a man can really see the beauty and the necessity of service, and that he can discover that the essence of life is

228

not in being served by others but in serving others. The world wants to make use of others for its own purposes; the Christian wants to be used for the purposes of God.

In regard to death, the Christian life should be characterised by certainty.

We are not thinking so much of death as it affects ourselves, although there is also the Christian who should be cleansed from all fear; we are rather thinking of death as it invades our circle and lays its hands on those we love.

When death comes, so many people are submerged in sorrow; so many are left in a state of collapse; so many grow bitter and resentful; so many live as if all that they were left with is memory and as if there were no hope.

The Christian is the man who in life's bitterest hour is still certain that nothing in life or in death can separate him or those whom he loves from the love of God in Christ Jesus his Lord.

SERENE   September 19

John W. Doberstein in *The Minister's Prayer Book*, makes three quotations, one after another, all on the same subject.

Of the first two the author is nameless! "The life of the clergyman is the book of the layman." "The life of the clergyman is the gospel of the people."

The third is from Kierkegaard: "Order the parsons to be silent on Sundays. What is there left? The essential things remain: their lives, the daily life which the parsons preach. Would you then get the impression by watching them that it was Christianity they were preaching?"

These three quotations are all saying something which has been said over and over again. They are saying that the most effective sermon is a life; they are saying that Christianity must be demonstrated in action rather than commended in words.

These three quotations all speak specifically of the parson. But this is to limit the matter far too much. It is not only the life of the parson which is a good or a bad sermon for Christianity; the life of every Church member preaches or fails to preach the faith which in words he possesses.

What then are the qualities which a Christian life should show? What are the qualities by which it ought to be distinguished and characterised?

In regard to life, the Christian life should be characterised by serenity.

The world is littered with people who, as one might say, are permanently disorganised. They are always fussing; they are always worrying; they are often in a near panic; they never quite catch up with their work. All their days are rushed and harassed and hot and bothered.

There should be in the life of the Christian a certain calm. A worried Christian is a contradiction in terms. A Christian is by definition a man who has that inner strength which enables him to cope with anything that life can do to him or bring to him.

There should be in the Christian a calm, quiet, unhurried and unworried strength which is the opposite of the feverish and fretful inefficiency of the world.

NEEDS TO MEET (1)   September 20

What would you say is the great characteristic of the work of a minister of the Church?

Raymond Calkins tells how, in the old provincial town of Saumur in France, there stood the great and ancient Roman Church of St. Peter. At its entrance, in the pre-war days, there stood a placard the object of which was to challenge young men to enter the ministry. The placard said: "There are just four days in anyone's life: birth, confirmation, marriage, death. Would you not like to be the one who would be needed on all four of those days?"

The one who would be needed. Here should be the first great characteristic of the ministry. The minister is a man dedicated to the needs of men. He is involved with his people in the great moments of joy and of sorrow; like Ezekiel, he sits where they sit. His people need him in their joys and in their sorrows alike. The true minister is one who is needed by his people.

On the arch of the gate of the seminary at Wittenburg there is an inscription directed towards students for the ministry. The inscription is a saying of Luther's: "Let no one give up the faith that God wants to do a deed through him." So then in the second place a minister is *a man whom God wants to use and who wants to be used.*

He knows quite well that of himself he can do nothing; but he also knows that God can do the most astonishing things with the most imperfect instruments, and therefore he never loses the confidence that God wants to act through him.

The minister is a man who wants to be needed and who wants to be used. Now clearly, here are very difficult tasks. Here are tasks which no man can perform in his own unaided strength.

NEEDS TO MEET (2)   September 21

There is a third thing about the minister.

One of the great Scottish preachers in the days of James VI was Robert Bruce. "No man, since the apostles," they said of him, "spake with such power."

Once Bruce was preaching in Larbert, as Adam Burnet tells. He was in the vestry before the service and someone was sent to fetch him when the time was near. The person who was sent returned saying that he did not know when Mr. Bruce would be free to come . . .

There was somebody with him, for he heard him many times say with the greatest seriousness that he would not, he could not, go unless he came with him, and that he would not go alone; but the Other did not seem to answer. And when at last he came out of the vestry to preach, and after he had taken that service that day, it was said of him that "he was singularly assisted".

Here then is the third and the dominating fact about the minister. He is a man who, if he will have it so, is always singularly assisted. God does not call any man to a task, and then leave him alone to do it. With the vision comes the power; with the call comes the strength.

Ministers and laymen should now and again set before themselves the ideal of the ministry. The image of the ministry can so easily become that of a man busy scurrying round attending committees and running the organisations of the congregation, in such a rush that he gets his visitation half done and his sermon half prepared.

The ideal of the ministry is a man whom people need; a man whom God can use; and a man who can meet the need of people and answer the challenge of God because he is at all times singularly assisted by the presence of his Lord.

THE CONQUEROR   September 22

Tolstoi somewhere has a story of a nobleman who always kept open house. At evening anyone could come and have a meal at his open and hospitable table. And when anyone came, he was never turned away, but there was one test. The nobleman always said, "Show me your hands," and, if the hands were rough and scarred with toil, then the man was given a seat of honour at the top of the table, but if the hands were soft and flabby, then his place was low at the foot of the table.

Dr. Jacks somewhere has the story of an Irish navvy. He was a simple soul, and one day someone asked him what he would say if, when he died, he was stopped at the heavenly gates and asked if he could produce any reason why he would be allowed in. He paused for a moment, and then he looked down at his spade with its blade polished and sharpened with constant work until it looked almost like stainless steel. "I think," he said, "I'll just show them my spade." And doubtless it would be a passport to heaven.

Jacks went on to say that when he wrote his many books he always wore an old jacket; and the right sleeve of it had become all tattered and worn with the constant friction of his desk as he wrote. "I wonder," he said, "if my old frayed coat sleeve will get me in."

One of the strange things about the ministry is that there are many people who do not really think that ministers do an honest day's work—and sometimes perhaps they could be right. There is nothing in this world more tiring and even exhausting than concentrated brain work and study, and there is nothing more emotionally draining than visiting people and trying to help them by nothing less than the giving of oneself. And in that sense there is no harder job in the world than the ministry.

But the minister is self-employed; he has no one to see that he does his work efficiently and conscientiously, and in such a situation it is perilously easy to rise late and to fritter time away.

It always takes self-discipline to be a workman who has no need to be ashamed, and I am certain that there is no job where that self-discipline is more essential and yet harder than in the work of the ministry.

Let us remember that the man who is prepared to do an honest day's work is indeed the conqueror. There are some victories that we cannot all win; but the victory of honest work is a victory that is open to all to win.

THE WORKMAN   September 23

Apolo Kivebulaya was one of the great saints of the African Church and in the book *African Saint,* Anne Luck has told his story.

One of the most characteristic stories of him tells how he arrived at Mboga in the Congo. He was not the first Christian missionary to arrive there. Two African missionaries had been there before him, but they had had to leave, because the people would not give them any food. These two former missionaries had been members of the proud Baganda tribe in which menial work is for women and slaves. So, when the people of Mboga refused them food, they had been far too proud to cultivate the land themselves and so they had to starve or go.

Apolo knew this, and he was well prepared to grow his own food. As he passed through the patches of forest on his way to Mboga, he stopped to cut some hoe handles to be ready to get to work on some patch of ground whenever he arrived. When Tabaro, the ruler of Mboga, saw Apolo coming into the village carrying his hoe handles at the ready he said, "Here is a man who is going to conquer."

A hoe handle may be an odd sign for a conquerer, and an odd crest for a victor, but the very sight of it marked out Apolo as the man who would conquer. And why? For the simple yet sufficient reason that here was a man who was clearly prepared to do a day's honest work. It is hardly an exaggeration to say that what the world needs more than anything else is men who are ready and prepared and willing to do an honest day's work.

But we can go a little further than that. Apolo's hoe handles made it clear to the Congo people that he was prepared to work as well as to preach.

Under the Jewish law the Rabbis were the greatest scholars and teachers of their day; they were the equivalent of the modern professor. But every Jewish rabbi had to have a trade. No rabbi could take any money for teaching and preaching at all. He had to earn his living by working at some trade. So we find rabbis who were tailors, carpenters, perfumers, barbers; and we know the trade of one who might have become one of the greatest of all Jewish rabbis, if he had not become one of the greatest of Christians, for we know that Paul was a tent-maker, or, as the word probably came to mean, a leather-worker.

The rabbi had to work with his hands as well as with his brain and with his words.

(R)EVOLUTION (I) September 24

Christopher Maude Chavasse, who was Bishop of Rochester, was a man with the gift of public utterance. He could say things and he could say them in such a way that people had to sit up and take notice, and so that they stuck in the memory.

Early in the Second World War he was talking about what was going to happen afterwards. He was thinking about the brave new world which everyone hoped would be born. He was remembering too the failure to build any kind of new world after the First World War, which he so well remembered. So he said that when it came to facing a new situation, people had three different attitudes—there was the reactionary attitude; there was the revolutionary attitude; and there was the evolutionary attitude.

Chavasse was right; these are the three possible attitudes to the challenge of any situation.

There is the reactionary attitude.

The reactionary attitude resents all change. It wishes to keep things as they are. It characteristically looks backward; and it has a built-in tendency to say No when any new course of action is suggested.

Very often, perhaps even as a general rule, the reactionary attitude springs from the determination to hold on to some state of privilege. The reactionary attitude was specially evident when, thirty or forty years ago, the social differences began to be ironed out.

I knew of one lady who was shocked to the core of her being that a servant girl should go out wearing silk stockings; and I knew of another lady who was staggered to find that her servant girl was able to play the piano, a thing that the lower orders should never aspire to do.

This is exactly the modernisation of Aristotle's attitude that by far the greater part of men are meant by nature to be slaves, hewers of wood and drawers of water, and that they existed simply to absolve the more cultured upper classes from the unpleasant labour of menial tasks.

That reactionary attitude is rampant in the Church. It may be seen in the desire to hang on to a certain form of constitution now long out of date; in the refusal to abandon a building from which the tide of population has receded; in the resentment of any change in an order of service; in the absolute refusal to experiment.

The reactionary attitude lives in the past; it tries to stop the tide of progress. And it has an inevitable result. If you try to stop a tide which should not be stopped with some defensive dam, in the end the dam will burst, and the end is disaster.

Change accepted is good; change refused can turn to explosive destructiveness.

(R)EVOLUTION (2)   September 25

There is the revolutionary attitude.

A revolution may be a good thing; it may in fact be an essential thing. All great nations have, somewhere in their history, a revolution.

But there is one thing to remember about a revolution—it is necessarily destructive—and it is necessarily temporary. It is not possible to live in a permanent revolution. A revolution can never become a routine. A revolution could be compared to a demolition squad. Here is some slum-infested area; a new transformation is dreamed of and worked out; the demolition squad is called in. That is the revolution. But you do not leave the area looking as if it had been hit by high explosive. You begin to raise the new buildings out of the rubble.

Revolution has to be followed by construction. That is why revolution can never be a policy; it must always be an emergency. There can be a savage delight in smashing things; but after the smashing there must come the building up.

We need our revolutionaries; but we need revolutionaries who can see beyond the revolution. Of course, there is plenty of demolition work to be done in the Church; but unless the revolutionary is ultimately prepared to turn into a builder, there is no future in his revolution.

We come to the evolutionary attitude, which is the attitude that is prepared to grow.

It is the attitude which is constantly willing to adjust itself to the challenge of changing circumstance.

In the physical world, it is the creature which will not adjust to changing circumstances which is ultimately eliminated in the evolutionary process. This can equally happen to the creature which is so perfectly adjusted to one set of circumstances that it cannot alter when the circumstances change.

Change and growth are the characteristics of life. The Church should be a growing and a changing Church. Since the grace of God is sufficient for all things, the Church can find the grace to deal with any situation—if it is living enough and flexible enough to take it.

Usually we have no difficulty in finding someone or something to whom or to which the blame may be attached.

We blame other people for our sins and our mistakes.

We blame someone else's influence for the mistake we have made, or for the trouble in which we have found ourselves. When Burns as a young man went to Irvine to learn flax-dressing, he fell in with an older man who led him astray. He said afterwards, "His friendship did me a mischief."

It is no doubt true, but it is also true that no one needs to say Yes to someone else's suggestions and no one needs to yield to someone else's seductions.

No one would wish to deny or to belittle the evil influence that a bad association can cause, but even in such a circumstance a man has still to say Yes to the tempting voice, and he might say No.

We blame life for our sins and our mistakes.

Sometimes we think that if life had been different there would have been things we would not have done and mistakes we would not have made. But the truth is that, if we are that kind of person, if life had been different we would simply have made other mistakes to match other circumstances.

Sometimes we say, "It's my nature. I can't change myself." But if there is any truth in the Christian claim at all, then any man who will submit to Jesus Christ can be changed and made new. We cannot change ourselves, but we can submit to being changed.

We can receive grace to live triumphantly in any circumstances and we can receive grace to make any life new.

We almost blame our sins and our mistakes on God.

Burns wrote:

> Thou knowest thou hast formed me
> With passions wild and strong,
> And listening to their witching voice
> Has often lead me wrong,

as if to say that, if God had made him differently, he would not have made the mistakes he did make. But a man is not so much what God made him as he is what he has made himself.

There can be neither forgiveness nor amendment until we admit our own fault and say that we are sorry.

The way to forgiveness and to betterment begins when we learn to say, "God, be merciful to me a sinner!" (Luke 18:13):

> I read
> In a book
> That a man called
> Christ
> Went about doing good.
> It is very disconcerting
> To me
> That I am so easily satisfied
> With just
> Going about.

In the Bible there are two kinds of "goings about" spoken of. Satan came to the assembly of the sons of God from going to and fro upon the earth (Job 1:7), and in Peter's letter the Devil is said to prowl about seeking whom he may devour (1 Pet. 5:8). And on the other hand Jesus of Nazareth was said to have gone about doing good (Acts 10:38). These are, as it were, the two opposite poles. The Devil goes about seeking whom he may devour; Jesus Christ went about doing good.

Kagawa in the poem speaks about "just going about". But in point of fact it is impossible to go about, as it were, *simpliciter*. A man's very presence brings something with it; a man has an effect on everyone he meets, even on everyone whom he passes on the street.

We can go about encouraging.

No man could desire a finer epitaph than: "He was a great encourager." "Courage! Keep your heart up!" was a word that was often on Jesus' lips, for the word which the A.V. translates, "Be of good cheer!" means just exactly that.

"Courage!" Jesus said to the man who was sick with the palsy (Matt. 9:2). "Courage!" he said to the scared woman who crept up and touched him in the crowd (Matt. 9:22). "Courage!" he said to the disciples terrified in the storm on the lake (Matt. 14:27). "Courage!" said the Risen Christ to Paul when he was up against it in Jerusalem and when there seemed every reason to despair (Acts 23:11). Anyone who encourages his fellow-men is walking in his Master's footsteps, and speaking with his Master's accent.

THE NECESSITY OF BEAUTY   September 28

Beauty, in our day, is not an optional extra, but a necessity.

Beauty in words is necessary.

There has been in the last thirty years a radical change in preaching. Preaching is no longer oratory; it is conversation. If the pulpit orator exists at all nowadays, he is quite out of fashion, and instead we have the pulpit conversationalist.

Now this has an attendant danger. Because of this new style, the preacher may think that he need not be nearly so detailed in his preparation as once he was; he may think that he need no longer carefully write out and prepare his sermons. Nothing would be further from the truth. It is an old paradox that nothing has to be so carefully prepared as an effective impromptu.

Preaching is like cooking. Two cooks can take precisely the same ingredients and out of them one can make a revolting mess and the other an appetising delight. All preachers use the same material. Out of it one can make something which would bore a saint to tears, and another can make something which would rouse the most hardened cynic to electrified interest. The difference is entirely in the presentation.

No preacher can afford to neglect beauty of words, except at his peril.

Beauty in worship is necessary.

No conscientious preacher will ever depend wholly on extempore prayer, for he will remember that, in the public worship of God, he is bringing to God not only his own prayers but also the prayers of his people, and to do that he must carefully prepare his prayers. And once he has prepared, only the finest language is good enough for the task of bringing the needs of the people to God.

Beauty in surroundings is necessary.

The drabness of so many churches is one of their greatest handicaps. It would be difficult to worship the Lord in the beauty of holiness in many of our church buildings.

We in the Church ought to remember that we are living in a time which has—perhaps even unconsciously—realised the importance of beauty. It would be a sad thing if, in a world which has rediscovered the importance of beauty, the Church alone neglected it.

SERVANT QUEEN   September 29

One day, Themistocles, the great Greek statesman and soldier, the leader of Athens, was looking at his baby son. "Do you know," he said to the person who was with him, "that little baby is the ruler of Greece!"

The friend asked him to explain this astonishing statement. "Well" said Themistocles, "this baby rules his mother; his mother rules me; I rule the Athenians; and the Athenians rule Greece; therefore this baby is the ruler of the whole of Greece!"

So Themistocles was another man fortunate enough to be ruled by his wife.

There are good reasons why the mother is bound to be the ruler of every home.

She is concerned with the most essential things.

The essential things are the simple things. The food, and health, the warmth, the comfort of the family are in the mother's hands. It is the hardest job of all; it never stops; there will be sheer disaster if ever women want an eight-hour day and a five-day week, and if they demand overtime for any hours worked in the home beyond these!

Fay Inchfawn was not one of the world's great poets, but she had a peculiar gift for writing about the home out of her own experience. So she writes about a woman's work:

> Lord of all pots and pans and things,
> Since I've no time to be
> A saint by doing lovely things,
> Or watching late with Thee,
> Or dreaming in the dawnlight,
> Or storming heaven's gates,
> Make me a saint by getting meals
> And washing up the plates.

That is a prayer which will be answered.

For another thing, quite inevitably, especially when they are young, the children have no one quite so important as the mother.

For the little child the world revolves round his mother. In the very nature of things the father's work takes him out of the home; and in the very nature of things the mother's work keeps her in the home; and therefore in the very nature of things the mother is needed in a way that no one else can be.

Within the walls of the home, Jesus's words come strangely true. He said, "Whoever would be great among you must be your servant" (Mark 10:43). And life has made a home such that in it the wife and the mother is at one and the same time the working girl and the boss, at one and the same time the servant of all and the queen of all.

A MAN   September 30

What are the qualities that you would expect a real man to possess?

I would want him to possess vitality.

Julian was the Roman Emperor who wanted to put the clock back. By this time Christianity had been accepted, but he wanted to go back to the old ways and to the old pagan gods. And his complaint, as Ibsen put it into his mouth, was like this: "Have you looked at those Christians closely? Hollow-eyed, pale-cheeked, flat-breasted all; they brood their lives away, unspurred by

238

ambition; the sun shines for them but they do not see it; the earth offers them its fullness but they desire it not: all their desire is to renounce and suffer and die." Swinburne turned the words of the same Julian into verse:

> Thou hast conquered, O pale Galilean;
> The world has grown grey from Thy breath.

Julian—and Ibsen and Swinburne agreed with him—saw in Christianity a colourless and anaemic thing. And the trouble is that it is often too true. The Christian Church is so often represented by people who are lack-lustre and depressed and depressing, preaching the Good News, as someone has said, like a wireless announcer announcing a deep depression off Ireland.

Even a man who is ill in body can still have a radiant vitality, if he really has Christ in his heart. Paul showed us that.

I would want him to possess virility.

Sidney Smith once said bitingly after taking the services in a certain church, "I have just been preaching to a congregation of old ladies of both sexes." It is all too true that there is in so much Christianity a kind of feminine streak and emphasis.

During the Peninsular War, Napoleon was confronted for the first time with the Duke of Wellington. It did not take him long to come to respect the courage and the skill of Wellington. "So," he said, "it seems that this Wellington is a man!" As Pilate brought Jesus out to the mob he said, "Here is the man!" (John 19:5)

Nothing does the ministry more good that a minister who is first and foremost a man able to get alongside men.

Jesus said: "I came that they may have life, and have it abundantly" (John 10:10); and if one thing is certain, it is that the bearer of the news of eternal life should himself be vitally alive.

Then, even if he is a minister, he will still be a man.

October

A true son of Abraham must have the humble mind.

The greatest necessity for the humble mind lies in the fact that there can be no learning without humility, for the very simple reason that there can be no learning without the prior realisation that we do not know. The man who knows all the answers already obviously cannot learn.

In learning there is one kind of humility which is both specially valuable and specially difficult. It is the humility to sit down in front of the facts and look at them just as they are.

One of the hardest things in the world is to rid oneself of one's prejudices and presuppositions. We so often make a fact mean what we want it to mean; we so often approach the facts with a preconceived theory already in our minds—and there is no one worse than the theologian for doing that.

A man will only begin to know when he has the humility to see things as they are, and when he is cleansed of the pride of seeing them as he wants them to be.

He must have the humble spirit.

No one can ever solve the problem of personal relationships without the humble spirit. For without the humble spirit two things are impossible. No one can see any beauty in service without the humble spirit. Service and pride are mutually contradictory; service and humility are almost synonymous.

It is only the man with the lowly spirit who really believes that he who serves is the greatest of all, and he does not think in terms of greatness at all.

So, the good eye, the generous eye, will give us the secret of right seeing; the humble mind will give us the secret of right learning; the lowly spirit will give us the secret of right relationships.

These things are worth praying for.

Abraham was the friend of God. To a Jew the highest compliment that can be paid a man is to say that he is a true son of Abraham. There is a Jewish saying which tells of the three things that a true son of Abraham must have. He must have "the good eye, the humble mind and the lowly spirit".

He must have the good eye.
Here the word good is not used in the physical sense of having good sight; it really means the generous eye. So a good man will look generously at people.

He will be generous with praise.
We have quite enough critics in this world; it is encouragers who are in short supply.

There used to be a regulation in the Royal Navy which stated that "no officer shall speak to any other officer discouragingly in the performance of his duty". I do not think that there are any people who perform a higher service than those who encourage their fellow-men.

He will be generous to give.
One of the most valuable things in the world is the sensitiveness which can see the need of people before they are compelled to ask for help. To see need sensitively and to help need quickly are great qualities.

He will be generous to overlook.
One of the most startling sentences in the Authorised Version is the sentence which tells us that God winked at the former times of ignorance. God in his mercy, when men did not know any better, turned a blind eye to their faults and failings (Acts 17:30).

Just as there is a gift in seeing, there is sometimes a gift in not seeing. The wise man knows what to see and what not to see.

There are times when the blind eye is as great a virtue as the seeing eye.

If we have God for our ally, then we have an ally for victory. But we must be quite clear what this means.

This does not mean that we are not going to have any trouble; it does not mean that we are going to have a peaceful and a protected life.
This very Paul who was so sure that, if God was for him, it did not matter who was against him, was the same Paul who wrote that he had been scourged five times, that he had been beaten with rods three times, that he had been stoned once, that he had been three times shipwrecked, that he had been in

prison, that he had looked death in the face often, that there was no kind of peril and no kind of weariness and no kind of exhaustion that he had not gone through (2 Cor. 11:23–28).

No, the fact that God is on our side does not mean that we will enjoy a comfortable trouble-free existence. What it does mean is that, no matter what comes to us, we can face it erect and foursquare and we can emerge triumphant from it.

If God is for us, then life will be no escape, but conquest.

If God is for us, it does not even mean that life itself is safe.

It will not necessarily save us or those we love from the last enemy. But it does mean that we will be very sure that not even that can separate us from the ally of victory.

This is precisely what Paul went on to say. He went on to affirm that in his belief nothing in life or death, in time or in eternity could separate him from the love of God in Christ Jesus our Lord.

To be able to say that God is on our side is not to say that we think that life is going to be easy, and protected, and trouble free: it is not to say that we will win the victories which the world counts victories; it is not even to say that we will go on living this earthly life. But it is to say that no matter what happens to us, we can bear it and face it and conquer it and transform it; and it is to say that even the last enemy has lost his terrors, for ours is the ally who has already conquered him.

ACTIONS   October 4

There are just two kinds of people in this world.

There are the people who talk and talk and better talk, but who never get anything done.

The world is full of wonderful word-spinners and wonderful planners but they never get past the words and they never get past the plans.

I am sure that there are desks and filing cabinets and pigeon-holes in government offices packed and piled and stuffed with the reports of committees and commissions about this and that and the next thing, and nothing was ever done about them and nothing ever will be done about them. And I'm sure that church offices are just the same as the government offices. Plans, schemes, proposals are there by the score but they have never got past being words on sheets of paper.

I think that my wife's way is much better—not to say anything *but* to go out and do it.

That brings me to the other kind of people, the people who do not say very much but who go and do the thing.

You remember the story of the Spartan king Aqesilaus, which we have quoted before. Greece was under threat from the Persians; the danger was real and the threat was dire. Aqesilaus had raised an army and was about to defend his native land. He sent a message to the king of another part of Greece. The other king shilly-shallied and put off a decision and finally sent a message that he was considering what he would do. The Spartan king sent back a message to him: "Tell him that while he is considering it we will march."

There are people—and we thank God for them—who are people of action. They act. It is quite true that they will often make mistakes, but then, as Robert Louis Stevenson once said, the man who is afraid to make a mistake will never make anything. In nine cases out of ten, it is better to do something than to do nothing.

Inaction induces a kind of progressive paralysis. My wife was right. She didn't talk; she went and did the thing. By doing it, she astonished herself and everyone else.

CRUELTY (1)   October 5

When I am writing, Rusty, the Staffordshire bull terrier who stays with us, is usually lying at my feet or across my feet. No one in this family ever comes in without a tumultuous welcome from Rusty. And usually at meal times he is sitting hopefully near the table just in case someone forgets the way a dog ought to be treated and throws him a scrap.

But Rusty is not here at the moment. He has had an experience which has wounded his heart!

Board and Lodging.

Within the next day or so we have to pay a visit to the south of England, and we cannot take Rusty with us. So Rusty had to have his board and lodging fixed up in kennels where they will be very kind and good to him.

One day last week Rusty was taken to the kennels, but Rusty refused to enter them. He shook and shivered and wept and slipped his collar and ran away, and in the end had to be bodily lifted and carried in and left.

Rusty was of course broken-hearted and terrified at leaving the people he knows and loves. But it is all right. We phoned to see how he was getting on (you would think he was an invalid in a nursing home) and he has settled down and is quite happy.

Roam the Streets.

I have just been reading an article in a newspaper which horrified me. This article says that every day strays and homeless cats and dogs are picked up.

But in the summer months, in June, July and August, every week they are picked up literally by the hundred and many roam the streets homeless until they starve to death. This is because there are people who, when they go on holiday, simply turn their animals out and make no provision for them.

This article goes on to say that quite often children get a present of a kitten or a puppy for Christmas or for a birthday. For a week or two, or a month or two, some of them are thrilled with their new friend. Then they get tired of it, and the animal is put out and left to wander and get lost and get run over perhaps or starve.

I hope no reader of this book will ever do this cruel thing to an animal. An animal cannot complain and cannot appeal for itself, and that makes the cruelty all the worse.

CRUELTY (2)   October 6

In reading Dr. Leslie Weatherhead's book *Why do men Suffer?* I came on this lovely prayer for the animals.

Hear our humble prayer, O God, for our friends the animals. In thy hand is the soul of every living thing, and we bless thee that thou carest for the dumb creatures of the earth. We bless and praise thee for thy joy in their beauty and grace, and we desire to share thy love for all of them. Accept our prayer specially for animals who are suffering; for all that are over-worked and underfed and cruelly treated; for all wistful creatures in captivity that beat against their bars; for any that are hunted or lost or deserted or frightened or hungry; for all that are in pain or dying; for all that must be put to death. We entreat for them all thy mercy and pity and for those who deal with them we ask a heart of compassion, and gentle hands, and kindly words. Make us ourselves to be true friends to animals and so to share the blessing of the merciful. For the sake of thy Son the tenderhearted, Jesus Christ our Lord. Amen.

That is a prayer that once in a while we might do well to pray in our churches and in our homes. God will not think it strange that we pray for the animals, for the prophet Hosea heard God speak to him about the last days when the golden age would come and heard God say: 'And I will make for you a covenant on that day with the beasts of the field and the birds of the air, and the creeping things of the ground" (Hos. 2:18, R.S.V.).

In the vision of the perfect time there was perfect friendship between man and the beasts.

Cruelty is always an ugly thing; and cruelty to animals in their dumb helplessness is specially an ugly thing.

The love of God is the love that stretches out over man and beast.

245

One of my difficulties in worship has always been that I have never been happy about the repetition of the Creed. The Creed is, of course, part of the service of the Church of England; it is not nearly so universally part of the service of the Church of Scotland, which is my own church.

My trouble has always been that there were certain statements in the Creed which I am not prepared to accept, and I have always felt that to repeat them as an act of worship was dishonest. But here is what Dr. Barry says: "In saying the creeds we identify ourselves with the total faith and experience of the Church, trusting that, as our Christian life develops, we may grow into fuller understanding of it. No one Christian can apprehend it all; and indeed the original form of the credal statement is 'We believe' rather than 'I believe'."

Here is something that is infinitely worth saying and remembering. And here for many years has been my mistake. Although it may be that I cannot say "I believe", it is blessedly true that I can say "We believe".

I can lose my uncertainty in the certainty of the whole Church, of the whole company of God's worshipping people. It will be a really notable day when we introduce our credal confessions not by "I believe", but by "We believe".

All this is a demonstration of the folly of thinking of oneself as an individual. As soon as we become Christians, there is a sense of which we cease to be individuals and we become members of a great community in Christ.

There can be no individualism in belief.

My own faith may be puny and meagre and inadequate, but when I enter into the Church, I enter into a tradition and a heritage which is far beyond anything I, as an individual, possess. I am no longer under the grim necessity of being unable to go beyond what I believe; I can remember what we believe, and I can take comfort in that.

I can even, in my belief, unite myself with the fellowship of all believers.

In a book he wrote many years ago now, entitled *Everybody's Calvary*, Alan Walker tells of a young minister in a little village chapel. He invited the congregation to wait for a communion service after the ordinary service was ended. Only two waited. So small was the congregation that he thought of cancelling the whole service, but he decided to go on. He followed the ancient ritual and he came to the passage: "Therefore, with angels and archangels and all the company of heaven, we worship and adore thy glorious name." He stopped; the wonder of it gripped him. "Angels and archangels and all the company of heaven . . ." "God forgive me, he said, I did not know I was in that company."

In worship, even where only two or three are gathered together, Jesus Christ is there, and all the company of heaven are there. You will remember how at Dothan Elisha opened the eyes of his servant so that he might see the unseen host which encompassed them from heaven (2 Kings 6:13–17).

When we worship, even with the two or three, we too are compassed about with a mighty cloud of witnesses (Heb. 12:1).

It is definitely so with the effort which Christian living and Christian service demand.

If we think at all, we are bound to think of things as they are and then to think of things as they should be. The difference is daunting, and sometimes we feel our own weakness and helplessness so much that we come to the conclusion that it is hopeless to do anything about it.

Once again, that is the result of thinking as an individual. At such a time we must remember that we are one of a great body and community of people, a Church scattered throughout every nation upon earth, and that there are so many besides ourselves who share our concern and who share our effort. And we remember that at the head of them, there is Jesus Christ.

Nothing is hopeless with a fellowship and with a leader like that.

Life alters when we lay down our foolish individualism and remember that we are one of the community of Christ.

CONTENTMENT   October 9

Last week I accidentally came across a copy of the *Strand Magazine* for Christmas 1894. In its day the *Strand* was perhaps the most famous of all magazines; it was in it, for instance, that the famous Sherlock Holmes stories first appeared. But what interested me was the advertisement pages.

It was interesting to note that, in the many pages of advertisements, there was not a single advertisement for cigarettes or for coffee, and very few for liquor. It seems that seventy-five years ago people were not the slaves to tobacco and to drink that they now so largely are!

The advertisements fell into certain classes, however.

There were many advertisements for *food* and for *clothes*. Here are the basic needs. Men need to know what they are going to eat and what they are going to put on.

There were many advertisements for *medicines*, for *toothpastes*, for *medicines for babies*, for *reducing treatments* and *slimming diets*, for *electrical machines* which were guaranteed to cure all ills. Men, then as now, were interested in their health.

From these advertisements it is possible to draw certain conclusions.

The basic needs of men do not change.

Throughout the centuries there are needs which remain the same and which will always remain the same.

But there were far fewer advertisements for luxuries.

The sophisticated and the affluent society has developed far more needs.

As time goes on, men's needs become more and more complicated and elaborate. The more sophisticated men become, the more they think they need to make them happy.

There was a radical difference in advertising technique.

For the most part, advertisements were announcements. They told the public that certain firms had certain things to offer. They were designed to meet an existing, already felt need. But modern advertising is designed to *create a need*. In doing so, inevitably it creates discontent.

The Bible is always right: "There is great gain in godliness with content." (1 Tim. 6:6).

I left school in 1925. About three years ago, because something rather important had happened to one of the old school class, some of us took steps to get the class together again for an evening. Since then we have been meeting for one evening each year.

These are nostalgic evenings. You can describe them in a single sentence— we eat and drink and remember!

What a perfect description of the great Sacrament of the Christian faith. At it, too, we eat and drink and remember.

The people who come to the sacrament are there for three reasons.

They share a common memory.

By far the commonest phrase when we meet is: "Do you remember?" So at the sacrament we share a common memory: "Do this to make you remember me."

At our dinner we are a fellowship because we share the memory of our schooldays; at the sacrament we are a fellowship because we share the memory of Jesus Christ.

Nothing creates fellowship like the sharing of a common memory.

They share a common gratitude.

At our dinner we share a common gratitude to our old school and our old teachers. That is why it was such a joy to have one of them with us at our last dinner.

The more the years go on, the more we know that we owe so much to the training and the tradition that we received more than forty years ago. At the sacrament we share a common gratitude to our Blessed Lord who loved us and gave himself for us.

They share a common loyalty.

At our dinner we still feel the tug of loyalty to Dalziel High School in

Motherwell, Lanarkshire, with its motto: *Summa Petenda*, which may be translated: "Seek the Highest." At our sacrament we have come because we share a common loyalty to Jesus Christ our Master and Lord, and we wish again to take our pledge to him.

A common memory, a common gratitude, a common loyalty—these are the things that bind men to each other and to Jesus Christ.

TO MAKE IS TO ENJOY   October 11

There are certain things in life that almost everyone can make, or at least can share in making.

We can make a home.
It was Robert Burns who said:

> To make a happy fire-side clime
> To weans and wife;
> That's the true pathos and sublime
> Of human life.

We often speak as if the making of a home depended entirely on the older members of the family, on the father and mother. Maybe we ought to remember more than we do that it depends on the sons and the daughters too. It may be that it takes a father's and a mother's love and care and toil to make a home, but a son's or a daughter's selfishness or thoughtlessness can go far to destroying a home.

Home-making is a co-operative effort in which young and old can and must join.

We can make a friend.
I have often quoted a verse of Hilaire Belloc's but it is so much one of my favourites that I want to quote it again:

> From quiet homes and first beginning,
> Out to the undiscovered ends
> There's nothing worth the wear of winning,
> But laughter and the love of friends.

"A man that hath friends must show himself friendly," as the old saying has it. No one can expect to have friends who will not go to the trouble to be a friend.

We can make a character.
When Sir Walter Scott was a lad, an accident kept him from the usual activities and sent him to the books of the old Scots stories and the old Scots

histories. Afterwards, an old friend who had watched what had happened said of him, "He was makin' himsel' a' the time; but he didna ken maybe what he was about till the years had passed."

We should always ask, not, "Why has God sent me this?" but, "What does God mean me to do with this?"

There is a joy in making things. We can make a home, a friend, and a character.

NO SUBSTITUTE . . .   October 12

I yield to none in my admiration and gratitude for all that religious broadcasting and those who direct it and practise it do for us, and do especially for those who are confined to their homes. And yet the fact remains that, at least as far as I am concerned, no broadcast or televised service can ever be a substitute for a service in a church. If I seem to raise this point frequently, I do so because it is important.

Why?

There is the very obvious fact that no picture can ever take the place of a person.

A photograph is no substitute for a presence. Take away the living, flesh and blood relationship between preacher and people and something quite irreplaceable is lost.

Nothing can really take the place of a worshipping fellowship of God's people. I know that at every broadcast or televised service there is an unseen fellowship. Many a time at the microphone I have experienced it; but the fact remains that an actual flesh and blood fellowship has something that an unseen fellowship can never quite have.

This is not in the least to belittle what broadcasting can do, but it is to say that there is no substitute for worship in the actual company and presence of the worshipping people of God. The day can never come when the actual church service will become unnecessary and irrelevant.

The advance of science and discovery could make it perfectly possible—has made it possible—for people to share in a church service without moving from their own fireside, but in such a service there is something lacking, and there always will be something lacking, which only the real personal, flesh and blood, physical contact, of the church service can give.

When a service is televised, we tend to be spectators of it rather than sharers in it.

We tend to look in rather than to be in. No man can really get all that a service can give so long as he remains outside it.

To spectate is not enough; nothing will do but truly to share; and it is difficult to be sharing without being physically there.

It should still be our aim, not to gather people round a radio or television set, but to gather them within the house of God.

In *An Introduction to Pastoral Counselling*, Dr. Kathleen Heasman talks of the ages of man. There are three main ages each with its own characteristics.

"The first reaches its peak in youth when the achievements are reached in spheres involving physical attributes such as strength and speed. The second is in middle age when a state of maturity and self-confidence has been reached and when the successful have attained the height of their profession or career. The third is in old age when mental attributes such as experience and systematic thinking are the crucial factors and when wisdom has been learnt."

One of the supreme mistakes in life is to try to remain at a stage from which we should have moved on.

It is a mistake to try to remain young.

There is wisdom in knowing when the time for competitive games has come to an end. There is still more wisdom in learning to leave young people to themselves.

Peter Pans who refuse to grow up, are tragic rather than attractive figures. Youth is a magnificent time—but it does not last. We must accept that.

Dr. Heasman says that *middle age* is the time when a man reaches the height of his profession or career. Here the temptation is to stay on too long.

There can be such a thing as the delusion of indispensability. There are few people who are immune from the conscious or unconscious desire for power. Power is difficult to lay down. To be able to leave the top is in its own way as great an achievement as to be able to reach the top.

Age too has its problems. Age has to have a care that it does not become self-centred and crotchety. It is no good "being yourself", if "being yourself" simply brings you into collision with other people.

One of the biggest problems in life is to remember that one's children and the people whom one taught are now grown up. The transition from authority to equality is something which is not always easy to make. But if personal relationships, and the closest personal relationships, are to be right, it must be made.

There is the popular saying, "Be your age!"

It is good advice.

When any new ideas are around, there are those who wave the red flag and there are those who wave the wet blanket.

There can be no possible doubt which is the right thing to do.

It is always a sin to discourage enthusiasm.

One of the surest signs of age in any man is when youthful energy and enthusiasm on someone else's part leave him feeling tired and disapproving.

W. L. Watkinson tells how once he was walking along the promenade in

Brighton with his little grandson. They met an older minister. The old man was sadly disgruntled. Nothing in this world was right; everything and everybody was all wrong, and to make matters worse he was suffering from a slight touch of sunstroke.

The little grandson had been silently listening. When they had left the gloom-stricken old man and had walked on for a short distance, the little grandson looked up at W. L. Watkinson and said, "Grand-dad, I hope that you never suffer from a sunset."

Maybe the little fellow hadn't got the word quite right, but he had got the idea all right. There are some people who suffer from a sunset. They live in a dark and discouraging world.

The Christian should be a man, not of the sunset but of the sunrise, a man of encouragement and not discouragement.

There are some people who have a very highly developed faculty of criticism. They see faults much more easily than they see virtues, and they find it much easier to criticise than to praise. There is one principle of criticism which we should always observe.

No man has any right to criticise any other man, unless he is prepared to do the thing better himself, or unless he is prepared to help the other man to do it better.

The world and the Church and life would all be infinitely poorer without the critics.

Only the man who is prepared to have a go himself, or at least to lend a hand, has the right to criticise.

Of all flags to wave, the wet blanket is the worst of all, and yet there are a large number of people in the Church and in the world, for whom the wet blanket is the national flag. We will not go far wrong, if we make it our aim to go through life always encouraging and never discouraging those who are willing to adventure and those who are doing their best.

PEOPLE MATTER   October 15

People are the most important realities in the world. We must remember this. And so must some others.

The scholar must remember it.

Kermit Eby, the great American teacher, in his book *The God in You* tells how he feels about teaching. "I know," he says "that research is important, yet I know also that a man is more important than a footnote."

He is.

The social reformer must remember it.

"Do not try to convert them," was the advice given to worker priests in Paris. "Love—for you are placed beside one another for this."

The social reformer can be tempted to forget people and concentrate on conditions. But it is people who matter. Change them, and conditions will change!

The ecclesiastic must remember it.

The ecclesiastic's danger is that he may begin to believe that the most important things in life are ecclesiastical systems, forms of church government, rituals, liturgies, vestments, etc! In fact it is living souls that matter.

However splendid forms of worship are, they are useless if men don't find, through them, the way to God.

The theologian must remember it.

The danger for the theologian lies in making an idol of a creed or so intellectualising Christianity that ordinary people feel lost from it. What a tragedy this is!

Let no one belittle the theologian, but the fact remains that it is the evangelist in the street who brings more men to Christ, for his concern is simply people.

NO ESCAPE

We all have this habit of calling something which we do not wish to face by a different name.

Men do this with God.

Men are often quite willing to speak of a First Cause, a Creative Energy, a Prime Mover, when they will not speak of God.

About the beginning of the century there was a famous poem by W. H. Carruth, entitled "Each in his own Tongue". Three of its verses run:

> A firemist and a planet,
> A crystal and a cell,
> A jellyfish and a saurian,
> And caves where the cavemen dwell;
> Then a sense of law and beauty,
> And a face turned from the clod —
> Some call it Evolution,
> And others call it God.

> A haze on the far horizon,
> The infinite, tender sky,
> The ripe, rich tints of the cornfield,
> And the wild geese sailing high;

And all over upland and lowland,
   The charm of the golden rod;
Some of us call it Nature,
   And others call it God.

A picket frozen on duty,
   A mother starved for her brood.
Socrates drinking the hemlock,
   And Jesus on the Rood;
And millions who, humble and nameless,
   The straight, hard pathway trod,
Some call it Consecration,
   And others call it God.

It is still true that there are many who will use all kinds of circumlocutions to avoid speaking and thinking of a personal God—but you cannot banish God by simply changing the name of God.

This is even truer of sin.

It is nothing less than characteristic of modern thought and speech to talk of everything except sin.

We cannot escape from God by changing the name of God; we cannot escape from our own responsibilities by talking of sin under names which are evasions. "A rose by any other name would smell as sweet." God by any other name is no less God; and sin by any other name is still nothing less than sin.

MEMORY'S ROLE   October 17

Never try to remember anything you don't need to remember. Resolutely refuse to clutter the memory with unnecessary things. Never try to remember anything on which at any moment you can quite easily lay your hands.

That is precisely the objection to a task like memorising the order of the books of the Bible. If you wish to find where any book in the Bible is, you can perfectly easily look it up in the index, and then turn it up. To carry the order in our head is to burden the memory with something which is quite unnecessary.

The time spent on memorising the order of the books of the Bible would be infinitely better spent on memorising great passages of the Bible—Psalm 23, Psalm 46, the Beatitudes, certain of the great parables, 1 Corinthians chapter 13, the end of Romans chapter 8, John chapter 14.

Suppose there comes a day, as there came to many in Germany in concentration camps and in solitary confinement, when we are separated from our

Bibles. It will be but cold comfort to rhyme off the books of the Bible in order; it will be the very staff and support of life to know the great passages by heart.

There is a sense in which we never forget anything.
Everything we have heard or seen in all our lives is buried somewhere in the subconscious parts of our minds.

There is a sense in which we can forget anything we wish to forget.
If the mind does not wish to look at a thing, it will quite unconsciously, as well as consciously, push it into the background out of sight. If, for instance, we forget to keep an appointment, the likelihood is that we either did not want to keep it or we were afraid to keep it.

H. G. Wells has said that there are three main faults which affect the mind and the memory. There is, first, inexact reception; second, bad storage; third, uncertain accessibility.

Inexact reception can be conquered by concentration on what we hear.

Bad storage can be helped by the very kind of thing we began by speaking about, by not cluttering the memory with things which it is quite unnecessary to remember.

It is no bad thing to make a habit of memorising some fine or useful thing each day.

In memory, as in so many other things, practice brings perfection.

KINDNESS   October 18

Long ago, Seneca said that what men need above all else is a hand let down to lift them up.

To be kind is always better than to be clever—not that the two things are mutually exclusive, but they so often tend to be.

It was Charles Kingsley who wrote in *A Farewell to C.E.G.*:

> Be good, sweet maid, and let who will be clever;
> Do lovely things, not dream them all day long;
> And so make Life, and Death, and that For Ever;
> One grand sweet song.

And I think that it was the same poet who gave the advice:

> Do the work that's nearest, though it's dull at whiles,
> Helping, when you meet them, lame dogs over stiles.

The world admires the clever people, but it loves the kind people; the memory of kindness lives on when the memory of cleverness has long since faded.

One of the greatest scholars under whom it was my privilege ever to sit was John E. McFadyen, who taught so many of my generation Hebrew, and who opened our eyes to the wonder of the Old Testament. But it is not "Johnnie's" scholarship that we who knew him remember; it was his almost Christlike kindness.

I remember a college football match at which Johnnie was present—he always came to them. One of our Glasgow boys was hurt—he was assistant in a certain church with responsibility for services in a mission. That evening there was a knock at his door. He opened it to find Johnnie on the doorstep. "You were knocked out at the match today," said Johnnie (it was Saturday), "and I've come to see if I could take your services for you tomorrow."

It is kindness that matters.

No one can think along these lines at all without the thought of the mind going back to the saying of Jesus: "Inasmuch as you have done unto one of the least of these my brethren you have done it unto me" (Matt. 25:40).

INCREASING KINDNESS   October 19

There are some people whose lot in this world owes almost everything to Christianity.

There is the child.

In his recent book, *A New Mind for a New Age*, Dr. Alan Walker tells of a plaque in a coalmining village near Manchester, commemorating a mining disaster. It reads as follows: "In the year 1832 the Lord terribly visited the colliery of Robert Clark and the above-named were called to meet their Maker," and there is a list of twenty-three persons who died in the disaster.

It is hoped that there would be few people who would ascribe a mining disaster to the visitation of the Lord nowadays. But, apart from that, the staggering thing is that every one of the twenty-three people who died in that disaster was under nine years of age. They were all children who had been working in the dark lanes and galleries of that mine.

That at least could not happen today, because now we care for the child.

There is the workman.

Aristotle was quite definite: "Master and slave have nothing in common; a slave is a living tool, just as a tool is an inanimate slave."

Varro is equally definite. Writing a treatise for the Romans on agriculture, he divides the instruments of agriculture into three classes—the articulate, the inarticulate, and the mute, "the articulate comprising the slaves, the inarticulate comprising the cattle and the mute comprising the vehicles".

The only difference between a slave and a beast or a cart was that a slave could talk.

When Lord Shaftesbury was asked why he toiled so hard for chimney-sweeps and factory workers and coal miners, he answered, "I have undertaken this task, because I regard the objects of it as being, like ourselves, created by the same God, redeemed by the same Saviour, and destined for the same immortality."

There is the woman.

Before Christianity, there was no such thing as chivalry. The difference in the status of women is one of the great differences between a Christian and a non-Christian community.

This at least we may say—where Christianity has been, no man can ever be regarded as a tool.

THE MIRROR   October 20

Looking in a mirror can produce many reactions!

You can look at yourself with a certain admiration.

Narcissus, the handsome young Greek, was not much concerned for anyone else, but he did like himself. Looking into a pool of clear water one day, he saw his own reflection and he fell in love with himself. He just wanted to keep looking and looking at his own lovely appearance. But he was so entranced with himself that, wholly occupied in gazing at his own reflection, he pined away and died. At death, he was changed into the Narcissus flower. And the truth in that story must never be missed. Self-admiration is the death of the soul. To admire ourselves as we are is to have no wish to change. And with those who don't want to change, the soul is dead.

You can look at yourself with a certain bewilderment.

A famous cartoonist drew a little man on a vast pile of books, looking into a mirror. The books were labelled history, philosophy, biology, theology, etc.

The little man was clearly an academic who knew the contents of all the books and probably understood them. As he looked in the mirror, there was sheer bewilderment, and above his head there was a question mark. He understood everything—except himself!

We are often a puzzle to ourselves.

You can refuse to look at yourself at all.

Too often in life, we refuse to take stock of ourselves, because we are afraid of what we may see. But this way lies hopelessness. Honest self-examination is sheer necessity in life.

It is wise to "look in the mirror" and take stock every now and then.

But we must not just look.
We must act.
And in Jesus we can.
He can give a new image to us all.

We are living in an age of power, an age when men control forces the like of which even their fathers never even dreamed of. The mind of man has penetrated the secrets of Nature. "The nature of the Universe," said Hegel, "hidden and barred from man at first, has no power to withstand the assaults of science; it must reveal and lay bare the depths of its riches before man, ready for his enjoyment."

Bertrand Russell once said, "Science as technique has conferred a sense of power; man is much less at the mercy of his environment than he was in former times."

Man has power today such as no other generation ever possessed. Distance has been annihilated, and space is on the way to being spanned. The means of mass communication make it almost as easy to speak to a continent as to a single individual. Speeds which would once have been thought incredible are commonplace. Measured in terms of sheer destruction, the power which man controls is like a devilish and satanic miracle.

It is this power which has presented man with a life and death problem.

The problem is not now the acquisition of power. The problem is the use of power. All power is in itself quite neutral. It is neither good nor bad. It is potential for goodness and for evil, for blessing and for destruction.

There is no use in abolishing distance and bringing the ends of the earth together, if they are to be brought together in bitterness and strife.

If speed of travel simply means that peoples and nations can get more quickly at each other's throats, there is little use in it.

If the greatest powers men ever commanded are to be concentrated on destruction, it were better not to have discovered them.

The important thing in relation to all power is the character and the quality of those who possess it. In the hands of good and loving men, power is a blessing; in the hands of selfish, self-seeking, reckless men, power is an evil.

I have come across two things which tell of very real threats to the life of man in the time to come.

The first is a reference to an article in the *Lancet* by Dr. Reginald Passmore, Reader in Physiology in Edinburgh University.

Dr. Passmore says that a new species of man is emerging in the West—a species which takes in too much food (often of the wrong sort), in relation to his energy output, and becomes diseased as a result. He calls this species *Homo sedentarius*, which literally means "sitting down man".

Here is the description of the kind of life that many people, perhaps most of us, lead. We drive sitting down to our work in a motor car; we do our work sitting down at a desk; we eat meals which are too large and too rich; we drive home again at night; and we spend the evening half-sitting, half-lying, in a chair, half-awake, and half-asleep.

The other thing I came across was in an article by the well-known journalist, Arthur Helliwell. Mr. Helliwell had been touring America and had been seeing life there. He tells us that on income tax returns and other returns by next year a new profession will be appearing, the profession of witness. "All over the United States," he goes on to say, "men are now employed as 'witnesses', and a witness is a man who does no work. He simply watches work being done! By giant robots. By Frankenstein monsters with iron hands and steel fingers that can work faster, more precisely and more efficiently than any man. By delicate machines that can assemble wrist-watches or wrap and pack fragile chocolates. And by electronic 'brains' with eerie memories that can perform half a million intricate calculations in sixty seconds.

"All the robot needs is to be started, stopped—and watched, by 'witnesses', men who for most of their working day never have to take their hands out of their pockets."

There are robots so sensitive that they do not even need to be switched off and on, but will respond to the sound of the human voice. So in Chicago there is a robot which can turn out one thousand transistor sets a day, and it needs only two men to tend it. In New York there is a bottling plant which can wash, refill, cap and crate two hundred thousand bottles a day with a total staff of three men to watch it.

The "witness" is a "workman" who can do his day's work by sitting watching, and never taking his hands out of his pocket.

GENERALISATIONS   October 23

Roy Larson once wrote an article he entitled "Memo to a Parson from a Wistful Young Man". In it he says he has tried all kinds of churches and has found none that he can like or find profitable.

"When I do go to church," he says, "what do I hear? From the pulpit, a semi-religious version of what Kenneth Galbraith calls 'the conventional wisdom'. From the choir loft, incredible Victorian anthems—the kind that Grandma used to love.

"From the pew, the attitude you discover at alumni reunions—'where there's not a single dry eye, but no one believes a word of it'. And from the button-niered ushers, the kind of mechanical handshake which makes me suspect that they would greet Jesus at the Second Coming by saying: 'It was nice of you to come'."

The average church, he says, stands for everything he despises, "false gentility, empty sentiment, emotional impoverishment, intellectual mediocrity and spiritual tepidity," and he has neither the wish nor the intention to associate himself with such a body.

It would not be difficult to argue with this verdict. But the answer to Mr. Larson's statements is not the point. The point is this: It is quite impossible to say anything that is true of the whole Church, any more than it is possible to say something that is true of all football teams or all hospitals or all concerts.

Generalisations are hardly ever true universally. To argue from one particular instance to a verdict on a whole institution is grossly unfair. It is no more fair to say that churches are packed because one is full than to say that churches are deserted because one is two-thirds empty.

There are very few statements made about "the Church" today which would stand up to a cross-examination in a court of law.

It is time that we all—ministers, laymen, journalists, authors, supporters and critics of the Church—stopped making large and general statements about the Church, often out of ignorance rather than out of knowledge. What we can do is to take the New Testament picture of the Church and compare our own congregation to it—and then we shall be compelled, not to criticism, but to search our consciences.

TAKEN AWAY   October 24

The Incarnation takes away our ignorance of God.

Long ago, Plato said that it was impossible to find out anything about God, and, if by any chance you did find out anything, it was impossible to tell it to anyone else.

The essence of Jesus Christ is that in him, we see what God is like.

The Atonement takes away the barrier of sin.

The Church very wisely has never had one official and orthodox theory of the Atonement. But every theory of the Atonement says one thing, although the different theories may say it in different ways. Through the life and death of Jesus Christ, the relationship between man and God was completely and totally changed.

The one idea that is common to all theories of the Atonement is the idea of Reconciliation. Because of what Jesus Christ is and what he did and does, the fear and the estrangement and the distance and the terror are gone.

We know that even to us the friendship of God is open.

The gift of Grace takes away our helplessness.

When we know what Grace means, more than one precious thing emerges clearly. We know that our relationship to God depends not on our merits but on his love. We know that he loves us not for what we are, but because of what he himself is. We know that we are no longer left to face and to fight life ourselves; but that there is open to us all the power and the strength of God.

In Grace there is release from the tension of unavailing effort, and the coming of power.

The gift of Immortality takes away the evanescence of humanity.

Jesus, through his glorious gospel, brought life and immortality to light (2 Tim. 1:10). We know ourselves now to be on the way not to death, but to life. We know that death is not the end, but the beginning of life. We know ourselves to be not the children of a moment, but the pilgrims of eternity.

Life has a new value, because it is not on the way to extinction and obliteration but to consummation and to completion.

CONSTRUCTION KITS   October 25

Construction kits, for me, are parables of life.

God does not give us a completed life; he gives us the raw materials out of which to make a life.

God gives us ourselves, with all our gifts and our abilities; he gives us the world, with all its beauty and its bounty, and its resources; he gives us the people we live with; and he says to us, "Out of all these things, make a life that is worthwhile."

It is never God's way to give us the finished article; he gives us the raw materials. It is never God's way to do things for us; it is always his way to enable us to do things for ourselves. God's whole method is to encourage and enable us to do things for ourselves."

But you would never get your construction kits to come out right unless you followed the instructions.

So it is with life. God gives us the raw materials of life, and God gives us the instructions how to turn them into a real and worthwhile life. He gives us his law and his commandments in his book; he gives us conscience within to tell us what to do and what not to do; he gives us the guidance of his Holy Spirit; he gives us Jesus to be both our example and our power.

God has given us all we need to make a life; God has given us the rules and instructions to follow; and God has given us his Son to help us to do the things we could never do ourselves, and to make the life we could never construct ourselves.

A HOUSE OF YOUR OWN (1)   October 26

Have you read the book for children called *A Little House of your Own?* It is by Beatrice Schenk de Regniers who says:

261

This is the important thing to remember . . .
Everyone has to have a little house of his own.
Every boy has to have his own little house.
Every girl should have a little house to herself.

Perhaps the house is under the dining-room table; or in the bushes in the garden; or in a big box, or even behind a false face. It doesn't really matter where. The important thing is that it is *our* house. And even our friends shoudn't come in unless we ask them.

Virginia Woolf said that all she asked from life was a room of her own.

James Agate, talking of the continual bustle of entertainment on a visit to America writes, "How the bustle takes the form of your not being alone; a continual restless button-holing goes on all the time . . . It doesn't seem to occur to anybody that one may like occasionally to be left alone for five minutes . . ."

The great souls knew the value of a house of their own—Francis of Assisi "loved mountains". Paul went to Arabia to be alone. Jesus was often alone.

We need to be alone to meet ourselves.

We are so often so busy making a living that we do not stop to think whether we are making a life.

We need to be alone to meet God.

We do not really know a person if we have only met him in crowds.

We need to withdraw to meet others better.

It is not so that we may live alone that we need a little house. It is to help us to serve others better.

A HOUSE OF YOUR OWN (2)   October 27

A family cannot really be a family until it has a house and a key of its own.

In this life we need at least sometimes to be alone.

It is one of the problems of modern life that people have lost the art of being alone.

Friendship is good, and doing things together is fun. Man is instinctively a gregarious animal. But there can get into life a restlessness, an inability to bear one's own company, which ends in making life a neurotic and a discontented business.

We have the example of Jesus.

After a busy day at Capernaum in which he gave himself unreservedly to people, he rose early in the morning and went away to be alone (Mark 1:35).

After the days of teaching and the feeding of five thousand he sent the crowds, and even the disciples, away on ahead across the lake that he might be alone (Mark 6:46).

It is necessary sometimes to be alone with ourselves and alone with God. It is not that this loneliness is an end in itself. Jesus did not want to be alone for the sake of being alone. He wanted to be alone so that he could meet God, and then come back stronger and calmer to meet people. His loneliness was only a withdrawal to fight the better. And so it must be with us.

We live in a nervous and a neurotic age; we live in an age with a fear, sometimes conscious, sometimes subconscious, that we cannot face life and cope with life. There is no doubt that we would be calmer, stronger, more serene, more master of the situation and of circumstance, if we learned to set apart a little time to be alone with God, for to be alone with him will give us serene and unafraid the calm strength which can cope with anything.

THE MEN GOD NEEDS (1)   October 28

At a recent conference I heard the story of an older minister who, when he was informed that a certain younger man was the possessor of a B.A. degree, said, "The only B.A.s we want here are those who are Born Again."

And I heard that the story sometimes circulated in the form that the only M.A.s who were wanted were those who were Marvellously Altered!

I have been reading the story of Father Herbert Kelly, the founder of Kelham, as it is told in the book *No Pious Person*, and there it is said that Kelly spoke of the needs of the Church. The Church, he said, needs men in numbers, still more in devotion, and hardly less, in training.

There, then, we have various views of what is needed to fit a man for the ministry of the Church. When we think about this, I think that we must come to the conclusion that a man must have five things before he can effectively serve the Church.

He must have a real religious experience.

No man can teach what he does not know; and no man can bring other men to Jesus Christ unless he himself has met Christ and knows Christ. It is not possible to introduce others to someone whom we do not know ourselves.

He must have a real training in thought.

No man will ever be an effective force as an evangelist if he can do no more than repeat like a parrot that which he has been told. Any real course of education must teach a man not only what to think, but far more, how to think.

Any man who is to become preacher, teacher, witness for Jesus Christ must know what the great minds and hearts of men have thought and said of Christ, and must also have thought the matter out for himself until he comes to a faith which is his faith.

The student for the Ministry must have a real training in the technique of communication.

Even if a man has a real religious experience, even if he has thought things out and through for himself, his experience and his thought are of no value to others, if they are expressed in language which no man can understand, or in a voice that no man can hear.

One of the most damaging of all mistakes is the idea that in the work of the minister and the evangelist and the witness for Jesus Christ, technique does not matter. Many a man's work has been spoiled and rendered ineffective for the simple reason that he never took the trouble to study the technique of how to get this material across.

He must have a real ability to understand his fellow-men and to get on with them and to get alongside them.

There was a great deal to be said for the Jewish regulation I have mentioned earlier, that a Rabbi must have a trade. There would be much to be said for making it the practice that all who seek to enter the ministry should have had some time at some ordinary work amidst men. Still further, the Jews had a saying: "An irritable man cannot teach." It is quite certain that the man who has never solved the problem of living at peace with his fellow-men will never be an effective servant of the Church.

No man who has failed to solve the problem of personal relationships has any right to preach. No man can in honesty preach love and practise bitterness; no man can proclaim the forgiveness of God and be himself an example of the unforgiving spirit; no man can preach reconciliation while he himself is at variance with his fellow-men.

To all this, there must be added staying power, the power to see things through, the power to persevere when there is very little to encourage and very much to discourage. That staying power can only be acquired by the ability daily to live close to God.

THE PASTORAL GIFT   October 30

The pastoral gift is a supreme interest in people and in *individual* people. This makes a man a great minister of a church.

This ability to remember things about individual people is not only the mark of a great minister; it is also the mark of a great doctor, and it comes first and foremost from sheer interest in people.

Paul Tournier in his book *A Doctor's Case-Book* says that sometimes a patient says to him, "I admire the patience with which you listen to everything I tell you." Then he says, "It is not patience at all, it is interest."

There is a kind of person about whom you have the feeling all the time you are talking to him that he is not thinking so much about you as about the next person he has to interview, and that his main aim is to get rid of you as expeditiously as possible. And there is a kind of doctor to whom, you are well aware, you are not a person but a case.

The great pastors and healers all have tremendous personal interest in people.

God is like that.

In another part of his book, Paul Tournier speaks of what he calls the personalism of the Bible. Most people find the long lists of names in the Old Testament and in the New Testament sometimes quite irrelevant. But Paul Tournier is fascinated that God should know so many people by name. "I know thee," God said to Moses, "by name" (Exod. 33:17). "I am the Lord," God said to Isaiah, "which call thee by thy name" (Isa. 45:3).

God, with a world to sustain, knows each one of us by name.

This was so clearly true of Jesus.

In one sense Jesus lived and moved amongst crowds; but you cannot read the story of Jesus without the feeling again and again that in incident after incident even in the middle of a crowd he was giving all of himself entirely to one single person, as if for the moment that person was the only person who mattered.

The great pastor and doctor, the great human person, is the person to whom no one is ever lost in the crowd, and to whom everyone is an individual, claiming and receiving his individual interest, attention and love.

PHILEMON   October 31

In many ways the letter to Philemon is the strangest book in the New Testament. What is a little personal letter about a runaway slave named Onesimus doing in the New Testament?

There is no doctrine and no theology in it; it is a little personal letter about a slave who had thieved from his master, who had run away and who, with Paul, had somehow made good again, so that at last he was living up to his name Onesimus, which means the useful one.

How did that letter get into the New Testament? We cannot tell for sure, but we can guess. Scholars believe that it was in Ephesus about A.D. 90 that Paul's letters were first collected and edited and issued to the public as a book. Now some years after that Ignatius, the Bishop of Antioch, was writing letters to the Churches of Asia, as he was being taken to Rome to be flung to the beasts in the arena.

Amongst the letters there is one to Ephesus which pays rare tribute to the Bishop of Ephesus and to his beautiful nature and to the usefulness of his life —just like his name.

And what is the name of this Bishop of Ephesus? It is Onesimus.

There are scholars who believe that the runaway slave, Onesimus, and the bishop, Onesimus, are one and the same person, and that when Paul's letters were collected to Ephesus, Onesimus insisted that this little letter to Philemon must go in, that all men might know what once he had been and what Jesus Christ had done for him.

November

Mothers never get tired!

If a so-called "working" man had to work a mother's day he would both strike and collapse.

Mother's day begins at 6.30 a.m. to get the family on the way by 8 o'clock and at midnight Mum will still be working.

An eight-hour day? Payment for overtime? These are things that mothers know nothing about. Mother works as long as her family need her.

Mother knows nothing about demarcation disputes.

We get a good deal of industrial trouble about who does what. Duties are strictly delimited and defined. But Mother is the cook who cooks the meals; the chambermaid who makes the beds; the cleaner who cleans the house; the laundrymaid who washes the clothes; the waitress who serves the meals; the dishwasher who washes up; the nurse who looks after us when we are ill; the child psychologist who knows what to do with the child; the teacher who helps the child with his first steps in learning; the priest who hears the confessional; the disciplinarian who keeps order; and at all times the lover and the friend.

Mother's don't stop to argue what is their duty and what is not. Where they are needed they act.

The Bible is rich in mothers. There is Rebekah the mother of Jacob (Gen. 27), There is Hannah the mother of Samuel (1 Sam. 1). There is the anonymous mother of Peter's wife who served Jesus with a meal (Mark 1:29–31). There is Eunice, Timothy's mother (2 Tim. 1:5). And there is Mary, the mother of Jesus.

Protestants are often angry about what they call Roman Catholic "Mariolatry". But I sometimes wonder if behind so-called Mariolatry, there is the recognition of what all mothers are and do; that, even if it has become debased and exaggerated, there is something of human value there.

Don't let us ever forget the tireless ones: Mothers!

MODERN PILGRIMS   November 2

I admire the adventurousness of young people today. They are ready to go off alone into the blue, without a tremor!

My grand-daughter Karen, when she was seven, went off to Ireland where she was to spend her holidays, by boat from Stranraer all by herself. True, she would be looked after on the boat and she would be met at Larne, but I'm pretty sure that at seven I wouldn't have made that journey!

My daughter Jane went off to France on her own when a teenager. True, we knew the people she was going to, and she was met at Paris, but I very much doubt if, at her age, I would have gone off with so much confidence.

I knew a young man who, when still at the university, made the most incredible journeys. On one occasion his brother drove him to the nearest motorway and left him to hitch a lift just anywhere. The boy finished up in Salonika! And the only money he spent on travel was for the boat from Dover to the Continent.

These modern pilgrims show faith in action.

There are three kinds of faith here. They have obviously *faith in themselves.* And there is *parental faith* too. There is *faith in the essential decency of other people.* For every one case where there is trouble and even tragedy, there are thousands in which everything goes well.

This is faith.

Again, all this adventure of pilgrimage does two things to young people.

It removes their insularity. And it ensures that there is growing up a race of young men and women whose outlook is international. It is part of an exciting new world.

I am convinced that it would be—thank God—very much harder to persuade people to go to war today than ever before, because no one wants to fight the people with whom he has eaten and drunk and hiked and swam and climbed and sung and talked.

The modern pilgrims are pioneers of a movement by which the world can become one.

Let us encourage them!

DO IT BADLY!   November 3

There is nothing quite like the D'Oyley Carte performance of the Gilbert and Sullivan operas. A performance by that company is as near perfection as any human production can possibly be.

In contrast with that, I well remember our school performances! There would be a girl singing Frederick's part in *The Pirates* because the school hadn't any boy tenors. The curtain would stick when it was supposed to open on the scene. And so on. But in the hearts of many of us in Dalziel High School it put a love for these operas that time has done nothing to lessen.

No school could possibly perform these operas like the D'Oyley Carte Company; *but if a thing is worth doing, it is worth doing badly.* We did them badly, but we got one of the treasures of life out of them.

We do not stop playing golf because we cannot score like Tony Jacklin. We do not stop playing the piano because we will never be concert pianists. We do not stop preaching because we will never be Spurgeons. It is worth aiming high even if it seems beyond us.

The choir *ought* to have a go at the really great music.

The preacher *ought* to attempt the great and difficult subject.

The congregation *ought* to launch out on this or that impossible scheme.

If it is worth doing, it is worth doing badly.

But—and it is a big but—it is also true that *the thing must be done, as well as we can possibly do it.*

The choir need not start on the big work if the members have come to a stage when they think they do not need to attend practices.

The preacher need not start on the big subject unless he is prepared to read and think. The congregation can hardly launch the big effort if 50 per cent of the members propose to do nothing.

If a thing is worth doing, it is worth putting our best into it.

Let us "have a go" at the big thing. If it is worth doing, it is worth doing badly, so long as it is done as well as we can possibly do it.

SPIRITUAL ECONOMICS   November 4

So far as the bank is concerned, you only get out what you put in. And so far as living is concerned, the same law holds good.

You only get out of life as much as you put in.

The unhappiest people in the world are those who always act in their own interests. They won't engage in public services. They won't help a choir or Sunday School. If voluntary work depended on them, there would be none. What can they expect to get out of life, who never put anything in?

"I want to be thoroughly used up when I die," said George Bernard Shaw.

The happiest people in life are the people who are too busy to pity themselves, too busy to think only of themselves.

Life pays its debts. The more you put in the more you get out.

You only get out of work as much as you put in.

No one will ever get a real, satisfying job, a job which grows with him, unless he has the qualifications and experience which discipline and study give.

How sad it is to see youngsters strain to get away from school. This world is not a charitable institution waiting to hand out money for nothing. To get back you have to give, in real, hard work.

You only get out of the Church what you put in.

Is your idea of church membership an hour on Sunday?

Have you realised that the congregation has as much to do with the service as the preacher; with the prayers as the pray-er?

Too often we are not church members but (as they said in war-time) "registered customers".

We are the church. The church is what we make it and put into it.

Spiritual economics are just as valid as those economics that refer to the bank.

WE NEED . . . November 5

There are certain things that we all need within the Church.

We need more co-operation and less competition.

It is far too often the case that churches which are close to each other are in competition with each other. There are a great many things which churches would do much more effectively, if they would do them together, yet in a kind of foolish pride, they insist on doing them separately.

If idolatry is the worship of wood and stone, then a great many congregations are guilty of it, for in their refusal to do things together they seem to worship their own building rather than their own Lord.

We need more sympathy and less criticism.

If only we would learn that there is no one way of worshipping God. There is no one way of celebrating the Lord's Supper. There is no one way of conducting the devotional part of the service; there is no one kind of church music.

There is such a thing as the tyranny and the intolerance of the expert. The liturgical expert is intolerant of everything which is not liturgical perfection; the muscial expert is intolerant of everything which is not musical perfection. The result is that we often regard each other's form of worship with criticism, intolerance, and sometimes even contempt, forgetting that what we despise may be very precious to someone else.

A wise tolerance and a kindly sympathy would go far to produce a new and gracious unity within the churches.

We need more appreciation and less jealousy.

As I search my own heart, I wonder how much of my criticism of others is due to the fact that I am at heart jealous of their success. The lesson of life is that it is much easier to sympathise with a man in his sorrow than to congratulate him on his success.

Maybe we have never quite learned the lesson that it is to Jesus Christ we want a man to listen—and not to ourselves.

A GOAL   November 6

A goal is an essential in life.

Without a goal to aim at, we never really get things done.
It is characteristic of the human spirit that we need something to focus an effort on, before we will make that effort. That is why it is very difficult to study any subject unless there is an examination or a test at the end of the course of study. That is why so many of us cease to be students when we leave our school, or college, or university.

In these places study had a goal, and we undertook it. Now there is nothing on which to focus it, and we do not do it.

To have a goal is the only way to have a test of progress.
It is the only way to see whether or not we are improving. The goal provides a measuring rod and a standard. It is when we set ourselves some definite target that we can assess whether or not we are on the way. To have a conscious goal is to be saved from the killing lethargy of a deadly content with ourselves as we are.

If we have a goal, then it is essential that that goal should be beyond our attainment, for that is the very essence of an ideal.
To have an attainable goal and to achieve it is to come to a stage in life when there are no more worlds left to conquer, and when life can sink into inaction and into stagnation. To have a goal which always shines ahead is to have something to which to the end of the day we may still strive.

The way of the Christian life can be summed up in one sentence. It is to walk "looking to Jesus" (Heb. 12:2). He alone is the goal, and he alone is the standard.

In him the Christian has a goal which will last beyond time into eternity.

BIBLE STUDY   November 7

How ought we to study the Bible so that we may overpass the barriers and come together?

We have to ask of the Bible first of all: What does it mean?
This is one of the great reasons—perhaps it is the only reason—why we

must never fail to teach our students and our preachers the original tongues, the Hebrew and the Greek, in which the Bible was written.

This is why the study of words is all-important. This is why the study of the background of the Bible is of intense importance, because we can never really find the meaning of a saying until we also find the circumstances and the situation in which it was written.

We must always study the Bible as a whole.

The battle of proof texts is a battle with no victory. Isaiah says, "They shall beat their swords into ploughshares, and their spears into pruning hooks; nation shall not lift up sword against nation, neither shall they learn war any more" (Isa. 2:4.). Joel says, "Beat your ploughshares into swords, and your pruning hooks into spears; let the weak say, I am a warrior" (Joel 3:10). In the Bible we are constantly being confronted with this kind of contradiction. Clearly, what we must do is to find the total message of the Bible and to think about it.

There must be an end of the belligerent hurling of texts at each other, and a real attempt to bring the whole gospel to the questions we discuss.

We must try to find out, not just what the Bible means in general, but what it means for us.

If we are to do this, there is one thing which, perhaps above all we must try to avoid.

We must try to avoid going to the Bible in order to find in it material to support ideas and theories which are in fact our own.

When we study the Bible we must sit down in humility before it and listen, not to our own voices extracting our own meanings from the Bible, but to the voice of God as it speaks to us in his book.

It will be an exercise in humility, but it will also be a path to truth.

WE ARE ONE!   November 8

I belonged to a small group of people who met together several times a year to work on a task which had been assigned to them. People who meet together might learn from this little group.

All the meetings of the group are begun with prayer.

It would be wrong to say that we ask for the presence of God, because we very well know that, even if we wished to do so, we could not get out of the presence of God; but what we do ask for is that we should be made aware that we are working in the presence of God.

How different many a meeting, even many a church meeting, would be, if we remembered that God heard and saw everything that was said and done!

No one in the group ever hesitates to express his opinion.

It may well happen that his opinion is very much his own, and that it is startling and unusual and even unlikely to meet with agreement. But everyone in the group feels quite free to say what he thinks.

If a man has something to say, he should say it at the right time and in the right place, and it is the reverse of helpful to be quite silent at the time when things ought to be said, and to be extremely talkative when the right time for saying them should be over and past.

There is always some hope of meeting a man's objections, if you know what they are.

The group is prepared to give anyone of its members a hearing.

There is never any impatience; no one is ever snapped at; no one is ever made to feel that he is a time-waster. The members of the group are prepared to listen to anyone who thinks that he has something to say.

All the members are prepared to admit that they were wrong.

On occasion it is the work of one of the group itself which is under the microscope and under examination; but no one ever resents criticism, however drastic. It often happens that a member of the group will express an opinion with conviction, but it may be that after he has heard the others speak, he will admit that he was in error.

Attendance at the group of which I have been writing is one of the joys of life.

I wish that all church groups were like this one!

RECEIVING   November 9

There is a royalty in receiving.

When a gift is offered, there are, I think three necessities.

A gift must be accepted.

There are few things more wounding than to have a gift refused.

People in this country do not wear their heart on their sleeve; they are not demonstrative. And I sometimes wonder, if, when we talk about unfriendliness, the fault does not lie in ourselves, for not accepting what is offered.

A gift must be appreciated.

This is where the courtesy of a thank you comes in. Sometimes we send a gift to a person and there is not a word, spoken or written, of thanks; and it is only long after that you can even be sure that the person got the thing at all.

Surely there can be few words easier to say than, "Thank you"; and surely there can be few words more uplifting to hear. We should pray, "Make me grateful, and make me remember to show that I am grateful." There was a time when even Jesus had to ask: "Where are the nine?" (Luke 17: 17).

A gift must be used.

Half the joy of giving a gift is to see the gift used by the person to whom it is given. This is where Jesus was so wonderful. He took the smallest and apparently most inadequate gifts and used them gloriously.

The giver whom Jesus praised most of all was a woman who put a couple of coins worth together less than a farthing into the Temple treasury (Mark 12:41–44). God, he seemed to say, can greatly use that gift.

There is a generosity in giving, but there is also a royalty in receiving.

DISCOURAGEMENT   November 10

Discouragement has three terrible consequences.

Discouragement kills a man's enthusiasm.

So long as a man is enthusiastic about something, life is bearable, but take that essential enthusiasm away and there is very little left.

If a man is enthusiastic about his work, his work is a joy; take away his enthusiasm and his work becomes a weariness to body and mind. Even if a man's work is wearisome and unrewarding and repetitive, he can still enjoy life, if he has some interest, some hobby, some gift, about which he can be enthusiastic. But continuous criticism, continuous discouragement, continuous lack of appreciation can kill the enthusiasm and then life becomes an intolerable thing.

Discouragement ends by making the person discouraged come to the conclusion that it is simply not worth trying any more.

A psychologist tells of being in a home where there was a small child. In a visit of an hour he heard that small child either told to do or told not to do eighteen different things, and told to do them or not to do them in a tone of the utmost severity. There can be only one result of that. The child is bound to come to think of himself, consciously or unconsciously, as a useless bungler who can do nothing to please his parents.

If that be the case, he will give up trying, and will become either a cowed and dispirited failure or a resentful and rebellious delinquent.

In the training of any child, in the running of any team, in the inspiring of any community, an ounce of encouragement is worth a ton of discouragement.

Constant discouragement can make a person lose all self-confidence.

There is a vast difference between the arrogant self-confidence which is based on an inflated idea of one's own ability and importance and the quiet confidence which knows that it can cope with life and with the situation. But constant discouragement can cause so much self-doubt that it can leave a person quite unable to face life at all.

There is nothing in this world which will pull the best out of a man as encouragement will. To feel that someone is with you, to feel that someone is willing you on to achievement is one of the great things in life.

Parents should encourage their children.

Let parents encourage their children. "Fathers," said Paul, "do not provoke your children, lest they become discouraged" (Col. 3:21).

Employers should encourage their employees.

If you want to get the best out of a man, the best way to do it is to give him some praise.

Praise from someone whose good opinion he values does not make a man proud; it makes him humble.

Congregations ought to encourage their ministers.

John Newton once said of his father, "I knew my father loved me, but he never seemed to want me to know that he did."

We are, in this country, and nowhere more so than in Scotland, undemonstrative people; we find it very difficult to show our feelings. No one could ever say that we wear our heart on our sleeve. In a way it is a good thing, because cheap and meaningless words of affection can be nauseating; but we can much overdo the reticence.

A word of encouragement to a preacher can be a thing of infinite value.

There is criticism enough in the world.
Let's try some encouragement instead.

Queen Victoria was almost entirely dependent on the Prince Consort, Prince Albert. When Albert died all too young, Queen Victoria was grief-stricken with a grief which lasted for many years; and all her sorrow was summed up in a thing she once said: "I have no one to call me Victoria now."

She had plenty of people to call her "Your Majesty", but no one left to do the little personal things which mean so much.

Here, there is something to be said about the modern set-up of life. This is one of the great problems—and even disasters—in the house and home in which the mother goes out to work. There is something fundamentally wrong with a home in which there is no one there to welcome a child when he or she comes home.

Sir James Barrie wrote about the days when he was young. In the old days in Thrums it was the men who had done the weaving in his home with true craftsmanship. Then there came the industrial revolution and the machine age and the hand-loom in the house was displaced by the power-loom in the factories. And it was the women who went out to work in the factories, and the home was left without them.

"It is there," said Barrie, "that I feel that my country is being struck."

I know that there may be cases when the mother has to go out to work to make ends meet, and sometimes even to give the children a chance. But I also know that there are even more cases in which the extra money earned to buy a television set or to run a car or the like costs far too much.

When money is earned at the cost of a child coming home to an empty house, that money is money dearly earned. Being a wife and a mother is not only far and away the greatest job in the world; it is also a whole-time job which takes everything any woman has got to give to it.

At the end of all the roads there is no empty house, but a home where we shall, face to face, receive the welcome of him with whom we have walked so long.

. . . SWEET . . .   November 13

The more "human" you are the more you love your home. It is a very strange person who does not love home. Dogs are next door to being human and they love their homes. I love cats, but I am bound to say that they are remote and inhuman animals, and home does not mean nearly so much to them, unless they are like Sammy the Siamese whom we still mourn and who was more like a dog than a cat.

The poets have all loved home. You remember Byron's lines:

> 'Tis sweet to hear the watchdog's honest bark
> Bay deep-mouth'd welcome as we draw near home;
> 'Tis sweet to know there is an eye will mark
> Our coming, and look brighter when we come.

Or you remember Robert Louis Stevenson's lines to S. R. Crockett, written away in the South Seas, far from the Scotland he loved and which for his health's sake he could never see:

> Be it granted me to behold you again in dying,
> Hills of home! and to hear again the call;
> Hear about the graves of the martyrs the peewees crying,
> And hear no more at all.

Or do you remember the story in the Bible about Hadad the Edomite who, when he was a little child, was taken in exile to Egypt? He was well treated there, but the day came when it was safe for him to go home. "Let me depart

276

that I may go to my own country," he said to Pharaoh. And Pharaoh, who had loved him and treated him well said, "What hast thou lacked with me that thou seekest to go to thine own country?" And Hadad answered, "Nothing, howbeit, let me go" (1 Kings 11:21, 22).

Let him who has a home thank God for it, and let him remember with sympathy and kindness those who have not.

. . . HOME   November 14

There are at least three reasons why in this age in which we live the home is supremely important.

We live in a worried age.

It is of supreme importance that we should have some place in which we can relax, in which we can find people to whom we can really talk and really open our hearts, knowing that they will neither laugh at our dreams, mock at our failures, or laugh our troubles out of court.

My old teacher, W. M. Macgregor, used sometimes, to talk of the work of the ministry and the importance of getting married in order to do it well! Thinking of the worries and the frustrations and the problems and the annoyances and the irritations that the running of a congregation is always bound to bring, he used to say, "Happy is the man who has someone at home to whom he can explosively unburden himself!"

There are many of us who simply do not know what we would do, if we had no one to talk to at home.

We live in a tired age.

One of the features of this age is the number of people whom one sees asleep! In buses, in trains, on any journey, in restaurants and in clubs you see people who obviously have been unable to keep their eyes open.

It is one of life's supreme gifts to have some place in which we can fully and completely relax.

Sometimes we may think that it would be pleasant to live for ever in some luxury hotel with all kinds of service at our beck and call. But experience teaches us that there is literally no place like home—and the supreme thing about a good home is that it is the one place where we can find the peace our souls desire.

We live in an age of insignificance.

Today, we all tend to be names on a card, numbers on a card index, specimens of some kind of class or group. The individual has come to matter less and less as an individual.

Jesus spent thirty years in fulfilling home duties and only three in the world of men.

Let us thank God for the home and for the family which, in his goodness, he has given to us.

CREATION   November 15

The joy of making things is one of the elemental joys of the human situation. The more ambitious the project, the better.

I have a friend who decided to try woodwork. Most people, when they embark on woodwork, start with something like a pipe-rack; my friend's first production was a most elaborate, built-in, fitted wardrobe for his and his wife's bedroom! There is nothing like starting in a big way!

To know the joy of creation is to share the joy of God, for it was at creation that, in Job's magnificent phrase (Job 38 : 7).

> The morning stars sang together,
> And all the sons of God shouted for joy.

Don't laugh at the person who tries to make something; he is finding the joy of creation.

It is something to hold in your hand, something which you have made. However many books an author may have written, he still gets a thrill when he holds in his hand the finished book. However long a craftsman may have been at his craft, his heart still beats faster when he sees something that he has made.

And once again this joy in the product is the joy of God. Again and again in the old creation story we come on the phrase: "And God saw that it was good" (Gen. 1 : 10, 18, 25, 31). "God saw everything that he had made, and behold it was very good."

There is joy in seeing someone able to use, or to be helped by, something we have made. Every craftsman finds joy in seeing that which his hands have made in use. And once again, we are back at the joy of God, for the old story tells how, when creation had been completed by the creation of man, God gave everything to man to use and enjoy (Gen. 1 : 27–31).

The man who refuses to use his gifts misses the greatest thrill in life, the joy of making something, the pride in the finished product, and the thrill of seeing others use what his hands or his mind have made.

RAW MATERIAL   November 16

Instinct is the raw material of life; and as with all raw material, everything depends on how you use it.

There is an instinct of acquisitiveness.

We can use it to develop a wise and prudent independence, to support ourselves and our loved ones by our own efforts, to build up a home, and to save something for the future and for all the things that can easily happen; or we can use it to become a miser gloating over our possessions, always keeping and collecting, never sharing and giving.

There is an instinct of self-defence and self-protection.

We can use it to seek a wise safety and to avoid a foolish recklessness; or we can use it to produce, within ourselves, a weak cowardice which will face nothing, and whose one policy in life is to run away from things.

There is an instinct of sex.

We can use it to ennoble life, to be in the closest and the most perfect relationship with someone else; or we can use it to become kin to the beasts, and even to ruin life for ourselves and for other people. It can lead life to the greatest of joys and to the deepest of tragedies.

There is an instinct of gregariousness, the instinct which makes us avoid loneliness and seek the company of others.

We can use it to build up friendship, to develop fellowship, to enter into the circle of those most dear; or we can use it in such a way that we are only happy when we are one of the crowd, and that we are quite incapable of taking an independent stand and of being alone. We can use it in such a way that we are unhappy if we have nothing but our own company to enjoy.

There is the instinct of motherhood.

We can use it to be the foundation of a home, to lead to one of the most perfect relationships in the world; or out of it we can make what someone has called smother-love, which saps the independence and stifles the life of the child.

God gave us the raw material of life. The question is, What are we going to make out of it?

A RESPONSIBILITY   November 17

There is no more delightful passage in Boswell's *Life of Johnson* than the passage which tells how a certain Mr. Edwards stopped Johnson one Sunday on the way home from church.

Fifty years before, he and Johnson had been fellow-students at Pembroke College and their ways had never crossed since. It was this Edwards who made the immortal remark, "You are a philosopher, Dr. Johnson. I have tried too, in my time, to be a philosopher, but, I don't know how, cheerfulness was always breaking in."

There stands philosophy condemned!

But in the conversation between Edwards and Johnson, there is a passage which must give every minister of the Church and of the gospel furiously and searchingly to think. It certainly did so with me.

Edwards is talking about what he wished he had done. "I wish I had continued at College," he said. "Why do you wish that, sir?" asked Johnson. "Because," answered Edwards. "I think I should have had a much easier life than mine has been. I should have been a parson and had a good living like Bloxham and several others, and lived comfortably." "Sir," said Johnson, "the life of a parson, of a conscientious clergyman, is not easy. I have always considered a clergyman as the father of a larger family than he is able to maintain. I would rather have Chancery suits upon my hands than the cure of souls. No, sir, I do not envy a clergyman's life as an easy life, nor do I envy the clergyman who makes it an easy life."

Johnson did not envy the clergyman who made his life an easy life. Surely this must make every minister of the gospel think. We have only to think of what the clergyman is.

He is the pastor.

He is the preacher.

He is the servant.

The preacher, who heralds the truth of God; the pastor, who shepherds the flock of God; the minister, who serves the men and women who are the children of God; that is the function of the clergyman.

It is no easy task.

IRRESPONSIBILITY   November 18

There are some people who claim that they live entirely by faith. They go off to the mission field, for instance, entirely on faith. It is their conviction that God will provide; they pray, and money for some needed purpose has an extraordinary habit of turning up.

I am becoming less sure that there is any virtue in that.

Recently I received a letter from abroad. The writer said that he had given up a good position in life to become a missionary. He had no financial resources, but that did not worry him. Somehow or other he got all he wanted; God never let him down. Then the letter went on to say that this man had heard of certain books. He would like to have them. Would I send them to him—"complimentarily"—or, to put it crudely, for nothing? Of course, the man got his books: I was very glad to send them to him.

But the incident set me thinking. People who rely on faith for everything, who never think of money, who trust God for everything, are in a very curious position. They are, in fact, completely dependent on people who *do* think twice about money and how to earn it.

A person goes out on faith; he needs money; a cheque arrives; but that cheque has come from someone who had had to think about how to earn and to save and to handle money with a sense of responsibility.

Those who are dependent solely on faith oddly enough are dependent on those who don't have that particular kind of faith. For the paradox is that, if everyone was dependent on faith, there would no one to supply the money to answer their faith!

Those who choose to live by what they regard as this kind of divine irresponsibility are dependent on those who accept the normal responsibilities of life. For if God wants to send money, he has got to get someone with money to send it!

Faith is not irresponsibility. The Bible does not really say, "Take no thought for the morrow," It says, "Take no anxious thought for tomorrow. Don't worry about tomorrow." "Do not be anxious about tomorrow," as the New English Bible correctly has it.

Stop thinking that there is any virtue in irresponsibility, for, in the last analysis, the irresponsible simply depend on the giving of those who have been responsible.

THE SIMPLE THINGS   November 19

It is a parable of life (as I have learned from the need to diet) that the things we miss most, are the simplest things.

There is home, for instance.
To go out in the morning with no one to say goodbye, and to come home in the evening with no one there to welcome, is one of the bleakest prospects in life. The worst home—if there is love in it—is better than the best institution. I will never belittle the work that is done in great institutions. But no institution can replace a home.

Home sweet home. How true!

There are friends.
I quote often the saying of the simple Greek who was on the edge, as it were, of the circle of Socrates and the great ones. One day someone asked him for what he most wished to thank the gods, and he answered, "That, being what I am, I have had the friends I have."

There is work.
Work is the most important of all. In the bleak day when sorrow comes and life is lonely, there is no consolation in the world like work.

Hugh Martin once wrote that the saddest words in all Shakespeare are: "Othello's occupation's gone." John Wesley prayed the famous prayer: "Let me not live to be useless."

To lose loved ones and to lose friends is grim; to lose the thing we work at is tragedy.

281

Let us thank God for the simplest things.

Let us thank God for home and loved ones.

Let us thank God for friends.

Above all let us thank God for a task to do, for the strength of body, the skill of hand and the ability of mind to do it.

DIETETIC DISCIPLINE

I am still thinking about the problems of dieting and slimming. I have learned a great deal of great value in doing so.

I have learned that to lose weight, the only way is to stop eating!

At least, I must stop eating the forbidden things. There is no short cut. Nor is there a short cut to anything worthwhile in this life.

I have learned that the supreme danger is little relaxations.

Someone hands you a plate of biscuits and says with a smile, "One won't hurt you!"

Someone offers you the chocolates and says appealingly, "Just one!"

Someone says, "Go on! Take a spoonful of sugar in your tea, just for energy!"

If you give in to this you're sunk!

There is no half-way house. You either take the things, or you don't take them. The little relaxations are fatal.

When you take a decision, you have to take it. No half-way house, and no let-up, just as in a diet.

I have learned that your worst enemies are the people who want to be kind to you.

They are the people who encourage you to take just one—"it can't do any harm".

How unwise love and kindness can be! I think that it was Seneca who said: *Ama fortiter!* "Love courageously." If you love a person, the love must be strong, not sentimental. The best sympathy is a bracing, not an enervating thing.

You must never invite temptation. Someone says: "Just one!" And I used to say, "I would love to, but I mustn't." And that in effect was to say, "I know I shouldn't do it, but I might be persuaded if you coax me!" The way to say "No" is to say "NO", and not to give any chance for a persuasive comeback.

We would fall far less often to temptation, if we did not put ourselves into a situation in which we are tempted.

Without discipline, there is no such thing as real life.

Let us thank God for the simplest things.

Let us thank God for home and loved ones.

Let us thank God for friends.

Above all let us thank God for a task to do, for the strength of body, the skill of hand and the ability of mind to do it.

DIETETIC DISCIPLINE

I met a man today who said rather a wise thing to me. He said to me, "I've been reading about your slimming successes!" "Yes," I said, "I've removed two and a half stones in three months." He smiled at me: "I think you ought to write a piece about pride!" he said.

He was quite right, because I was really much too well pleased with myself! And we are all very apt to be pleased with ourselves for the wrong things.

There is no point in being pleased with ourselves for doing the things which it is our duty to do.

In my own case it would have been better to be ashamed of letting myself get overweight rather than to be proud of myself for having taken weight off!

Jesus had something to say about this. He said, "When you have done all that is commanded you, say: 'We are unworthy servants; we have only done what was out duty!'" (Luke 17:10).

Too many people seek praise and thanks for doing what it was only their duty to do. No man has any right to be well pleased with himself when in fact all that he has done is what he ought to have done.

Jesus wanted to know what cause for pride a man had if he loved the people who loved him, and if he greeted his brothers enthusiastically. That is the kind of thing anyone does. So Jesus asked, "What more are you doing than others?" (Matt. 5:47).

This is the really Christian question. There are a great many people who will claim: "Well, I'm as good as the next man anyhow." But the whole point of the Christian life is that the Christian should not be as good as the next man; *he should be a great deal better than him!*

There is no point in Christianity unless it has the something extra special.

Not only has the Christian the obligation to be something special. He has also the power to be something special. For he has God.

This is his real reason for pride. "Let him who boasts, boast of the Lord," said Paul (1 Cor. 1:31). The only thing about which the Christian can have a just and legitimate pride is the fact that God so loved him that he gave his Son to die for him.

That is the pride which brings with it the obligation to be a little more worthy of that love.

There are three possible attitudes which a man may adopt towards the world and towards society.

He may adopt an attitude of withdrawal.

That was the attitude of the monks and the hermits, and it is still, in some cases, the attitude of the man or the woman who withdraws to a monastery or to a convent.

Very early in the history of the Church, there are those who decided that they could only be Christian by withdrawing to the Egyptian deserts and living in seclusion there.

These people prayed for the world, but at the same time they withdrew from the world on the principle that it was impossible to be a Christian in the world.

He may adopt an attitude of indifference.

That is to say, he may not withdraw from the world and he may live in the world; but he takes no part whatever in anything beyond his own private activities and his own little circle.

That is, in fact, the attitude of at least 90 per cent of ordinary men and women. They live their own little lives, in their own little circle, and are quite indifferent to anything beyond. They are quite prepared to enter into the benefits that the efforts of others bring them; they are totally unprepared to serve the community in any way themselves.

He may adopt an attitude of involvement.

The New Testament word for a church member is the word which the A.V. translates "saint". It is *hagios* in Greek. It is also translated "holy"; and its basic meaning is "different". The Christian is different from other men. But the whole point is that that difference is expressed, not by withdrawal from the world, but by involvement in the world.

It is the duty of the Christian to be involved, involved in his trade union, involved in industrial relationships, involved in local government, involved in national government.

The Christian who withdraws from the world, and the Christian who is indifferent to the world, are failing God.

Only by involvement can Christian vision become Christian fact.

At home we are too busy practically ever to go to a "show", but there is time on holiday. And I shall not forget packed audiences reduced to helpless laughter by Jimmy Edwards and Wyn Calvin in Llandudno.

Beyond doubt there is a ministry of laughter.

I know well there is laughter and laughter. There is a wrong kind of laughter, the bitter laughter of the cynic laughing someone's faith away, the snigger of the dirty mind laughing at some smutty joke, the cruel laughter which can find delight in someone else's pain. But beyond doubt, laughter is one of God's great gifts to men.

"Laughter," as Thomas Hobbes the philosopher said, "is nothing else than a sudden glory".

There is no doubt that the great laughter-makers are exercising one of God's ministries.

I am profoundly grateful to the great laughter-makers; they too are serving men and serving God, for he who brings sunshine into the lives of men and women, if only for an hour, is doing something well worth while.

Another thing no one can forget about Wales is singing.

I think that the thing about Llandudno that I will remember longest is community hymn-singing with the town brass band on the promenade at the bandstand on Sunday evening. There must have been far more than a thousand people there. The bandmaster was a genius at getting men and women and children to sing. "The Church's one foundation", "Onward, Christian Soldiers", "Pleasant are thy courts above" and, of course, "Guide me, O thou great Jehovah" to the immortal "Cwn Rhondda"—these and many another hymn sounded out in the summer evening sunlight.

There was a ministry there.

LAUGH . . .   November 24

Laughter is one of the greatest of God's gifts. And here are three questions.

Can you make others laugh?

There are some people, and if they are in a group or company, you can be sure that very soon everyone will be laughing; you feel happier just for meeting them. There are other people who are like a douche of cold water, or a black cloud, or a deep depression over Iceland; you feel chilled just for meeting them.

Alice Freeman Palmer was a great American teacher, and one of her students said to her, "She made me feel as if I were bathed in sunshine."

The laughter-bringers are doing God's work.

Can you bear being laughed at?

There are some people who are deeply offended if they are laughed at. There are some people who promptly lose their temper if they are laughed at. One of the most difficult things in the Christian life is to be regarded as a fool for the sake of loyalty to Jesus. It takes humility and it takes courage—maybe the two greatest virtues—to enable a man to bear being laughed at.

Can you laugh at yourself?

In many ways the greatest gift in life is ability to laugh at oneself. If we can really see how silly we are sometimes, if we can really see how ridiculous we often are, and if we can laugh at ourselves with all our queer ways, life will be very much easier.

Laughter is always a cleansing thing, but it is never so cleansing as when it is directed by ourselves at ourselves.

A novelist tells how once she told her little daughter not to do something. "I was never allowed to do that, when I was your age," she said. And the little girl replied, "But you must remember, Mummy, you were then and I am now!"

This is the parent's and the educationist's problem. No two generations speak the same language, and no two generations have the same experience.

This is why youth and age get out of sympathy. We cannot expect the young child to see this problem and to make the necessary allowances. It is therefore we who are older who must remember and allow for the difference, for, unless we do, education can hardly begin, in any real sense of the term.

But there is a bigger problem here. It is the problem of religious language and thought forms

There is a real sense in which to the twentieth-century child the Bible is a completely strange book. Today's child knows all about motor cars, but he knows little about sheep and corn and vineyards and all the rest of an agricultural civilisation.

If Jesus had lived and taught in the twentieth century, he would have constructed and told very different parables. They would have been about shop assistants, and typists, and secretaries and garage mechanics and engineers. He started from the here and now in A.D. 28 and he would start from the here and now in 1972.

No translation can do anything about this. It is not the words that are strange, it is the whole world in which the thing moves.

It is usually the case that, to understand a gospel parable properly, we need instruction in Palestinian manners and customs. I wonder if there should not be an attempt, not to rewrite the Bible, but to re-express the Bible in terms of the 'seventies, especially for children. Jesus would have remade his own stories for the "now".

We must seek the guidance and the help of the Holy Spirit to enable us to re-express the eternal and the unchanging truth for the child of today.

For the adult too, of course.

INFECTION November 26

Do we take as much pains to guard our children from moral and spiritual infection as we do from physical infection? Do we try to be as sure that they are kept safe from so much that threatens their minds and souls as we do in relation to danger to their bodies?

For there has never been an age when children are so exposed to spiritual infection.

We have for example, what seems to be a cult of violence in the entertainment world. That cult has invaded even the games children play and the language they use.

One of the strangest features of our mid-twentieth-century society is the amount of advertising directed to creating the worst possible habits! Modern advertising does not only aim to satisfy an existing need: it aims to create a need to be satisfied. And sometimes the needs so created are anything but desirable.

One of the worst features of life today is the flood of pornography pouring from our printing presses. This is a quite deliberate stimulation of that which is worst.

Life is full of infection. It is impossible for young people to escape contact with this infection, but it is neither possible or desirable to isolate the young person from life.

Parents have a great responsibility in these difficult days on this matter of spiritual infection.

FARES, PLEASE!   November 27

In life, you progress in proportion to the fare you are prepared to pay.

This is true of Knowledge.

In getting knowledge, the price of the journey is work. If we are not prepared to work really hard, we only get a smattering of a subject, a superficial knowledge of it, a nodding acquaintance with it, admission to the fringes of it. If we are prepared to pay the fare in the coin of work, we can travel far.

No one can learn without paying the fare—in sheer hard work!

This is true of Friendship.

Real friendship is a costly thing.

It was said of one wealthy man, "with all his giving, he never gives himself".

Friendship means far more than getting; far more than using the other person for our convenience. It means self-giving. This is the fare that friendship asks.

This is true of Life.

It is easy to stay in the shallows in life.

There are those who wonder why they do not get more out of life: why they never get on or succeed in making something worthwhile out of their lives.

But there is a kind of rough justice in life. We get out of life what we put into it. If we always live as if life owes us something, we will receive nothing.

This is true of the Christian life.

Jesus said that if we tried to save our lives, we would lose them, but if we threw them away, we would find true living.

Are you prepared to pay the fare?

GIVING   November 28

A small church I know has raised ten thousand pounds to renovate their church building. This I find incredible, knowing their limitations as I do.

How have they done it?

They had an aim and an object.

That object was the reconstruction and the rebuilding of the sanctuary, of the church.

It is easier to raise money for a concrete cause than for a general appeal. That which catches and fires the imagination is the way to the heart.

The whole parish was brought into this, not just the congregation.

In other words, the project became a community undertaking and ambition.

A community effort is always more successful than a congregational effort. The work of the church, in the sphere of the care of the aged or work amongst youth, should lend itself to this.

There was the full support of the minister.

It is true to say that the leadership lay largely in the hands of lay people. When there is lay leadership at the top, everything becomes much more attainable.

There is a leadership which only the lay part of the church can give.

The congregation called in the experts.

If a job is to be done it is wise to get the expert to do it.

The expert will only achieve his best results when the spiritual tone and atmosphere of the congregation is also high.

A church is not a business, but that is no reason why it should not be run in a businesslike way.

DIFFERENCES   November 29

I have just been reading two interesting books. The first is the life of Sir Halley Stewart, churchman and industrialist, founder of the Sir Halley Stewart Trust, who was born in 1838 and died in his hundredth year in 1937.

The other is the *History of the Highland Railway* by O. S. Nock.

These two books have shown the wide difference between the Victorian and Elizabethan ages.

There is the difference in the family.

Halley Stewart's father, Alexander Stewart, was one of twelve children; he married a girl who was one of a family of seven daughters; he himself had fourteen children, of whom Halley was the tenth. To use an Irishism—if Halley Stewart had been alive today, the chances are he would never have been born at all! Here we have three marriages with a product of thirty-three children—common enough a hundred years ago, almost impossible today.

There is the difference in the Sunday.

Alexander Stewart ran a school, and we are told of the time-table of the ordinary Sunday: 7 a.m. prayer meeting for the scholars and the family; 8.00, breakfast; 9.00, School Scripture class; 9.30, Sunday School; 11.00, church service; 1 p.m. dinner; 2.30, Sunday School followed by a walk; 5.00, tea; 6.30, church service; 8.00, singing in the home.

That was a Sunday in a pious home a hundred years ago. Today it would be incredible.

There is the difference in the employment of so-called servants.

Halley Stewart did not run a very big house, but there is a photograph of the house staff taken about 1896 or thereby. There are three gardeners, a coachman, a cowman, cook, scullery maid, parlourmaid, housemaid, washerwoman and two other assistants who were gardeners' wives.

For the fourth difference I turn to O. S. Nock's railway book.

In the new Elizabethan age the child-bearing mother becomes the wife who goes out to work; the regimented Sunday becomes the day for golf and a run in the car; the servant in a big house has become the wage-earner in the factory; the disciplined work has become the permissive society. It may be that in the Victorian age the pendulum swung too far to one side and in the Elizabethan age it has swung too far to the other. Our task is to get discipline and permissiveness into the right proportion.

LAWS OF GOD   November 30

The most astonishing and significant fact about space travel is this. When the scientists prepared things for the space flight which encircled the moon, they made every possible calculation; and they made their calculations on the basis that the laws which operate here on earth operate in exactly the same way a quarter of a million miles away. They assumed confidently that the scientific laws which operate here operate there too. And they were right.

Now, where there are laws, there is mind; and the mind which imposes laws on the whole world must be external to the world; it must be, in other words, the mind of God. Space travel proves that not just the earth, but the universe, is God's, that God is not a figment of earth-man's imagination, but that his mind and his laws are operative everywhere.

Two things we already knew about God have been confirmed.

God is universal.

The Psalmist was profoundly right: "Whither where shall I go from thy Spirit? Or whither shall I flee from thy presence?... If I take the wings of the morning and dwell in the uttermost parts of the sea, even there thy hand shall lead me, and thy right hand shall hold me" (Ps. 139:7–10).

Jonah crossed half a world to get away from God—and found God still waiting for him. From the universality of God there is no escape.

God is dependable.

In their calculations, the scientists trusted the laws of nature, which are the laws of God, in part of the universe where no man had ever been—and the laws worked. The astronauts literally bet their lives on God—and they did not lose.

If the scientific laws of God are operative everywhere and utterly to be depended on, we can trust the laws of God's love too.

As Whittier puts it:

> I know not where His islands lift
> Their fronded palms to air:
> I only know I cannot drift
> Beyond his love and care.

December

HOW GOD IS SEEN

God has three problems.

God has to ask, "How can I get men to know me?"
Man, being man, cannot achieve the knowledge of God, being God. Knowledge of God cannot be had by man reaching up, unless God also reaches down. It is through revelation, not speculation, that man must know God.

There are three ways in which God reveals himself to me:
He reveals himself in the beauty and the bounty of the world.
He reveals himself in people.
He reveals himself in Jesus Christ.

God has to ask, "How can I get men to heed me?"
The experiences of life are designed to turn the thoughts of a man to God. Sometimes God speaks in suffering or in weakness.

Leighton, you remember, said in a time of illness, "I have learned more of God since I came to this bed than I did in all my life." Sometimes God speaks out of failure and loss. Sometimes a man has to lose the non-essential things to be driven back to the things which are essential.

As the poet heard God say, "If goodness lead him not, then weariness may toss him to my breast."
The experiences of life are meant to turn a man's thoughts to God.

God has to ask, "How can I make men love me?"
It would never be enough for God to subject men to himself by force. The only compulsion that God can use is the compulsion of love; and the only submission that God desires is the submission of the loving heart. So, when we see the love of God in life and in the world, and supremely in Jesus Christ,

surely in the end we ought to come to say, "We love him because he first loved us" (1 John 4:19).

December 2

There are certain things we should see to it that we never lose.

We should never lose our temper.

The people who fly into a temper are a problem in life. If we know they are like that, we have to handle them as carefully as a stick of gelignite or there will be an explosion. Any man in a temper will say things and do things for which he will afterwards be profoundly sorry.

When a man wished to enter the famous Qumran Community, from which the Dead Sea Scrolls came, the first question that they asked him was about his personal relationships with other people. In other words, the most important question was: How do you get on with other people? I should certainly say to any man contemplating entering the ministry: If you don't get on well with people, stay out! And if you have got a temper, get it cured—or don't begin!

We should never lose our head.

When anything dangerous or disastrous happens, the biggest problem is not the people who are injured; the biggest problem is the people who panic.

Kipling said that the sign of true manhood was this: "If you can keep your head when all about you are losing theirs and blaming it on you."

We should never lose heart.

It is easy to lose heart about ourselves, about our work, about the Church, about world in general.

Most artists have painted Hope as young and eager, with head thrown back and face laughing to the wind. But Watts knew better. He painted Hope as battered and bleeding and tattered, with only one string left on her lyre, but with eyes alight.

This is the hope that matters—the hope that has seen all and still hopes on. For the Christian it is literally true that where there is life there is hope. He has a hope which goes even beyond life and which is immortal and eternal.

Our temper—our head—our heart—these are things we should never lose.

December 3

A great deal of our Christianity is colourless, and a great many of our alleged Christians are colourless.

It begins with clothes.

Is there any very good reason why a parson should wear a black suit, a black hat and a black raincoat? Is there any good reason why a messenger of the good news should be permanently dressed as if he was going to a funeral?

A wholesale revolt from the more clerical kind of clerical dress might do the image of the Church a vast amount of good.

It goes on to a whole attitude to life.

Religion is for so many a colourless thing, a thing of negatives. There are nuns who to this day are saints in their treatment of the sick and of the poor. But I can well understand the feeling of the teenager who saw a nun, dressed in her habit, with her thick shoes and stockings and the pallor of the convent on her face, who exclaimed involuntarily: "Boy, give me my sins!"

Would that there were more Christians who gave the appearance of really enjoying themselves.

There is a Jewish rabbinic saying which has a wealth of truth in it: "At the judgment day a man will be called to account for all the good things he might have enjoyed and did not enjoy." And, when it comes to the bit, the kind of Christians who are really remembered, and the kind of Christians who really attracted men and women into the faith, were the laughing cavaliers of Christ like Francis of Assisi, who lived in a world in which God had made all things well, and in which a man could not help singing for joy.

Let Christians stop being colourless and start being colourful, so that men may see again the sheer radiance of the Christian faith.

VERDICTS (1)   December 4

In his book *The Day before Yesterday*, James Moffatt set down some verdicts on religion, and on what religion is.

Religion is madness.

Robert Owen spoke about "the various phases of insanity called religion".

Religion can be madness in the wrong sense and in a right sense. It can be madness in the wrong sense when it issues in that fanaticism which launches into persecution and savagery.

Madame Roland made the famous statement: "Liberty, what crimes have been committed in your name!" But when we read back into the history of the Church, it would often be true to say: "Religion, what crimes have been committed in your name!"

The days when the Church burned its so-called heretics, and when it preached the love of God in hate, were, and are, days not of religion, but of madness.

But it can also be madness in the right sense. There was a time when the friends of Jesus said: "He is beside himself." (Mark 3:21). The unswerving loyalty of the Christian, the complete self-forgetfulness, the selfless service, the sacrificial giving, the love which will lay down its life for its friend, can, and do seem like madness to the man who can see no further than the world and the material tests and standards of the world.

Sometimes the man who tries to live like God will seem mad to a godless world.

Religion is delusion.

Gibbon made his famous and cynical statement about religion in the early days of Christianity. He said that all religions seemed to the people equally true, to the philosophers equally false, and to the magistrates equally useful. To the philosophers religion was no more than a delusion. So there is a certain type of psychology which will hold that any idea of the fatherhood and the love of God is simply man projecting his own sense of need into a series of ideas which are not more than wishful thinking.

But the great argument against that is that all delusions have a way of being found out in the end, for they simply collapse when a man tries to support life upon them. There are, on the other hand, millions in every generation to witness that religion works.

VERDICTS (2)   December 5

There were these two hostile verdicts on religion, and now there are two very different verdicts that James Moffatt gives.

Religion is challenge.

Religion has not by any means always been this. George Meredith's objection to religion was that "it belonged to the ambulance corps rather than to the fighting line of life". He felt that religion as he saw it was concerned rather with picking up the pieces of failure than sending men out on a gallant adventure.

Sometimes religion has been other-worldly in the worst sense of the term. It has been so concerned with the life to come that it has been less than concerned with this present life, and in its ideas of the life to come it has been no more than what Stevenson called "the fairytale of an eternal tea party".

But real religion is bound to be challenge. Real religion is bound to awaken in a man dissatisfaction with himself and dissatisfaction with the world. It is bound to give a man at one and the same time a judgment on things as they are, and a vision of things as they should be, and a summons to turn the one into the other. Real religion presents a man with a challenge to change himself and to change the world.

Religion is power and peace.

Ibsen spoke contemptuously of "the puny and the pious life", as if piety and ineffectiveness went hand in hand.

But it is the witness of the centuries that time and time again religion has made the coward into the hero, and the weakling into the strong man, and the defeated into the victor, and the frustrated man into the master of life. And this is so because the peace of religion is not the peace of withdrawal or the peace of acceptance; it is the peace which comes of the certainty of being able to cope with any situation which can possibly arise in time or in eternity, the peace which is the flower of power.

Madness, delusion, challenge, power and peace—these are the verdicts on religion; and there is no way to show what real religion is other than by demonstrating it in life.

ACROSS THE MILES   December 6

Charles Wesley was one of the most attractive of men, and the full charm of the man meets us in Frederick C. Gill's biography of him. Unlike John, Charles was ideally happily married, to his wife Sally.

Like John, Charles was much on the road, but even on the road he had a way of meeting his wife across the miles. The idea was that they should agree both to pray exactly at the same time each day and at a certain time on certain other days, and that, though separated, they should at these times meet, as it were, at God's mercy seat.

So during one of his visits to Ireland, Charles writes to Sally, "Remember to meet me always on Monday noon, and every evening at five." At twelve o'clock on Mondays and on each evening at five they kept their pact of prayer, and across the miles they met.

Everyone of us has friends from whom we are separated. Now in real friendship you can take it up again after years of separation as if things had never been any way different. But at the same time, Dr. Johnson's advice is always valid, "A man, sir, should keep his friendships in constant repair." Friendship is like any other plant—it flourishes with nurture and it wilts with neglect. There are certain very simple things that we can say.

How often do we write to our friends when we are separated from them?

I fear that most of us are bad correspondents. Happy is the home where there is one person who is the family letter-writer.

Nowadays, there is something better than a letter, there is the telephone.

There are times when I cannot make up my mind whether the telephone is a blessing or a curse! When it rings mercilessly all evening up until midnight you begin to wonder. I am about the country a good bit; when I am away I phone my wife every night without fail. It makes opening the envelope with the telephone account a terrorising experience—but it's worth every penny of it to meet across the miles. Time and money are never wasted in keeping touch with someone you love.

There is just thinking about each other.
There are more things in this world than our philosophy dreams of, and there are things which defy explanation. I am convinced that there is more than something in telepathy, in establishing contact across the miles by the power of thought.

The letter, the telephone, the thought, the prayer—all these can be used to annihilate the miles.

HALF TRUTHS   December 7
There are things we say which are dangerous half-truths.

We sometimes say, "God will provide".
True, but only if we do something to help ourselves. When we pray, "Give us this day our daily bread", we do not think that we can sit back in an arm-chair and comfortably doze and find not only bread but cake there, too, when we wake up. We know quite well that we have to plough and reap and sow and grind and bake and pay for it all before the bread arrives.
One of the truest things that was ever said is that God helps those who help themselves. If we want God to provide, it is not a bad idea to give him a helping hand.

It is often said—I have said it often myself—that if God gives a man a task to do "he will give him the strength to do it".
We have a half-truth here.
One of the truest things that was ever said is that consecration is what makes drudgery divine. Commitment does not absolve a man from the duty of training; it lays the duty of training inescapably upon him. Once God has called us, then we must give him a hand.

It is often said that "a way will open up".
This is true, but only if you set out to look for one. God never encouraged either laziness or irresponsibility.
Often God shows us the door; but very often we ourselves have to find the key; and perhaps always we have to open the door and go through it ourselves.

296

There is a right and a wrong trust. The wrong trust waits on God to do it for us; the right trust sets out to do it with God.

With God, all things are possible. What God so often gives us are possibilities which we must turn into actualities.

A Christian and a Communist were in a group run by a pastor in France. It was a group where people of different beliefs and backgrounds could get together and talk—"a house of dialogue". They had been reading the story of the woman of Samaria, and after they had finished the pastor asked each of them what struck him about the story. So he said to the Christian, "What strikes you about this story?" The Christian answered, "What strikes me is that Jesus should ask a favour of that awful woman—an adulteress." So the pastor said to the Communist, "What strikes you about the story?" The Communist answered, "What strikes me is that the woman had to come to the well because she had no running water in her house."

Now here are two people speaking from different points of view.

The point of view of the so-called Christian was the point of view of respectability.

Respectability was his touchstone—and it certainly is not the Christian touchstone.

You will remember R. B. Duncan's famous saying to the woman at the sacrament. She was plainly hesitating to take the cup. "Take it, woman," said the old saint. "Take it. It's for sinners. It's for you."

The church is the place for sinners, and Jesus Christ is the friend of sinners.

The test of the Communist was social service.

His aim was to give people better living conditions and better homes to live in. But neither will that do. We have all seen people transferred from a slum to a new house and we have seen them make the new house into a slum in a very short time. That is very far from always happening, but it can and does happen. You do not change a person by changing his or her house.

The real Christian aim is not the collecting of respectable people and not primarily the construction of new conditions. It is the making of new people.

Once you make new people, once you change the heart, then the true goodness and the true holiness follow, and then the new man makes the new conditions.

The Christian aim is not a conventional respectability, not simply the changing of a material situation. It is the re-creation of the individual man and woman.

In the last analysis nothing less will do.

It is much easier to define and describe the abuse of anger than it is to describe and define its use. But there is one sure way to see the proper use of anything, and that is to see how Jesus used it. Let us then see how Jesus used anger. What were the things which incurred the anger of Jesus?

Jesus was angry with anyone who was a hypocrite.

In Greek the word for *hypocrite* is the same as the word for an actor. A hypocrite is a man who plays a part, a man who puts on an act, a man whose whole life is a deception. A hypocrite is a man who says one thing with his lips and quite another in his heart. A hypocrite is a man whose actions give the lie to his profession.

Jesus would prefer honest godlessness to hypocritical piety. The man who is one thing to your face and another behind your back, the man who is ostentatiously pious on Sunday and completely worldly on Monday, the man who professes a religion of love and of service and who lives a life of bitterness and selfishness—that is the man who incurred the anger of Jesus (Matt. 6:2, 5, 16; 7:5; 15:7; 22:18; 23:13–29).

Jesus was angry with irresponsibility.

There are not many cases in which Jesus in so many words condemns a man to hell, but he does just that in the parable of the Rich Man and Lazarus (Luke 16:19–31). What had this rich man done? His fault was this. Day after day Lazarus was laid at his door. He did not order him to be removed; still less did he kick him in the passing; he simply accepted him as part of the landscape. It never struck him that there was anything wrong in the fact that he was disgustingly rich and Lazarus desperately poor. It never occurred to him that he had anything to do with Lazarus. He had not the slightest feeling of responsibility for a fellow-man in trouble.

As it has been succinctly put: "It was not what Dives did that got him into gaol; it was what he did not do that got him into hell."

Jesus's anger is kindled against selfish irresponsibility.

Jesus's anger was against those who loved systems more than they loved human beings.

There was the day when there was a man in the synagogue, and the orthodox Jews stood and watched to see whether or not Jesus was going to heal him, for it was the Sabbath day. Jesus looked round with anger (Mark 3:1–6).

Jesus was angry with any man who loved a system of theology or a system of church government more than he loved God and his fellow-men. To be more devoted to a system than to God is a common enough fault in the Church, and it incurs the anger of Jesus.

Jesus's anger was kindled against all exploitation.

This is the background of the cleansing of the Temple (Mark 11:15–19), the story in which John presents us with the terrifying picture of the Jesus with the whip (John 2:13–17). At the back of this is the simple fact that the money changers were charging exorbitant rates for changing the pilgrims' money, and in the Temple booths a pair of doves was costing seventy-five pence while outside they could be bought for four pence. Jesus's anger blazed against the exploitation of poor people in the vested interests of the rich.

Hypocrisy, social irresponsibility, the love of systems more than the love of God and man, the exploitation of any human being for someone else's self-interest—these were the things that roused the anger of Jesus. "Be ye angry and sin not," wrote Paul (Eph. 4:26). It is against such things as these that anger is still a virtue and a necessity, not a sin.

CORRUPTION OF THE BEST   December 11

"Lilies that fester smell far worse than weeds."

It is one of the tragedies of life that the best things can be perverted into the worst.

Take, for instance, the four virtues which Hitler singled out.

There is love of country.

Patriotism can be a noble thing. But love of country can be perverted into the idea of a *herrenvolk*, a master race, which despises all others. Love of country can turn into *apartheid*, which looks down on all others. Love of country can turn into the desire for conquest and the lust for power. Love of country can beget the mailed fist and the jackboot and the merciless ambition for mastery.

There is courage in the face of adversity.

Courage in the face of adversity has kept men on their feet through thick and thin. But courage in adversity can turn into self-centred stubbornness which is based on selfishness and which will not realistically face the situation.

There is loyalty to one's leader.

Loyalty to one's leader sounds like a wholly admirable quality. But Paul saw loyalty to one's leader tearing the Corinthian church apart, when men claimed that they were loyal to Cephas and to Apollos and to Paul himself. Loyalty to a leader had become a disruptive and divisive force within the church.

In the church what is required is not loyalty to one's leaders, but loyalty to one's Leader. There is a loyalty to Jesus Christ to which all secondary loyalties must yield.

There is the willingness to accept discipline for the sake of some great cause.

It is perfectly true that no great object can be achieved without discipline; but there can come a situation in which discipline becomes discipline for its own sake and not for the sake of some end in view. Asceticism can become asceticism for the sake of asceticism, just as in the army what the army calls "bull" can become discipline for the sake of "bull".

No discipline is valuable unless it looks beyond itself to a greater end in view.

It is frightening to see how easily the best can become the worst; and the only way to avoid this is to keep Jesus Christ in the centre of the picture, for, when he gets his proper place, all other things will get theirs.

SELF CRITICISM   December 12

On his eighty-first birthday Archbishop Garbett wrote in his diary, "People have been undeservedly kind, they have formed an ideal picture of myself—the devoted pastor, the kindly old gentleman, and the courageous prophet! They don't see me as I really am, selfish, self-centred, seeking and enjoying the praise of men, lazy, possessive and timid. With old age one sees how many opportunities have been lost."

Garbett had the gift of self-criticism—and it is one of the greatest of all gifts.

"Know thyself," said the Greek wise man. Most of us see ourselves through very rose-tinted spectacles, and most of us can be very blind to our own faults. To be able to criticise oneself, and to be able to see one's own faults, is an essential part of the road to self-amendment.

How shall we learn self-criticism? How shall we see our own faults? We can only learn to do this when we have a standard against which to compare ourselves.

There have been men who have had such a purity in them that they made others feel their impurity. Bernard of Clairvaux was like that, and in the days before Bernard had learned gentleness, many of his monks were afraid even to come into his presence, for in his presence they learned how far they fell short.

Alcibiades used to say to Socrates, "Socrates, I hate you, for every time I meet you, I see what I am."

We have this standard in Jesus.

There is no man alive who cannot benefit from criticism, if he receives it in humility. There is no man alive who would not benefit by learning self-criticism. A man can only see what he is by realising what Jesus is, who with the humiliation gives grace to us to rise above ourselves.

300

One of the best tests of any man is just how he accepts criticism.

He may receive it with resentment.

Anyone who has resented criticism has put himself under three great disadvantages.

First, he can never be a servant of any leader or of any cause, for to himself, he is the most important person in the world.

Second, he can never co-operate in any joint effort, for no one but himself can ever be right.

Third, he will never be able to learn or to improve, for no man can learn, and no man can become better, who refuses to admit that he has any ignorance or any faults.

He may receive it with petulance.

There are certain people who, if they are in the least criticised, simply throw up the job on which they were engaged, like children who sulkily "won't play". It is no good at all to "pet" people like that. If they want to go, let them go. We are far better without them.

There are people who receive it with undue sensitiveness.

There are people who have one skin fewer than other people. They are very easily hurt, very easily discouraged, and very easily depressed. When they are criticised, they do not give up in petulance; they give up in discouragement and even in despair.

There are those who receive it in humility.

As the ancient wise men used often to say, the really wise man is the man who realises that he does not know. The man who will make real progress is the man who knows that a job could be done better, and who is anxious only to find out how it can be done better.

The real enemy of all good work is complacency. The man, who will never make any progress is the man who is content with everything which he produces.

There is not only an art in accepting criticism; there is an art in giving criticism.

Criticism can be given almost solely with the desire to hurt.

The psychologists will tell us that almost everyone has in some way or other the desire for power; and there are those who criticise acidly or savagely because, whether they admit it to themselves or not, they like to see the other person wince. There is never anything to be said for cruelty and there is nothing to be said for that.

Criticism can be given in conscious superiority.

It is possible for us to stand above the other person, and to look down, and to point out his faults, as if we had none of our own. One thing is certain—no man is faultless.

Criticism given in conscious superiority is seldom effective, because it lacks sympathy. When a man has to criticise, he should remember George Whitefield's famous saying as he saw the man going to the scaffold: "There but for the grace of God go I."

There are two kinds of right criticism.

There is the criticism which is prepared to try to do better itself.

When the young Isaac Watts was returning from church with his father, he complained about the dreariness of the hymns. His father retorted, "Then give us something better, young man." In time for the next Sunday, Isaac Watts started on that career of hymn-writing which made him one of the two or three greatest writers of hymns in the English language.

There is the criticism of love.

Love is not blind; there is nothing so clear-sighted as love; and love cannot rest content watching its loved one living a life which is below the level of what it might have been, wasting the talents which might have been splendidly used, following some course of action which may end in sheer disaster.

But in such criticism there is gentleness, there is sympathy, there is understanding.

LEAVE IT ALONE! December 15

In the days of the 1914–18 war, a body of British troops were besieged for a long time. Boredom more than actual danger was the problem. Among them there was a man who was a man of culture, but an atheist.

In the siege he missed above all something to read. In despair he went to the chaplain, thinking that he might have some books. All the chaplain had to offer was the Bible.

At first the man declared that the Bible was useless to him; but out of sheer boredom he took it and began to read it. It opened at the Book of Esther.

Now whatever else Esther is, it is a great story which would make a magnificent film scenario. The man could not lay it down until he had finished it. If the Bible was like this, it was worth reading! So indeed he read on—and he was converted. And it is literally true to say that it was the reading of the Book of Esther which led directly to his conversion.

I have been told of an army doctor who was converted by the reading of Leviticus, because its regulations for sanitation and for hygiene were so eminently sensible.

Now, if there are two books which, it has been said, could be removed from the Bible without loss, these books are Esther and Leviticus—and yet in the two cases I have instanced these two books were the means towards conversion.

There is a lesson here. To put it simply—it is safer to leave the Bible alone! Almost the first person to criticise Scripture and to pick and choose the parts he was going to keep and the parts he was going to dispense with was Marcion, who, as Tertullian said, criticised the Scriptures with a pen-knife.

There is a tendency to do just that. No one is going to claim that the Book of Esther has the religious value of, say, the Gospel of John, or that Leviticus has as much of the gospel of grace as Luke.

But the lesson of experience is that there is a place in Christian experience for all the books of the Bible, and even the books which seem most unlikely have been for some the way to God and grace.

Leave the Bible alone in its entirety, for no one knows out of which book in it the Spirit of God will speak to the heart of some man.

A PARADOX   December 16

Every man is capable of being hero and coward, saint and villain, kind and cruel, gentle and hard, sympathetic and callous. Every man is a walking paradox.

This means two things.

It means that we should be very careful in our judgment of other people.

There may be another side to the man we know; he may be another man with other people. It can work both ways. A man may be charming in public and selfish and inconsiderate in his own home. A man may appear to be as hard as nails in his public life and may be gentle and kind at home. But, no matter which way the change lies, there can be a change, and we ought not to be too quick to judge when we know only one of the two sides.

If this be so—and it is so—what human nature wants above all is someone who can recognise its possibilities, and who has the power to release them.

Someone has said that, if he had one request to make to others about himself, it would be—always think of me at my best. And, if we have one need, it is for someone to take us and make us able to live always as we do in our highest and best moments.

This is what Jesus Christ does. He sees the hidden possibilities in a man; he sees the side that no one else can see. And by his grace, he can make a man live always more nearly to his best.

With none of us is this process complete. No man is always his best self.

But the more we submit to the power of Jesus Christ in life, the nearer we come to it.

THE IMAGE OF THE CHURCH December 17

There is a common image of the Church. It is the image of a place whose main clientele is old ladies, whose main aim is the maintenance of respectability in sexual matters, and whose preaching is on the level of a twelve-year-old child. Is the Church really like that?

There is enough truth in this to make it sting.

There is no doubt at all that there are far more women than men in the average Sunday congregation, and that the age level is high.

There is no doubt at all that the Church's view of sin has identified it with drinking, swearing, gambling, adultery and fornication.

There is no doubt that there are preachers who under-rate their congregations and who deliver pious and harmless essays instead of grappling with the problems which are matters of life and death.

All this may not be typical of the whole Church, but the situation does exist.

Here is the remedy.

The Church must become fearlessly involved in the world.

It must show where it stands on great subjects like peace and war, industrial relations, social justice. Then will youth return to it—for to be young is to be ready to crusade.

The Church must realise that there are greater sins than the sins of the flesh.

There can be a pride, a callousness, a personal and social selfishness, a sheer materialism which are terrible and deadly sins. There can be an external veneer of respectability with a complete godlessness underneath it.

This is just not good enough in Christ's Church.

The Church must be completely honest in its preaching.

There must be no evasions of issues, because to face them might cause trouble.

Preaching must not be following popular opinion, giving people what they want to hear. It must be the statement of inner convictions, even if these convictions are not what some people want to hear.

The Church need not have the image it has acquired, if it has the courage to think and to speak.

CROSS ROADS December 18

The Church is at the cross roads, and the Church has to make certain great decisions.

Is the Church going to look back or forward?

Is the Church going to go on forever speaking in seventeenth-century English, or is it going to use contemporary language to contemporary men and women?

Is the Church going to make an honest attempt to think out its message in the categories of the day in which it is speaking?

Are we going to go on saying that something must be good and great because it has been used or done for the last five hundred or a thousand years, or are we going to say that, if a thing has been used for five hundred or a thousand years, then it is near certain that it does not speak relevantly to today?

I am not answering these questions—I am asking them!

Is the Church going to look out or in?

Is the Church going to become more and more a "gathered" community for a comparatively small, and almost certainly dwindling, community, or are its eyes to go out to the millions who have lost touch with the Church altogether?

Is a congregation to be concerned more with keeping itself together, more with its own congregational activities, than with the hundreds in the parish or area with whom it has completely lost contact?

The greatest problem of the Church today is whether to withdraw within itself and become a gathered and separate community, or whether to go out adventurously to those to whom at the present moment the Church means nothing.

Once again I am not answering these questions—I am asking them!

Is the Church going to agree to some extent to conform to the world, or is the Church going to insist above all on its difference from the world?

What, for instance, in a new housing area, often a slum clearance area, is the Church prepared to allow young people to do on a Sunday night?

Is the Church to allow activities and modern ways of enjoyment which may shock many of its members, in order to establish some kind of human contact with the lost generations?

The Church stands at the cross roads. The first step to finding the right way is to face the questions with which the present time is confronting us, to stop running away from them and to stop taking refuge in doing precisely nothing but preserve the *status quo*.

HOPE   December 19

The Church must nevertheless be the one institution which cannot know despair.

In the Christian faith, there is hope for the world.

It is possible to look at the world and to feel that men are possessed by a kind of suicidal insanity which cannot end in anything other than a disintegrated chaos. But, as Bengt Sundkler tells us in his fine biography of Nathan Söderblom, Söderblom used to say often, "The only remedy is to give the commonwealth of nations a Christian soul, because without that soul it is a dead body and with a non-Christian soul it is a beast or a devil."

Christ has the remedy for the human situation. The application of that remedy is the business of the Church.

In the Christian faith, there is hope for men.

Time and again I have quoted that sermon title in one of Fosdick's volumes: "No man need stay the way he is." Often a person will defend himself or herself by saying, "I can't help it. I'm made that way. That's my nature. I can't change myself." That is sheer heresy.

Yes, it is true that a man cannot change himself. But if Christ cannot change him, then the whole claim of Christianity is a lie.

But if the Church is to change the world and to change men and women, it must be changed itself.

The more one sees of the Church, the more one senses a deep down attitude of defeat. There are so many people in the Church who have simply accepted the situation. Diminishing and ageing congregations, an increasing irrelevance in the eyes of the common man—there are many who are well aware of these things, but they have simply accepted them as things about which there is nothing to be done. A church which has accepted the situation like that is a church which is on the way to death.

God give us, not the defeatism which accepts things as they are, but the divine discontent which, in the life and the strength of Jesus Christ, will battle to change them.

BLACK AND WHITE   December 20

At a conference in St. Andrews I met a very charming Nigerian called Agwu Oji. Agwu Oji was going back to Nigeria to be a bishop of the united Church there. He was going back to his own land and his own people to be one of the chosen leaders of the Christian Church in West Africa.

After evening prayers one night Agwu Oji and I were leaving the chapel together and I suddenly had an idea. I said to him, "Before you go back to Nigeria, would you not like to go and stand for once in the pulpit from which John Knox preached?" A Church of Scotland missionary, who has served for more than a quarter of a century in Nigeria and who was one of Glasgow's brilliant classicists in his student days, was standing beside us. "Oji," he said,

"is far too humble a man to go and do that by himself, unless you take him."
So I took Oji by the arm and the two of us walked up to the pulpit, and went up the steps of it and stood for a moment in that very pulpit from which John Knox had preached.

For me that was one of the great moments of that conference, and I think that, at that moment, among the unseen cloud of witnesses, the spirit of John Knox looked down and was glad.

In that moment ancient and modern came together.

There are moments when a great tradition can be the greatest inspiration in the world.

In that moment black and white joined hands.

There is only one place in which there can be a true united nations organisation—and that is within the Church of Jesus Christ.

GO TO CHURCH! December 21

There are at least five reasons why we ought to go to church. And even if we have been over some of these before, they are worth noting again at the end of the year.

To go to church, and to let others see us going is to demonstrate to the world where our heart lies.

Every time we go to church we tell the world where our loyalty is directed.

To go to church is to share in the fellowship of Christian people.

To go to church is not only to make a demonstration to the people outside; it is to find the people inside, and with them to be united members of the Body of Christ.

To go to church is to uphold the hands of the preacher.

Any minister will tell you that the congregation is far more responsible for the "feel" of the service than he is. It is the people who can create the attitude of eager expectancy in which things really can happen.

To go to church is to worship, to wait upon, and to listen to God.

Perhaps we connect going to church far too much with hearing a sermon. This is specially so if we belong to the Free Churches. This is a mistake that the devout Anglican will not make. But in a service there are prayers; there are scripture readings; there is music, hymns and psalms; there is an offering; there may be a sacrament; there ought to be silence. And it will be our own fault if in some part of the many-sided worship we do not meet God.

To go to church can be, if it is nothing else, an act of discipline.

It is fatal to get into a way of life when we only do what we want to do, or when we only do a thing when we want to do it. There is room for that spiritual discipline which, even when the spirit within us is arid and dry, and even when we feel our hearts cold and unresponsive, sends us out on an act of spiritual discipline. And it has often happened that just on such a day God all unexpectedly has broken into life.

To worship God in God's house is a privilege, but it is also a duty, to neglect which is to weaken and truncate the spiritual life.

It is nearly Christmas. Why not plan to go then?

QUALITY, NOT QUANTITY   December 22

In Deuteronomy 20:1-9 there is an interesting passage. It is a list of those who in time of war are to be exempted from service. Those who have built a new house or planted a new vineyard are to be exempt, lest they do not live to enjoy it. Those who are newly betrothed in marriage are to be exempt, lest they die too soon. And those who are "fearful and faint-hearted" are to be sent home, lest they infect the others with their craven and their cowardly spirit.

Clearly, the leaders of Israel worked on the principle that quality, and not quantity, is what matters. And it might well be better for us, if we thought more along the same lines.

In this twentieth century, there are few of us who are not the victims and the slaves of statistics. When we want to see what a congregation is like, we look up the Church Year Book, and we see how many members it has, and how many members its organisations have. But paper membership is no test at all of the vitality of a congregation. We want to know, not how many members are on the roll, but how many are committed to Jesus Christ and to his Church—which is a very different thing. It may well be that we would be well advised to pay more attention to the quality than to the number of the members of a congregation.

In regard to any profession, it is again surely quality more than quantity which matters.

When there is a shortage of candidates for any profession—as, for instance, in teaching—it is very tempting to introduce a policy of dilution, and to lower the standards of entry. It has to be remembered that there is a kind of inexorable law that dilution is a policy which is very hard to reverse, and that dilution tends to beget further dilution. It may well be that we would be better with fewer and better teachers and shorter hours of education for the child, than a diluted profession.

This is a problem which has to be faced in regard to the supply of candidates for the ministry.

In any sphere, a mere handful of picked and dedicated troops will be more effective than a faint-hearted, uncommitted, indisciplined rabble. It is better to have a few who are the best rather than many who are inferior and un-dedicated to the work; for, once a standard is lowered, even if the lowering is meant to be temporary, it may never be possible to raise it again.

SHARING December 23

There are only two kinds of people in the world—the people who want to share, and the people who don't want to share. There is no doubt which of the two are taking the Christian way.

It is a duty to share material things.

As Luke tells the story, the crowds came to John the Baptist, asking: "What then shall we do?" And John answered: "He who has two coats, let him share with him who has none; and he who has food, let him do likewise." (Luke 3:10, 11).

But there is another and a different kind of sharing. The good leader shares and delegates work and responsibility.

It took me thirty years of work to learn this, for I was one of those people who wanted to do everything for myself. To try to do that is grossly unfair to oneself, because no one can do everything. It is the sure way to some kind of breakdown.

But it is still more unfair to the people who work with us. To despoil them of the opportunity to work and to carry responsibility is to deprive them of their right. It is to fail to train them for the work they ought to be handling.

In the Church there is often a complaint that we cannot get leaders. Could it be true that this situation has been produced throughout the years because there are so many ministers who do try to do all the work themselves? If it is so, then the sooner the process is reversed the better.

When we share our possessions and share our work, then a new element of fellowship and partnership will enter into life, and life will be happier for ourselves and for others.

THE CELEBRATION OF CHRISTMAS December 24

The *Sunday Telegraph* once gave the results of a specially commissioned Gallup Poll about Christmas. Thirty-five per cent of the people consulted thought of Christmas as a religious festival. Twenty-six per cent of them thought of it as a holiday. Twenty-three per cent thought of it as an opportunity to meet family and friends. Five per cent thought of it as an opportunity for eating and drinking. Eleven per cent thought of it as none of these things.

Now before I read the details of the poll, I naturally read the headline. The headline was, "65 *per cent leave Christ out of Christmas*". Clearly, this was something to make a Christian think. Then I read the poll, and I am not at all sure

that the headline is the only way that the results can be summarised. The headline could equally well have read: "*More people think of Christmas as a religious
Festival than in any other way.*"

It could have been pointed out that about 10 per cent more people think of
Christmas as a religious festival than think of it as a holiday or as an opportunity to meet family and friends.

The fact still remains, however, that only a third of the people think of
Christmas as a religious festival, and 65 per cent of the people consulted think
that Christmas is less religious than it used to be.

Christmas watch-night services were very few and far between in past
years, at least in my native Scotland. Now, even in Scotland, they are celebrated everywhere, with churches filled to overflowing with people who have
come to sing the old carols and hymns and to hear the Christmas message.
Then there were very few services on Christmas Day. Now there are many.
In my day in the church of which I used to be the minister, there was neither a
Christmas watch night nor a Christmas Day service; now there are both. There
seems to me more to be said on the other side than at first appears.

If the result of commercialism is no worse than to make a husband give
a gift to his wife, and a father a gift to his child, and to enable us all to
be extravagantly generous for once, then there could be much worse
things.

ONE SOLITARY LIFE   December 25

Some time ago, when I was staying in the Y.M.C.A. in Skegness, I saw a
most unusual notice on the notice-board. It was a quotation taken from a
newspaper printed in Hamilton in Ontario, and the author is not known. It
was headed "One Solitary Life", and it ran thus:

> Here is a man who was born of Jewish parents in an obscure village, the
> child of a peasant woman. He grew up in another obscure village. He worked
> in a carpenter's shop until he was thirty, and then, for three years, he was an
> itinerant preacher.
>
> He never wrote a book, he never held an office, he never owned a home.
> He never had a family. He never went to college. He never put his foot inside
> a big city. He never travelled two hundred miles from the place where he
> was born. He never did one of these things that usually accompany great-
> ness. He had no credentials but himself.
>
> He had nothing to do with this world, except the naked power of his
> manhood. While still a young man the tide of popular opinion turned
> against him. His friends ran away. One of them denied him. He was turned
> over to his enemies. He went through the mockery of a trial.
>
> He was nailed to a cross, between two thieves. His executioners gambled

for the only piece of property he had on earth, while he was dying—and that was his coat. When he was dead he was taken down and laid in a borrowed grave, through the pity of a friend.

Nineteen wide centuries have come and gone, and today he is the centrepiece of the human race, and the leader of the column of progress. I am far within the mark when I say that all the armies that ever marched, and all the navies that were ever built, and all the parliaments that ever sat, and all the kings that ever reigned, put together, have not affected the life of man upon earth as powerfully as has that solitary life.

This is a very beautiful description of the life of Jesus.

BASIC RELIGION (1)   December 26

Judaism has always had its saints and its thinkers; and one of the supreme thinkers of Judaism was Maimonides. It was Maimonides who laid down the thirteen basic principles of the Jewish faith.

They can be found in that fascinating book, old now but still of very great value, *The Jewish Religion*, by M. Friedlander. Maimonides's principles are well worth setting down:

(1) The Creator exists; there is a God.
(2) The Unity of God; God is One.
(3) The Incorporeality of God; God is spirit.
(4) God is Eternal; God has no beginning and no end.
(5) The Creator alone is to be worshipped; there are no other and no secondary gods.
(6) There is such a thing as prophecy. There have been men who had such moral, intellectual and spiritual power that they reached a knowledge not attainable by others.
(7) Moses is the greatest of all the prophets, greater than any before and than any since.
(8) The Law is divine. The Pentateuch, the first five books of the Old Testament, were divinely delivered to Moses, both in their legal and their historical parts.
(9) The Integrity of the Law. Nothing may be added to, or subtracted from this divinely-given Law.
(10) God knows the deeds and thoughts of men, and marks them.
(11) God rewards those who keep his commandments and punishes those who transgress them.
(12) The Messiah will come at a time when we cannot tell. He will be of the house of David and will have extraordinary wisdom and power.
(13) The dead will be raised and the soul is immortal.

These principles are like so much that is in Judaism; there is very little in them that is not timeless and for ever valid.

There are probably only two things with which a Christian would wish to differ. The Christian would say that in Jesus the Messiah has come, and that the Law has been superseded by grace.

BASIC RELIGION (2) December 27

Friedlander points out that the thirteen principles can be reduced to three great claims, and these three great claims are the very foundations of religion.

There is the fact that God exists.

We cannot prove that by a neat series of logical steps at the end of which you can write Q.E.D. But the final argument for God comes not from logic but from experience. To know God is not to know him as one knows a theory, but to know him as one knows a person. And the person who has experienced the help and the love of God needs no other argument.

There is the fact that God has revealed himself.

The Jew would say that God has revealed himself through the prophets and in the Law; and the Christian would say that God has revealed himself uniquely in Jesus Christ. But the basic principle remains. For the Greeks, God was hidden; for Jew and Christian alike, God is a God who wants to be known. God is offering to all men nothing less than himself.

There is the fact that this world is not the end.

So far from making this world less important, this makes it far more important; for this means that every action in time is eternally important, and through every action man is either winning or losing life eternal.

That God is, that God reveals himself to men, that life points beyond itself to eternity—both for Jew and Christian, these are the foundation stones of religion.

POWER HOUSE December 28

How is a church to be a Christian power station?

The first necessity is, quite simply, work.

It could be said that work is the most under-rated activity in the world. There is a kind of delusion that things can happen without work.

I read of an interview with Sir William Walton, the great composer. Now we may think of a composer sitting down and waiting on the melodies to flow into his head by a kind of divine inspiration. But Sir William Walton says:

"Nothing occurs to me unless I sit down and really work at it; and sometimes a lot of effort produces very little." "Most days," he went on, "I work at my desk from nine to one, lunch, go for an afternoon walk and work again from six to eight. If there is extra inspiration I might work after dinner."

Inspiration does not replace work, but involves work. It comes not when a man is sitting waiting, but when he is sitting at his desk.

The second necessity is prayer.

There can be no work without prayer and there can be no prayer without work. The two things go hand in hand. *Laborare est orare*, to work is to pray, work is prayer, says the old Latin tag.

Teilhard de Chardin, mystic and scientist, always insisted that adoration and research are one and the same thing.

Prayer adds God's strength to our effort.

The third necessity is vision.

In many cases, the great fault of the congregation is that it is concerned above all with keeping things as they are. The struggle to keep things as they are has taken away the vision of what could be. An ingrowing congregation cannot be a power house.

To work to the limit of one's strength; to pray with all the intensity of one's being; to lift up one's eyes and to see the harvest to be reaped—these are the things which will make a congregation a real power house for Christ.

THE CURE December 29

I once read an article by Andrew Wilson on lions and lion taming. Mr. Wilson relates a very interesting story.

One day, a young man called Bobby Ramsay turned up at his zoo asking for a job; he wanted, of all extraordinary things, to be taken on as a lion tamer. When asked why, his reason was still more extraordinary. He was in fact in serious danger of a nervous breakdown, and his doctor had told him that the only thing that would cure him would be to get so nerve-racking a job that he would forget the other fears which haunted him. So he applied for the most dangerous job he could think of, and he became a very well-known lion tamer. His nervous breakdown was cured!

The way to get rid of nerves was to tackle something that demanded nerve.

The way to lighten one's own burden is to help someone else with his.

Teilhard de Chardin tells how on his expeditions in the wilder parts of China on horseback, the load would be hung on one side of the horse and on the other there was a stone to balance it. And it is well known that African carriers carry loads on poles laid across their shoulders and that they hang a stone on the other end of the pole as a counterbalance.

We may well ourselves have found that two suitcases are easier to carry than one, for one balances the other.

The way to bear someone's sorrow is to share someone else's.

We remember the way that Josephine Butler found her life work. One day when she came home, her little daughter ran out of an upstairs room to greet her. The house was built round an open space, and the little girl leant over the railing to see her mother. She overbalanced and crashed to the ground floor and was killed instantly. Josephine Butler was broken-hearted. To her in her sorrow there came an old Quaker lady. The old lady said to her, "I have spent most of my life looking after girls taken from the streets. I am old now and I can no longer handle the work of looking after the home where forty of them live. Come and take my job, and you will forget your own sorrow."

Josephine Butler went. True, she could never wholly forget her own sorrow, but by taking on her shoulders the troubles and the care of others she made her sorrow bearable.

To forget one's own burden in the burdens of others, to lighten one's own sorrow in the sorrows of others, *that* is the cure.

THE LORD IS RISEN!   December 30

The central fact of this Christian faith of ours is the Resurrection.

We would never have heard of the Cross had it not been for the Resurrection.

Without the Resurrection, the Cross is the tragic death of a good man. A whisper of it might have come down the centuries, certainly no more, probably not even that.

It is because of the Resurrection that we know of the Cross at all. It is the Resurrection which makes Christ Christ.

There is a stage in life when the Resurrection will make an impression on a person that the Cross will not.

This is specially so when people are young. It takes the years to awaken that vivid sense of sin which the Cross alone can relieve. But there is no stage in life when the child, the youth and the maiden, the teenager, will not thrill to the message of the possibility of a great companionship with the most heroic soul who ever walked this earth.

There is a time in life when the note of preaching should be the reality of the presence of this princely figure more than anything else. I would be the last to suggest that there is any kind of necessity to choose between the preaching of the Cross and the preaching of the Resurrection; but I do say that the common proportion between the preaching of the Cross and the Resurrection is wrong.

We cannot preach the Cross too much. This is not untrue. But perhaps some of us preach the Resurrection too little.

It is clear that very early in the second century, and probably before the end of the first century, the Lord's Day had taken the place of the Sabbath. Ignatius speaks of the Christians as no longer keeping the Sabbath but observing the Lord's Day.

Now the Sabbath, the last day of the week, commemorated God's rest after the six days of creation; the Lord's Day, the first day of the week, commemorates the Resurrection.

That is why the day came into being. It is the day on which the Christian Church remembers that the Lord is risen.

Here is the proof, if proof were needed, that the Resurrection ought not to be the subject of an annual sermon on Easter Day, but the basic memory of every Sunday.

THE END   December 31

Life has an end. No one knows when that end will come. So life is for ever saying, "*Now* is the time."

Life has an end.
The time that is given to any man is limited. Nothing then that can and ought to be done today should be put off till tomorrow. For none of us knows if tomorrow will ever come.

So often we live as if we had all the time in the world: as if life were endless and limitless: it isn't.

If there is something that ought to be done, it ought to be done *now*.

In life we ought to have an end.
The Greek word *telos* means an "end", but it does not just mean the time when something stops. It includes the sense of a "goal", an "aim", a "consummation".

We must have an "end" in that sense. Life must never be an aimless stroll down all kinds of byways. Without an end, you drift.

With an end, life does become a pilgrimage.

Life is not finished until it comes to its end.
The danger of life is that, even to the last moment, disaster can come. To the end there is the possibility of failure, falling to temptation, undoing all the years have built up. "Eternal vigilance is the price of liberty." We must be watchful to the end.

The ultimate end is meeting with God.

"Prepare to meet thy God," said Amos to Israel. The end of time is eternity. The end of life is God. The last step of life is the step which leads into the presence of God.

What consummation!